Vince Copley AM, a proud Ngadjuri man, was born on an Aboriginal mission in South Australia. As a young boy he attended the now famous St Francis House in Adelaide, a home for First Nations boys that produced many future leaders, including civil rights activist Charles Perkins. A star footballer and cricketer, Vince later devoted his life to advancing the rights and improving the lives of First Nations people. He worked closely with Charlie, and with everyone from community leaders to premiers and prime ministers. Along with other Ngadjuri people, he was also active in recovering and protecting Ngadjuri cultural heritage.

Lea McInerney grew up in the Clare Valley on Ngadjuri Country. Her ancestry is Irish-Australian. Lea's writing has been published in *Griffith Review* and other literary magazines. Lea met Vince in 2016. As well as this book, she worked with Vince on several Ngadjuri projects he led.

The *Wonder* of Little Things

VINCE COPLEY
with Lea McInerney

ABC
BOOKS

Aboriginal and Torres Strait Islander readers are respectfully advised this book contains names, images and descriptions of people who have died.

 The ABC 'Wave' device is a trademark of the Australian Broadcasting Corporation and is used under licence by HarperCollins*Publishers* Australia.

HarperCollins*Publishers*
Australia • Brazil • Canada • France • Germany • Holland • India
Italy • Japan • Mexico • New Zealand • Poland • Spain • Sweden
Switzerland • United Kingdom • United States of America

HarperCollins acknowledges the Traditional Custodians
of the land upon which we live and work, and pays respect
to Elders past and present.

First published in Australia in 2022
by HarperCollins*Publishers* Australia Pty Limited
Gadigal Country
Level 13, 201 Elizabeth Street, Sydney NSW 2000
ABN 36 009 913 517
harpercollins.com.au

A catalogue record for this book is available from the National Library of Australia

ISBN 978 0 7333 4244 8 (paperback)
ISBN 978 1 4607 1483 6 (ebook)

Cover design by HarperCollins Design Studio
Cover artwork: Detail from *Minyma Kutjara* © Venita Woods/Copyright Agency, 2022.
Courtesy of Japingka Gallery, Fremantle.
The photographs are from the Copley family collection, except where individually acknowledged. The family collection has been gathered over many years and includes copies of photographs from family and friends as well as other sources.
Author photos by Kathryn Sutton
Typeset in Bembo Std by Kelli Lonergan
Printed and bound in Australia by McPherson's Printing Group

For Kara and Vincent:
What their dad did

Contents

Prologue

'The red car'

South Australia, 1940s

We head down to the beach – me, my sisters Maureen and Josie, and my brother Colin. I'm nearly four, big enough to reach the pedals of the red car. The others are running along beside me, and Colin drops back and pushes me every now and then. He's six years older than me and a really fast runner. Our aunties call him Old Phar, after Phar Lap the racehorse. He wears one of those jockey caps all the time too. Mum's back at the house, and our oldest sister Winnie's staying with our relatives at Point Pearce, forty miles down the coast road. Dad's not around because he died when I was one. He was a fast runner too. Mum says Dad died of a broken heart.

We take a short cut where the road goes down to the bridge over the railway line. To get onto it you go down three steps, and once you're across to the other side you go down some stairs to the ground. Colin pushes me in the red car all the way. My feet slip off the pedals, and they keep turning and hitting

1

my legs. When we get to the bottom I'm crying because my shins and ankles are skinned raw. The others just laugh.

We keep on going along the road, and when we get to the jetty we walk out to the end and watch people fishing and a ketch loading up at the port to take the wheat and barley to Adelaide. There's a clipper there too with a load for England.

We come home the same way, and Colin carries the red car up the stairs and across the bridge and up the last few steps, then I get back in and he pushes me home. When Mum finds out what happened she gives Colin a hiding. He's meant to look after me.

* * *

We're living in Adelaide now. It's a year or two later. A local politician helped Mum find us a place to live in Mile End. It used to be a shop, and Mum covers up the display windows on each side of the front door with curtains. Mum's got regular work cleaning people's houses.

Just up the road from us is the town hall, where they show movies on Saturday nights. I'm usually asleep before the movie's over, and Colin piggybacks me home – it isn't far but it's far enough for him to be carrying me. My feeling about him is that he's my big brother. I look up to him.

When the summer school holidays come we go over to the mission at Point Pearce and stay with my grandfather Papa Joe, grandma Maisie and our cousins. Mum's there too. Every morning we head off and play all day around the paddocks and sheds. Every evening at teatime we come back to Papa Joe's for a feed and bed.

One day, Colin and his mates are over at the shearing shed, chasing each other and mucking about. There's a stone wall around the shed just high enough to stop the sheep getting out and low enough for young lads to think they can jump over it. Along the top of the wall are iron droppers, and strung through a hole near the top of each one is a line of barbed wire. Colin jumps the fence and tears his knee on the wire. But he just carries on and doesn't tell anyone about it.

A few days later Mum sees him limping and asks him what's wrong. He shows her his knee, all swollen and hot. The closest hospital is ten miles away in Maitland, but that's taboo for us — they don't take Aboriginal people. We have to keep going up the road to the hospital in Wallaroo, fifty miles away.

No one's got a car we can use because very few people at Point Pearce have them and petrol's expensive. In the horse and cart it will take about six hours to get there. Papa Joe and Mum work out that the bus going to Adelaide leaves soon and will get us to a hospital quicker. Papa Joe brings round the horse and cart and takes Mum, Colin and me along the road to The Gate where the bus stops. We jump on.

As the bus heads down the Adelaide road, Colin gets sicker and sicker. He opens the window and leans out and vomits all down the side. The bus driver isn't happy. We get to the Adelaide depot and the hospital's just across the road. We go straight over and they admit him, but the infection's set in too far.

It's just so sad when he dies.

* * *

Welcome to my story.

It's a simple story of a simple person, who's lived a long life now.

Losing Colin and my dad when I was young are two of the sad parts of my story. But there have been a lot of happy parts and funny parts and enjoyable parts too.

Bad things have happened to me, like they happen to everyone. Being a black person living in these times meant I experienced some particular sorts of bad things, and I've done my best to turn that around for myself and my family, and for other black people too.

In this book I'll tell you a bit about how I worked my way around racism, and how I made sure I kept on enjoying life. How I often just ignored people's ignorant comments, or made crazy jokes about them with my friends and family. How if someone was trying to stop me from enjoying myself or from making a living just because of the colour of my skin, I'd just keep going until I found someone who treated me right. And how once one person treated me right, others soon did too.

I'll tell you about how I worked behind the scenes with my Aboriginal and Torres Strait Islander friends to change the laws and policies that meant a lot of white people saw us only as the colour of our skin and not as people just like them.

I'll tell you about some of the other struggle times in my life and what I learned as I went along. I didn't learn a lot in school, not in the classroom anyway. But I learned a lot all through my life, and I'm grateful for the people who showed me things and taught me things and let me do the things I knew I was good at.

In this book you'll meet Mr Vickery, my high school headmaster, who used to love watching me play football when I was a teenager. At the end of my matches he'd take up a collection from his mates and give it to me, to give me a taste of being a professional sportsman.

You'll meet my friend Charlie Perkins, who I was at the boys' home with. Charlie went on to be a bit famous for stirring things up so that Aboriginal and Torres Strait Islander people could have the same rights as other Australians. I worked for him for a lot of years, and we travelled together a lot. I got to see what a good operator he was with people and how he was making the changes that needed to be made, especially at that time in history. It was because of Charlie that I met Muhammad Ali.

You'll meet my Curramulka friends Frank and Pat Joraslafsky, who invited me to tea at their place when I was seventeen years old and new to the white farming community they were part of. And you'll see how that set the ball rolling for other people to do the same, and how I ended up living there for fourteen years, and how I met Brenda and we fell in love, and how on the Peninsula there were dances every week in the big halls and the little ones, and how I learned to do waltzes and foxtrots, and became one of the most stylish dressers around. The Currie people didn't care about the colour of my skin – they just saw me and what I had to offer, and they enjoyed my company and I enjoyed theirs.

And you'll meet my mum, a really strong woman who taught her kids to 'always remember you're as good as anybody else'. She died when I was fifteen, which is another one of the sad times in my life I'll tell you about. But what she said to me when I was young has stayed with me all my life.

Anyway, I better not tell you everything that's in the book!

How I've made my story into this book is by telling it to my friend Lea. I got to know Lea a few years ago when she came to my place to ask me about my Ngadjuri culture. We had a few cups of tea that day, and Brenda had made a big spread of her homemade scones and curried egg halves and sandwiches, like she always did for visitors. Brenda being the daughter of farmers, well, country-style hospitality and catering was par for the course for her.

Since that first visit of Lea's, we've had a lot of cups of tea together. And as well as making this book, we've worked together on other projects. But it's always a cup of tea first, and the business after.

So if you feel like it, make yourself a cup of tea and I'll have one too, and we can be having one together while you read.

I can't know how you'll feel when you get to the end of the book. What I'm hoping, though, is that the first time you read it, it gives you a different impression of what life's about. It might make you conscious, in a small way, of the existence of other people in the world. I wouldn't say it will change your life or other people's lives. But it might give you a taste of a life that's different to yours, and the same as yours in some ways too.

I hope you enjoy my story.

1

'I think my mum should know'

In the beginning my name was Vincent Gilbert Warrior, but that wasn't what I was called. At Point Pearce, the government mission where Mum and Dad were from, they had a white book with all the details of the births and deaths. Mine said something like: 'A child born to Fred Warrior and Kate Warrior: Boy.'

From then on, my aunties called me Boy. 'Boy! Boy!' they'd say. Then Boy became Boyd and then Boydie. That stuck. My nieces and nephews still call me Uncle Boydie.

I was born in the government hospital at Wallaroo on the twenty-fourth of the twelfth month, 1936. My mum said that's when I was born, but the government said I was born on the twenty-third of December. If you look at my passport, you'll find that the government won. I still celebrate my birthday on the twenty-fourth, though. I think my mum should know.

I'm the youngest of six. Winnie was the eldest. Valda, the next one, passed away at an early age, before I was born. Then there was Maureen, Colin, Josie and me.

My mum was Katie Edwards and my dad was Fred Warrior. They grew up at Point Pearce on the Yorke Peninsula, about two hours' drive west of Adelaide, or a few hours by boat across Gulf St Vincent. The Peninsula's in the shape of a boot and on the other side of it there's Spencer Gulf.

As far as I know, when I was born Mum and Dad were still considered residents of Point Pearce but they were living in Wallaroo, the main town at the top of the Peninsula. These days it takes an hour to drive from there to Point Pearce, but back when they were young parents, they did the trip by horse and cart. I have some small memories of us living in Wallaroo. Mum used to do cleaning work for a lady called Mrs Venning, and our house wasn't far from a square in the town. Another memory is of Colin pushing me too fast in the red car that day we went down to the jetty.

But I have no memory of my dad. He was thirty when he died. I never knew anything about him when I was a young kid, but later on I heard a story about how the young men at Point Pearce would go down to the sheep shed to play cards or two-up or just spend time together, and a creature – some sort of ghost – used to come along and scare the hell out of them, so they'd all take off. Dad was the fastest runner – no one could beat him.

Once he was gone, Mum had to be the person looking after all of us. Every time I asked her what he died of, she'd say, 'A broken heart.'

'How can you die of a broken heart?' I asked her one day, when I was older. She said Dad was a sprinter and he used to run in athletic races around the place. Each win was worth

Here's my dad, Fred Warrior, acting in a school play at Point Pearce when he was about seven. He's third from the left. *(South Australian Museum)*

twenty-five silver dollars, or something like that – it was good money, anyway. A lot of my uncles used to be good runners too, and they'd all go away to different races and try to get that little bit of money. I think probably what Mum was saying was that Dad had strained his heart.

Much later I found out he'd died from tuberculosis or what they call TB. In the year before he died he'd been in and out of Wallaroo hospital with a condition that made his heart muscles weak. So Mum was right in what she said, that his heart was broken.

* * *

The next place I lived in was Point Pearce, on the mission. I was around four years old. I don't remember the day we moved, but I remember being in one place and then the other. Mum was away working a lot, and we mainly lived with our grandparents Joe and Maisie May Edwards. They were Mum's mum and dad.

At that stage my sister Josie would have been about seven. She had friends and cousins she used to take off with, and it was the same with Maureen, who was around nine. Colin was ten and had his mates too, and Winnie would have been about thirteen. I don't remember seeing her much. She'd probably left school by then and was working on the mission, maybe in the dairy. I think she used to help Mum with cleaning jobs sometimes too.

Dad in the Point Pearce football team in the 1920s. He's in the back row, second from the right, wearing a cap.

Me being the smallest of us kids and not able to hide quickly like the others, I spent most of the time with Mum and my grandparents. That's what was needed so welfare didn't take me away – they used to just turn up and take kids from unmarried mothers or from mothers who were trying to look after what welfare saw as too many kids.

Papa Joe never talked a great deal about where he came from and his connections. I found out later he was a Narungga man – they're the traditional owners of the Yorke Peninsula area – and he was the grandson of King Tommy. King Tommy was an important Narungga man who had a lot to do with negotiating with the white people when they first came to his Country. He seemed to be well regarded by both the Narunggas and the whites.

Papa Joe was very well respected in the local community. There must have been something in him that outshone anyone else on the mission at that time. People had respect for him because of his attitude: the way he knew he had to do the things he had to do and wouldn't complain or get angry. He was a really good fencer, a master haystack builder, and he'd been the captain of the Point Pearce football and cricket teams.

Papa Joe was also a god-fearing man. Every Sunday he'd get dressed in his three-piece suit and head off to church. I never saw him get wild, and I don't think he drank. He'd cut a block of tobacco with his pocketknife then put it in his pipe and light it up. He seemed to be in control of himself. For a big man, he was very gentle. He spent a lot of time looking after his grandkids and never complained about it, and I never saw him raise his voice or his hand to us. He showed me how to harness a horse and put it in a dray, then he let me drive it. We'd do fencing and get dead wood from the trees for the kitchen stove and the fireplace. I enjoyed my times with him.

The sandhills between the beach and the mission weren't far from Papa Joe's house. One time he told me about a group of old ladies who lived there. 'Don't ever go there,' he said. He reckoned these old ladies had enormous breasts, and if you went there they'd chase you, hit you on the back of the head with their breasts and knock you down. I took notice of him, of course, and never went to those sandhills.

As well as looking after all us kids, Papa Joe was looking after my grandmother. Her name was May, but to me she was Grandma Maisie or Grandma Maisie May. I didn't see much of her – she was bedridden with diabetes. Later on I worked out that she had important connections too, like Papa Joe did. Grandma Maisie was an Adams and her mum was the granddaughter of Kudnarto, who was a teenager when the white people first arrived. Kudnarto was pretty well known because in 1848 she married a white man called Tom Adams and it was the first approved marriage between a black and a white person in South Australia.

I knew some of my aunties on my mum's side, like Aunty Amy, Aunty Doris, Aunty Viney and Aunty Mary. And there were cousins older than me who I called Aunty too, like Aunty Gladys. Then there were these other ladies who I used to see – Aunty Annie, Aunty Bessie, Aunty Flossie and Aunty Nellie – and I often wondered who they were and how we all fitted together. They'd give me a big hug and I'd be thinking, *Who are you?* I noticed that the way they talked was a bit different to most of the Point Pearce locals, like they had an accent. But when you're a kid, you're busy doing everything else and I didn't ask them about it.

One day it dawned on me that these other ladies were my father's sisters. Whenever I saw them, they didn't talk about my dad or their parents Barney and Mary Warrior – they just talked about me and what I was doing. And they'd feed me up. If it was teatime, they'd give me more than they gave to their kids. I don't know whether they thought, *Oh, this poor little boy's got no dad. We'll have to look after him.* Aunty Annie would hug the death out of me. She had a little shop in her home that she used to make lovely lollies for. She'd give me free ones while everybody else had to pay. I thought that was really good – it was just a special sort of treatment, I suppose.

These aunties had all lost their big brother Fred. Their dad Barney had lost his only son who'd made it through childhood. Their mum Mary had died a few years before. You don't go through those sorts of losses without some grief.

All of my aunties had their own battles. They were living on the mission and trying to feed their kids while being controlled by the government, which meant they had to get permission to come and go, and they had to do what the mission bosses told them to. Sometimes they didn't have time to worry about others. But like I said, some of them always seemed to find that little bit of time to give me an extra hug.

2

'Our lives were controlled by a bell'

Point Pearce was home to a lot of people. The village had four rows of houses all made of brick or stone, with about fifteen houses in each row. The houses in the row furthest away from the water had two rooms – a kitchen and a bedroom. As their families got bigger, people would attach a sleep-out at the back.

The houses in the second row seemed a little bit bigger, then there was a fairly wide gap between that row and the next one, and a big shed in between, where an old man by the name of Banks Long lived at one end. He was what we called a traditional man – I think he was the last of the river people who came over from the Riverland, near where the Murray crosses into South Australia from Victoria. Close to the big shed was a little round building they used as the butcher shop.

The third and fourth rows were nearest to the water and a plantation of gum trees. Those rows had bigger houses, and Papa Joe's was in the last row. Up the top end there were some other bigger houses for the superintendent and for the stock manager and the farm manager – we called them the bosses. Further up the top was a big implement shed for all of the ploughs and headers. Just across the road from there were the stables for the horses, and near that was the milking shed. A little further out was the oval and the school, and from there, there was nothing. If you went any further you'd run into the sandhills and then Spencer Gulf.

We had a big hall where they held dances and functions. It had a stage and a picture screen, and a man from Port Victoria used to come once a week to show movies. Attached to the hall at its northern end was the church for all denominations. The different preachers used to come from outside: one week was Lutheran, the next Methodist, then Church of England, then Catholic.

The village had a shearing shed too, with eight or nine stands for the shearers. In those days they sheared the sheep with the old hand shears. Just across the road was the piggery. Point Pearce used to win prizes for its sheep and pigs at the local shows on the Peninsula.

The cemetery wasn't far from the shearing shed and the piggery. At Point Pearce everything was fairly close.

Our lives were controlled by a bell. In the mornings it would ring to tell you the milk was ready. It would ring again a bit later, and you'd see the men drift from their houses up to the office to find out where they were working for the day. Then it would ring for lunchtime, then for after lunch, then for knock-off time. Sunday it would ring for church. Us kids would hear it ring and we'd say to each other, 'Hello, something's on.'

A lot of our food came from what we had on the mission. Every week they'd kill some of the sheep and hang the meat in the butchery, then people would go up and get their rations. The butchers were Point Pearce men and you'd go there and they'd ask if you wanted chops or a leg of the lamb. People took mainly chops. The milkers would milk the cows, and when the bell told you it was ready you'd take your jug up to a little window and they'd fill it up and off you'd go. They brought bread in from outside and you'd go get a loaf from the window at the office. Papa Joe used to make milksops for us kids: bread boiled in milk and lots of sugar.

We'd go down to the bay to fish. Mum would throw in a line. The men would be there carrying three-pronged harpoons on long handles, and they'd walk out into the sea until it was up to their waist. All they'd have on was their shirt and a belt with a rope tied to it. You'd have three or four men walking around in the water looking for the butterfish. They'd spear one, tie it to the rope, then spear another and tie it, then another, until they had half a dozen or so. Then they'd drag them all along behind them and bring them in to shore. They'd gut them all, cook one and sit around and eat it, then take the rest back to the mission to give to everybody. There were no fridges then, so once you got them you had to eat them quickly. We all loved the fish.

One or two of the Point Pearce mob had a boat, so they'd often fish from that. Swans used to come into the bay, and sometimes there were sharks but nobody worried about them.

Sometimes the men would run a net out. My uncle Syke, Dad's cousin, was a real short bloke, and they used to think it was funny to put him in the deep end of the bay. When they ran the net out, the water would be up to the other men's waists but it would be up to Syke's neck. It always made me laugh.

Rabbits were a big go at Point Pearce too. My cousins and I would head out with what we called waddies: hunting sticks we made out of iron bars from old bedheads, the ones with knobs at the end. We'd look for the track the rabbits had made back to their burrow and then try and find the squat — that's the name for the place part way along the track where the rabbits stop and have a sit down. They'd squat under a tree or a bush, and as far as the rabbits were concerned they were hiding. We'd hunt them out of their squat and as they came out we'd throw the waddies and try and knock them over while they were moving. If you were lucky enough to hit one, well then you had a rabbit.

We became experts at throwing the waddy, because if you missed you mightn't have dinner. Sometimes you could get a bit of extra pocket money selling them, but you had to work for it, of course. As well as getting them with the waddies in the daytime, sometimes we'd camp overnight and set traps and catch fifty or sixty pairs. We'd sell them to the rabbit boy, who used to come round and collect them up. I think we were getting a shilling a pair at that stage.

In those days we'd go in the bus to the other towns on the Peninsula or to Adelaide. The bus driver would pick us up at The Gate and he'd let us off there when we came back home. Papa Joe would be waiting for us in his horse and cart to take us the few miles into the village. We'd go down a gully and then up over a hill and see the village and the bay that went out to Spencer Gulf.

* * *

Being at Point Pearce seemed pretty good when you were a kid. But for the adults it wasn't so good. The Chief Protector of Aborigines lived in Adelaide, and the government had all these rules and regulations that stopped you from moving outside the mission unless you got an exemption. You were under their control.

The superintendent and the managers at Point Pearce were white. Some of them would say they knew how to handle farm work – sheep and cows, crops and reaping, sewing wheat bags, that sort of thing. Which was sometimes laughable. If you asked them to tail a lamb a lot of them wouldn't know which end was which. When it came to shearing, they were supposed to know how to shear a sheep or class the wool but a lot didn't. When it came to harnessing up the header to the horse to harvest the wheat and barley crops, they didn't know how to do that either.

But the people living there knew how to do all of those things. And yet the houses built for the managers were ten times better than the houses we had. It was ridiculous in some cases.

Still, if something happened that upset the people and they didn't like whoever did it, they had a way of dealing with it. The toilets weren't the flush ones like we have now. Instead they were a wooden seat with a hole, and the you-know-what would land in a basin below where you'd sit. The toilets were down the back of the houses and each night a few blokes would come round with the night cart, which had big bins on it, and they'd grab the basins and tip the stuff into the bins. If these blokes were annoyed with one of the staff, they'd get a bin full of you-know-what and they'd lean it against the door of that person's house so when he opened it, the stuff would all go down his passageway. It was a way of showing their disgust about the bloke being in the job. It only happened sometimes.

When they got a person who was really good and they could trust, it was different, of course. One bloke had been a policeman before he came, and he taught the boys boxing and he'd take them to other towns for competitions. People liked him.

Point Pearce was only a little way up from Port Victoria, where most of the shopping was done. It's where the police station was too. The police knew most of the people at Point Pearce. Of course all of the people at Point Pearce knew who the policemen were – they'd see them at Port Victoria, and the police would often come out to the mission and just wander around. They had that control over you. It was under the guise of protection. That's what they said, anyway.

There were also the Kadaitcha. In different places 'Kadaitcha' means different things. In some places it can mean spirits that come and cause you trouble if you've been causing trouble. For us, we knew they were traditional men who were hunting people who'd done the wrong thing and were going to spear them.

At Point Pearce I heard stories about some younger men who were working on the new railway lines the government was building in the west and north of the state. They were accused of mistreating some young ladies in the communities near where they were working. A story spread around Point Pearce that the Kadaitcha were looking for these young fellas and they were going to punish them.

One night, around two o'clock in the morning, my cousin and I were sitting talking in the shadow of one of the homes, and along came these three tall men carrying spears and shields. They had very little clothing on and were all painted up. We froze and wondered whether they were here to spear the blokes we'd heard had been playing up. They went to the house next to where we were and tried to get in but couldn't, then they went off to another house. It fitted in with the stories we'd picked up about the Kadaitcha.

It was the first time in my life that I realised there were people different from me who were part of the traditional Aboriginal system – people who lived under different sorts of structures to the Point Pearce one we were living under. Around that time I also heard that sometimes people would come down from the APY Lands – the Anangu Pitjantjatjara Yankunytjatjara lands in the north of the state – and they'd pick up a young kid from the mission and take them away to be initiated. One time one of my cousins was taken, and he spent a lot of time going through the traditional system. Later I heard that in some cases going through it changed people's lives: they went from wandering around the place with nothing in life to being much calmer people.

I wasn't initiated. I was frightened I might be. If you were naughty, your mother or one of your other relatives would say to you, 'You'd better behave or you'll be taken away.' It became a threat, a good one. It scared me, anyway.

I knew we weren't traditional people like the Kadaitcha were and like Banks Long was, but I could see that they existed and had some different ways to us.

3

'Come the night, you'd go back to Hollywood'

I think Mrs Venning in Wallaroo might have told some people in Adelaide that Mum was a good cleaner, because Mum started getting work there. She'd go across to the city for a week at a time. Sometimes she'd take Winnie with her to help out and sometimes I'd go too. She had some pretty big jobs at big houses. They'd have a room in a shed at the back where whoever they called 'the help' stayed. I didn't go in the house while Mum was cleaning. She made sure I was comfortable where I was. I'd play or I'd sleep. I was young, but I must have been grown up enough to stay where I was told.

Mum was spread around a bit. They always got her back, so they must have been satisfied with what she was doing. I remember a very big house in North Adelaide that had its own ballroom down in the basement where they used to have dances. Then there was another big house at Kent

Town, and another one at Glenelg. When the week was up we'd go home. Sometimes we'd catch the bus all the way, and sometimes we'd catch the train going north as far as a railway station called Bowmans, where we'd stop for a cup of tea and a pasty, then swap over to the bus.

If I didn't go to Adelaide with Mum I'd be at Papa Joe's with the other kids. We'd get up in the morning and sit at the table and Papa Joe would get us all breakfast, and then we'd go outside and play all day. The big kids would look after the little kids. When it came to teatime us kids always knew where to come. We'd always have a feed and a bed.

Part of the reason Mum took me with her to Adelaide was because of what welfare was up to. It didn't matter that you were being looked after by your family like we were: the younger you were the easier it was for them to grab you. Josie, Maureen and Colin were that bit older, and as soon as they saw the car coming they'd head off down the beach to some hiding places they had.

When I was about five Mum decided to move us to Adelaide to live more permanently. She had more chance of getting work there, and a lot of people from Point Pearce were doing the same, because the government had brought in exemption certificates for Aboriginal people.

If you wanted to leave Point Pearce and live somewhere else you had to get an exemption, which declared you to be an honorary white person. Once you signed the exemption form you could get a house in Adelaide and a job. You could go to the pub and drink inside. You could stand in a queue and you didn't have to be at the end of it. That's what the bit of paper was saying.

None of that happened, of course. You'd end up in the worst houses or flats, and the rent was sky high. If you went to the hospital or the shops you were always served last. The only thing an exemption did was stop you going back to the mission to stay. Because once you signed that paper and left, that was the end of it. You could visit your relatives in the daytime but you couldn't stay overnight. For a while, that's what the rules were. A lot of us wanted to go back for more than a day to visit our relatives who were still living there, but we couldn't. Which is how Hollywood came about.

Just on the boundary of the mission and the beach, the Point Pearce people set up a little camp so the people with exemptions could meet up with their families and stay for a while. They built little huts out of galvanised iron and anything else they could find. They were pretty simple, with a sand floor, a bed and a stove. You'd go in to Point Pearce in the daytime and see your families, then come the night you'd go back to Hollywood.

We did it a few times with Mum. One time the bus dropped us at The Gate and it was late in the day. Papa Joe was there to pick us up. A big policeman from Port Victoria was checking everyone. 'Where's your forms?' he was saying. He had a list of all the exempted people and we were on it and he told us we couldn't go in. That was his job, whether he liked it or not. We couldn't argue, otherwise you'd end up in jail. Papa Joe took us down to Hollywood that night.

I never heard Papa Joe talk about the exemptions and the police. He could have, but not to me. He was settled there. In his mind, I think how he saw it was, he's a Narungga man, he's got a home that he built, he's got a job, he's looking after his wife, he's got all his grannies around him, and so he's happy. He was going to keep living his life the way he'd been living it. He was a strong man and he knew who he was.

And that got passed on to Mum too. She wasn't the sort of person who was going to sit in a corner after my dad died and feel all sorry for herself. She'd work for people to get enough money to look after us kids. Nothing was going to deter her from that particular line.

* * *

At that stage the houses that people like us could get in Adelaide were dilapidated, but there was an MP by the name of Cecil Hincks who lived in Port Victoria and he helped find us a good place near the city centre. It was on Henley Beach Road in Mile End, about fifty yards from the Mile End Hotel and straight across the road from a little deli that sold newspapers and a few groceries. Because our house had been a shop it had a little alcove you'd step into off the footpath, and on either side of the front door were big windows. Mum put up curtains and made those rooms into a lounge and a bedroom. Down the passage on either side were a couple of other bedrooms, and at the end was the kitchen. I slept in one bedroom with Mum, because I was young. I think Josie and Maureen slept together in a room, and Colin had his own room. Winnie didn't come with us. She stayed on at Point Pearce because she was working by then. Outside the kitchen there was a long backyard that was too big for us – the grass just grew wild and we had no way of cutting it.

I remember my first day at school in Adelaide very clearly. An Italian boy gave me a good hiding. At that time there was a big Italian community around Mile End, where we lived, and Thebarton, the suburb next to us where the school was, and this boy was king of the hoop with the other kids. After he belted me I ran home, crying all the way. When I told Mum what had happened she gave me another hiding and took me back to school and made me front up to the kid and fight him. *Oh, crikey,* I thought, *how many hidings am I gonna take in one day? I'll have to show a bit of heart I suppose.* I gave the kid a towelling and things changed. I didn't have any more problems.

I remember going to school with Josie, but I don't remember Colin and Maureen being there. They might have been close to finishing primary school, and that was as far as we went back then.

Josie and I used to walk to school together. We'd go through the back gate and along a lane where the night cart used to come, then into the gate at the school. Along the way we'd both be making jokes, and at school she'd stick up for me. We had a few fights too, although not many. One morning we were getting ready to go to school and something happened, and she flicked me over her shoulder somehow. I bashed my ear on the chair and split my ear. It's still there, a little mark. She was bigger than me and she was just starting to learn how to play netball. That was going to be her life.

Back then I used to faint a lot. I had a mate I played with who lived not far up the road. Often we'd go to some paddocks across the railway line and kick around a strange rubber ball he had that was shaped like a rugby ball. One day we were in the kitchen at his house and I fainted but didn't fall down. When I came round his mum said to me that my chin had got caught on the table and I'd been swinging there for a while. Another time I fainted at school assembly, and that time I fell and my face hit the bitumen and it busted my front teeth. Mum took me to the dentist. When we got there I put on a show and I wouldn't sit in the dentist chair. The dentist had to come around from behind and grab me. After a lot of screaming and hollering from me, he pulled the teeth out.

On the way home Mum said, 'Here's a shilling for being such a good boy.'

Oh well, I thought. *That's not bad*. It was a fair while before I got my teeth fixed.

* * *

We used to go back to Point Pearce a lot – around this time they had another system in where if you had an exemption you could get permission from the Aborigines Protection Board to go back and stay for a while – and I can remember going to school there sometimes. My cousins used to call me 'the professor' because I'd been at school in Adelaide. But they knew more than me. I never really felt frustrated about it – I just thought I must be stupid because I couldn't do the things they were doing. I couldn't work out sums. I didn't know where London was. Simple things that I didn't have any interest in or didn't care about. I could read and write, though.

For a while I sold newspapers outside the Mile End Hotel. It wasn't long after I'd started school at Thebarton. A friend lived across the road from the pub and I used to go and see him. One day on my way there I saw a bloke standing on the corner yelling out, 'Newspaper! Newspaper!' He had a bag full of them and he asked me if I wanted to take over sometimes. I said all right, and I filled in for him for a while. I made a little bit of money, and I'd take a newspaper home and read it.

I used to read a lot. That's one thing I was interested in — being able to read, and read properly. A couple of aunties said they remembered me as a kid reading the newspaper. I'd be sitting at the table and looking at the newspaper and reading out what was in it. Colin helped me a lot to get the words right. I think he and Mum were pleased I had a job at that age. 'Ooh, he's gone out and got his own job!' they'd say. They thought I was pretty productive.

But I was still too dumb with sums to understand what sort of money the bloke was paying me. It wasn't great. In the end I worked out he was robbing me so I gave it up.

4

'Sometimes I'd see an old man'

Mum had some good friends in Adelaide, especially two ladies she'd grown up with at Point Pearce, Aunty Glad and Aunty Pearl.

Aunty Glad was Mum's cousin through Kudnarto. As well as being famous for being the first Aboriginal woman to marry a European man, Kudnarto was given some of her land back – for a while, anyway. Kudnarto and her husband Tom Adams had two sons called Tom Jnr and Tim. I'm from Tom's side and Aunty Glad is from Tim's.

Aunty Glad had grown up at Point Pearce, and she was a bit older than Mum. She got married there and had two sons. Her first husband was a Hughes, but he died when their boys were young. Aunty Glad moved to Adelaide a year or two before we did, and at some stage she married a soldier called Fred Elphick and she became Gladys Elphick.

Aunty Glad was a fighter. Back then she was involved in a group called the Aborigines Advancement League of South Australia, which had started up in the 1940s to get better conditions for Aboriginal people. It had been set up by a group of people including Charles and Phyllis Duguid. He was a Scottish medical doctor and she was a teacher, and they'd helped set up the Ernabella mission in the APY Lands. Dr Duguid used to travel around the state seeing how conditions were for Aboriginal people. The league would hold meetings and get people to talk about their experiences with the laws and what the conditions were like for their houses and work, and they'd be calling on the government to fix the policies.

At the time mostly white people were involved. Aunty Glad might have been there, to try and set up a bridge for better understanding between white and black people.

I think Aunty Pearl's real name was Ellen Newchurch, but we mainly called her Aunty Pearl or Aunty Pearlie. I'm not sure of the connection but I think she'd been married at one time to one of my uncles and now she was living with a white man who might have been in the army too. She was a chirpy little thing. She was very fair skinned, which helped her lose herself in the crowd, which a lot of Aboriginal people with fair skin did at the time.

Aunty Glad lived behind the West Torrens Hotel, and on Sunday afternoons we'd walk around to her place, and Mum and Aunty Glad would have a cup of tea and a yap. Aunty Pearl would be there some of the time too – I'm not sure where she was living then. The three of them would be having a good laugh. About what, I'm not quite sure. I was too young to understand adult things at that stage.

They were pretty good-looking women, and they all dressed really well. Mum always looked very smart – she was fairly particular about that. She wore nice dresses, and if we went somewhere she'd get dolled up in a hat and gloves and her shoes would be spot on. Aunty Glad and Aunty Pearl were the same. They'd be all dressed up in the fashion of the day and they'd meet up at places like Light Square in the city, which was a meeting place for everybody from Point Pearce and Raukkan, another mission south of Adelaide that the mission people called Point McLeay.

To me as a young boy they seemed to be three really strong women who were fighting against the odds at that time. They thought having an exemption form would allow them to do this and do that. But it didn't allow them anything. They had to go through all that period, which wasn't easy.

Sometimes on a Saturday, Mum and I would go to the horseraces at Cheltenham, and she'd meet up with lots of relatives there. Josie would be off with friends, and Mum would get me dressed up and she'd be dolled up. We'd catch the tram into the city and then the train to the racecourse, and she'd meet up with different cousins and spend a pleasant afternoon with them, and I'd meet up with my cousins and muck around with them.

On the way back home on the train you'd sometimes get smarties who'd be half full of lunatic soup and they'd say some stupid things. 'Oh, look at that little black boy,' they might say. Then you'd hear them say the n-word. They'd make sly digs just loud enough for us and a few other people to hear.

Mum wouldn't let them get away with that. The train would be about to pull into our station and she'd stand up then suddenly turn around, and before they had a chance to say anything she'd tell them she didn't appreciate the comments they'd been making and who did they think they were and we lived in this country too and we were as good as they were. I'd be standing there amazed. I could see that the person she'd said it to was really embarrassed. Mum didn't care. She'd just dress them down.

We knew a few other people in Adelaide who we used to visit. One was another big family from Point Pearce. They lived in an old double-storey place with a stone staircase between the two floors. The stone steps were all worn down, and one day I slipped on them and broke my right arm. I had to get a plaster on it, so I started using my left hand for everything. Just as my arm was starting to heal and the plaster was off, I did it again – same place, same stairs, same arm broken. Then it happened again another time. So that was three times that I broke that arm and had to have it in plaster. I just became left-handed, although it took me a fair while and a lot of concentration.

Sometimes Mum and us kids would catch the tram up to Light Square. Some days I'd see an old Aboriginal man there and I'd think that he must be from the mission at Raukkan, because a lot of people there were from Raukkan. Later I found out he was my grandfather Barney Warrior, my dad's dad, and that he wasn't from Raukkan but that his wife, my grandmother, was. She'd died before I was born. I didn't know it then, but this man Barney Warrior became pretty important to me later on in my life.

From Light Square, we'd sometimes walk up to another aunty's place in the city. That was Aunty Edie. She kept bobbing up in my life over the years. Later on I learned she was connected to Barney Warrior, although I'm not sure how.

My grandfather Barney Warrior, around 1940. His surname was
sometimes spelt Waria. *(South Australian Museum)*

Aunty Edie was fairly light-skinned and for a long time she
and her family escaped any racial abuse because of that. They
lived what you'd call a normal life and were part of the wider
community.

Back in those times some Aboriginal people passed as
white people or they let people think they were from other
countries. I remember hearing about some Aboriginal people
in Western Australia who wore turbans so they'd be classified

as Indians. That way they could get jobs or be allowed to go into hotels and do things that, if you were known to be an Aboriginal person, you weren't allowed to do. Because of the laws at the time a lot of Aboriginal people all over Australia did that. But it meant you could go through life not wanting to let anyone know who you really were. One thing I learned living in Adelaide was that we Aboriginal people come in all shapes and sizes and colours.

* * *

One day a man knocked on our front door. When I opened it he frightened the hell out of me because he was dressed up in a bowler hat and suit and he was carrying an umbrella.

I slammed the door and ran back to the kitchen. 'This goonya's at the front door,' I whispered to Mum.

'Did you let him in?' she asked.

'No!' I said.

Mum went to the door and let the man in. His name was Allan Copley, and that was the start of their relationship. From then on he was a constant visitor, and next thing I knew he was living with us.

With Allan Copley coming into our lives, I started to work out that it was taboo for an Aboriginal woman to have any association with a white man, in the sense of being in a relationship with them. She could work for one, but she wasn't allowed to extend that to a relationship. At that time there was no way that black and white could mix without some repercussions. If you had an exemption certificate then legally you could, but if you were dark like Mum was, and the bloke was white, well a lot of people didn't care what the certificate said. This was the 1940s and Aboriginal people weren't even counted in the census – that didn't come until 1967.

One day, when I was five or six, I went across the road to the deli and there was Mum's photo on the front page of a newspaper called *The Truth*. Some not very nice things had been written about her. A long time later I found out more about why her story made it into the papers like that.

What I hadn't known back then was that when Mum and Allan got married in May 1942, Allan was already married. A few months later there was a trial, and I think he went to jail for a while, for a year or more. The newspaper story must have been about him being a bigamist as well as about a white man and an Aboriginal woman being together. When Allan came out of jail, he and Mum got together again, and she took his name and became Katie Copley. I was still Vincent Warrior at that stage.

I think Mum and Allan must have had a relationship prior to him coming to the house at Mile End that day. It was the same situation with Aunty Glad being with an army man, and I think Aunty Pearl was with one too. This was all during the war. They might have met at Light Square or in the park next to the River Torrens. They wouldn't have met at a hotel because Aboriginal people weren't allowed to drink or be served in them.

As far as I know, when Allan came to Mile End he didn't have a job but he'd signed up as a volunteer soldier. I worked out recently that he was ten years younger than Mum, so when they'd got together he was nearly twenty-five and Mum had just turned thirty-five.

We'd go back to Point Pearce in the holidays. Mum probably had to get permission each time from the Aborigines Protection Board.

I spent most of my time with my cousins, the Grahams – that's my Aunty Doris, Mum's sister, and Uncle Cecil and their kids. Their house wasn't far from Papa Joe's, and I'd bunk in with my cousin Bradley.

It was during the summer holidays in 1944 that Colin cut his knee on that wire and it got infected. He died on the fifth of February, when he was thirteen. I'd just turned seven. I can remember going to Colin's funeral, although I can't remember very much about it. I think we were at Aunty Edie's place and we left from there to go to the funeral parlour. Then we went to the West Terrace Cemetery, close to the city, and that's where he was buried.

Now Mum was in the situation where Colin was no longer around. Before, I'd been watching him grow up and hearing different ones talk about what he was going to be, what with him being the eldest boy, and whether he'd be a good runner too. And of course that was all gone now.

Mum was busy working, and Allan might have still been in jail, so Josie and I had to do our own thing. Josie was ten by then and a mad netballer so she'd do that. I liked going places. Mum might have thought I was staying home, but if I wanted to do something I'd just do it. The tram was really easy because I didn't have to pay – they'd just let me get on. It used to stop outside our door on Henley Beach Road. I'd jump on it and away I'd go, sometimes to the city and sometimes down to Henley Beach for a swim. Some days when I'd go into the city I'd walk down Hindley Street to the Metro or one of the other movie theatres. The ladies at the door were always nice to me and they'd let me in for free. Sometimes I'd sit there all day and watch the same movie over and over. Then come five o'clock, off I'd go home in time for tea.

I remember being in the city the day the war ended in 1945. King William Street was crowded with people, and everybody was jumping around and kissing and hugging. I was standing there watching it all, and people were grabbing me and dancing with me too.

* * *

One day, Winnie and a gentleman came walking up the long backyard. I was about nine and Winnie would have been seventeen or eighteen. Mum saw them coming and ran out of the kitchen and down to meet them.

Winnie was pregnant. At that time having a baby out of wedlock was taboo, and Mum gave them both the works. She told them to take off and not come back. Winnie was crying and I felt a bit sad for her to have Mum act like that. We didn't know why Mum was being so strict. But that was the go in those days: you couldn't be pregnant and have a baby without being married.

Mum was tough, really tough. It might have had a bit to do with her husband dying at such a young age. I've tried since then to think about how she must have felt and how she managed to get over it and keep doing all she was doing to look after us kids. Was she being hard with Winnie or strong? I'm not sure.

Sometime after Winnie brought that news, Mum packed us up and we moved again. I don't know if she might have just wanted to get away and forget about a lot of things. Colin had died and Allan was back and she'd been through all the kerfuffle with marrying him. Me, I was the youngest and I just followed wherever she wanted us to go.

5

'Next thing I was standing in the corner'

Allan had bought an old buckboard ute and away we went – Mum, Allan, Josie and me – to a place call Leigh Creek north of the Flinders Ranges. I was nine and Josie was eleven. Winnie and Maureen were still at Point Pearce – Maureen was staying with Papa Joe and Grandma Maisie, and Winnie was on the verge of living her own life.

My only memory of the trip from Adelaide was waking up and it was cold and foggy and we'd stopped at a church in Salisbury, which wasn't very far out of the city. Allan might have stopped to put water in the radiator. Anyway, we eventually got to Leigh Creek.

The government was opening up a brown coalmine, and Allan got a job drilling for water. We lived north of the town, about a quarter of a mile out, in an old campsite. It had a massive tent where all four of us slept and we could have a bath. Alongside it was a corrugated-iron shed where we'd cook and eat. That was it.

Once those mining towns like Leigh Creek got going they had everything – shops and good accommodation and a big dining area they called the Mess, where the people working at the mine got fed. They had a small hospital too with doctors and nurses. For a while Mum worked at the Mess, cleaning up after the men had their meals.

Not long after we moved to Leigh Creek, somebody said to me, 'What's your name?' I decided then to call myself a Copley. I don't know why – I just changed it myself from Vincent Warrior to Vincent Copley and that's what people started calling me. Josie was never a Copley: she kept the name Warrior. People couldn't work out how we were brother and sister. It never ever came up about adoption. I just carried on with that name. In my mind I never classified Allan as a father. I always called him Allan, never Dad. I don't have a lot of memories of him. As far as I know he never bashed my mum, and I hardly ever heard them arguing. But I didn't grow to like him, not really.

When we first came to Leigh Creek it didn't have a school, so we went to one in a small town called Copley, near Leigh Creek. People would ask me if they named Copley after me or if they named me after the town, and I thought that was funny.

Josie and I would walk the quarter mile from our campsite into Leigh Creek, and we'd joke around a lot while we were going along, like we always did. Once we got into town one of the blokes who worked in the mine would take all us schoolkids to Copley in his truck. He set up rows of planks on the truck's tray for us to sit on, and he'd take us there and bring us back every day.

It was a one-teacher school with one classroom. The Grade One kids and the Grade Seven kids and the kids in between were all in together. A lot of country schools were the same. We had about fifteen kids there, and as well as Josie and me there was a couple of other Aboriginal kids. The rest were white.

The teacher wore R.M. Williams boots with a big high heel at the back. He did all right coping with Grade Seven stuff and bringing it down to Grade One, and then to the in-betweens. Those teachers were pretty versatile.

One day at recess time I was out in the yard playing rounders with the other kids. I happened to be standing alongside a girl who was suffering from earache, and she had a scarf wrapped around her head to cover up her ears. I yelled at somebody else who was playing, and it hurt the girl's ear and she started crying.

The teacher came over and she told him why she was crying. He reprimanded me and made me apologise to her. 'What am I apologising for?' I asked him. 'All I did was this.' And I screamed again.

Of course that set her off again, and the next thing I was standing in a corner of the classroom. Josie tried to tell the teacher I didn't mean to hurt the girl, but he wouldn't listen to her. I stood there for the rest of the day and sort of whistled away, looking at the bricks. When the time came for the truck to take us home, I was the first one out the door and up there on the tray waiting to go.

When I think about it now, I didn't think I was hurting anybody, but of course I'd never had earache. There she was with a scarf wrapped round her head, poor little thing. She must have been in pain.

Eventually they built a school at Leigh Creek, and we stopped going to Copley. That was probably a year or so later.

* * *

One day when Mum was working at the Mess, three Adnyamathanha men from Nepabunna came in for a meal. Nepabunna's about eighty kilometres east of Leigh Creek, and back then it was in its early days of being an Aboriginal mission. A group called the United Aborigines Mission had set it up in the 1930s for Adnyamathanha people who'd been pushed off their land when the pastoralists came and started up the stations. Nepabunna's also where the inventor of R.M. Williams boots learned how to make them. The people at Nepabunna taught him how to make leather and then how to do the stockwhips that he made a lot of his money from. A lot of people don't know that story.

The three Adnyamathanha men were working at the mine and living in the single men's quarters. When Mum saw them and they saw her, it twigged between them who she was and her connection to my grandfather on my dad's side – Barney Warrior, the old man I used to see in Light Square. Barney was a Ngadjuri man who'd been initiated by the Adnyamathanha elders because there were no Ngadjuri elders left. Because these men knew Barney, Mum had a connection with them, and we all became really friendly. They were lovely people. One was an old gentleman called Jack Coulthard, then there was a man called Frank Jackson, and the other name I can't remember.

On long weekends and holidays we'd drive to Nepabunna and meet up with everybody and stay in one of the three Adnyamathanha gentlemen's homes. The bloke in charge of the mission kept a fairly tight rein – he was a religious bloke, and I remember he only had one arm.

Sometimes the three Adnyamathanha gentlemen would come out to our place at Leigh Creek for Sunday lunch, and we'd travel around the local area with them. One time we went out shooting for kangaroos. Frank Jackson was the shooter, and when he saw one he sat cross-legged on the ground and shot the gun, and the bullet hit the spot where the kangaroo's tail connects to its body. Then he cut its throat with a knife.

He had a special way of getting the meat ready to eat. First, he cut off a piece of steak from the kangaroo's rump, which meant it was a fairly big piece. Then he folded it in two and got a thin stick and poked holes around the edge of the steak. The tail was still partly attached to the body and all these sinews were sticking out. He cut some of them off and put them through the holes in the steak to sew it all up. Then he left one little hole open at the top and poured blood from the kangaroo's throat into it. Then he threw it on the coals and cooked it. When I was in Point Pearce we cooked rabbits on the coals, but this was the first time I'd ever seen meat done the way Jackson cooked the kangaroo. It was the best steak I'd ever eaten.

When we finished eating, Mr Jackson cut the kangaroo's tail off and gave it to Mum, and a few days later she cooked it up for them when they came to have tea with us. That was my first experience of eating kangaroo, and it gave me more understanding of how different people can be in how they live and the food they eat and how they cook it.

* * *

After we'd been at Leigh Creek for a while, Mum got a new job looking after the kids of a white bloke, Mr Knowles, who worked for the government as a water contractor. He was single and had about five kids. I don't know what had happened to their mum. They had a big house in the town, and the four of us moved into it with them. Mum became the housemaid and made sure the kids were fed and looked after. A couple of the older kids were going to school, and there was a baby who was about one.

One time we'd been to Adelaide and we had the baby with us. We were in Allan's old ute and it was stinking hot. On the way home the ute broke down just outside of Copley, which in those days was south of Leigh Creek, before they moved the town in the 1980s. Allan said he'd walk into Copley and get the mechanic to come out and fix the car up. While he was gone we all sat in a dry creek bed under a big gum tree. Allan was taking a long time, and the baby was starting to be in a bad way because we had no water. Mum said Josie and I better take off into Copley and see what was holding Allan up. So off we went, and halfway there we met Allan and the mechanic coming out. They had some water and we raced back to Mum. She washed the baby and he came good.

Another time Mum left me to look after the baby while she was away from the house doing something somewhere else. There'd been a bit of rain and one of the creeks close to us had water in it, which meant all the kids were in there swimming. Mum had told me to stay at home with the baby and not go anywhere. So what happened? I went down to the creek and took the baby, because everyone else was there. All I did that day was sit on the bank of the creek with the baby and watch the other kids swim. I had my arm around him so he wouldn't run away and get in the water. He just sat there watching too. But when I got home and Mum found out, she gave me a hell of a hiding. It wasn't good. But I never did that again.

Mum didn't care where we were when it came to giving me a hiding. If I was playing up, it was no problem for her to make sure I got what I deserved. I felt her wrath a couple of times: that time at Leigh Creek with the baby, and then another time I remember in Adelaide on the corner of Hindley and King William streets. We'd been waiting for the bus to Port Adelaide to see our relatives and I must have done something wrong – I can't remember what. Next minute she was giving me a hiding and people were looking at her as if to say, 'You shouldn't do that.'

Of course, she told them to mind their own business. 'I'll do what I want,' she said. 'He's my son and he's misbehaving and he needs a hiding.'

That's how strong she was. Other people didn't put her off. Sometimes I wished they did but they didn't. She didn't go with the status quo – if she wanted to do it, she'd do it. It was the same with Aunty Glad and my other aunties. If they thought something wasn't right in how Aboriginal people were being treated, well, they said something about it or they did something about it. The more I learned about Papa Joe, the more I could see he was like that too.

We'd been with the Knowles family for a few months when Mum and Allan started talking about moving again. I think Allan's job had run out and they thought Alice Springs would be a better place for him to get work: it was bigger than Leigh Creek, and Mum could get work there too.

Mum's connections with some women she knew in Balaklava might have had a bit to do with her and Allan deciding to go to Alice too. Balaklava's not far from Adelaide and back a few years ago, during the war, these ladies and their kids had been evacuated from the Northern Territory to a special camp there, in case the Japanese invasion spread south to places like Alice Springs. Every now and then some of the Balaklava ladies would catch the train to Adelaide for the day and go to Light Square and that's where Mum would have met them. When the war finished, and the women were going back to their homes, one lady from Alice said if we ever wanted to move there we could stay with her until we found our own house.

We didn't have Allan's ute anymore, but in those days the Adelaide to Alice Springs train went through Leigh Creek so we caught that. It took more than a day, and the only thing I remember about the trip is that we couldn't go in the dining car because we hadn't made a booking before we got on. Luckily, they made some sandwiches for us.

Leigh Creek had been the beginning for me of understanding how people can be different and still be connected. It stuck in my mind that the three Adnyamathanha men and Mum had a rapport straight away because of my dad's dad, Barney Warrior. While I didn't really remember him much back then, I hadn't forgotten him either.

6

'The white people classified us all'

To get into Alice Springs we had to go through the mountains that wind around the town. They're called the MacDonnell Ranges and there's different gaps you can go through. When we came in from the south, we came through Heavitree Gap, but everyone just calls it The Gap. There's Emily Gap to the east and Simpsons Gap to the west, and some others too.

We moved in with the lady Mum knew from the Balaklava camp, who lived just over the road from the Todd River. Most of the time there's no water in the Todd – it's just a wide sandy creek bed with big gum trees all the way along.

One day I was standing out on the road and I heard some dogs barking. All of a sudden about ten or fifteen men came along the Todd carrying spears and woomeras. They were wearing shirts that hung down around their backsides and they had belts on. They might have had underpants on, but I couldn't see because of the shirts hanging down.

It frightened the hell out of me. I ran inside and watched them through the window. I think I'd got scared because of what I'd heard when I was in Point Pearce, about people coming down from the north to get kids and take them back up and initiate them. If those men caught me out the front of the house they might take me away. That's why I'd shot off when I saw them.

I asked the lady we were living with what was happening and who they were and whether they might be at war with some other people. She told me they weren't at war, that they were the traditional people who lived through the Gap and they were going hunting. A little later in the day, around four o'clock, I heard dogs barking again and there they all were, coming back and carrying four or five dead kangaroos they'd caught to eat.

The traditional people would very rarely come into Alice. They were allowed to make visits in the daytime, but then they had to leave and go back to their own communities at sunset. They'd started setting up town camps on the outskirts of Alice and through the Gap. All around central Australia, pastoralists and miners had been moving in and taking over people's traditional lands. A lot of them had guns. People from the Western Desert, Arrernte, Pitjantjatjara, Warlpiri, and other lands were losing the food and water they'd always had available to them and they were coming into town and staying in camps with their own groups. I remember seeing one of the town camps called Amoonguna, where the people had built two-bedroom corrugated-iron huts to live in.

As well as the people in the town camps, traditional people from the Hermannsburg mission, a Lutheran mission west of

Alice Springs, used to come and stay at a mission place the church had in town. They'd do some shopping and sell a few paintings then go back to Hermannsburg.

Non-traditional Aboriginal people like us lived a bit of distance from the main shops, where you really weren't a part of the town. After a while staying with the Balaklava lady, we got a home of our own in a group of houses they called the Cottages. There were about fifteen or sixteen of them, each one made up of two houses joined together. They were all painted white, and they had a lounge, two bedrooms and a sleep-out.

The Cottages were behind an abattoir. When they'd kill a cow they'd strip the guts and all the things they didn't need and just throw them out on the side of the road. Of course after a week or so it didn't have a very good smell, and that smell would float over the Cottages. Back then there was no sewerage either. Instead, the night-cart people would come with a horse and dray with 44-gallon drums on it, the same as in Point Pearce and Adelaide.

The Cottages were run by the government. I don't know how Mum and Allan got housing there, whether there were forms you had to fill in. How it all operated wasn't in my mind – I was busy looking around, meeting all the other kids and learning about how we were classed.

The white people classified us all like this. The 'full bloods' were the 'real Aboriginals'. These were the Aboriginal people who still walked around wearing loincloths and carrying spears and eating witchetty grubs – things like that. Another category they had was 'half-caste', where you had a white father or a white mother. They saw that as the half-educated situation. In their minds you were a little bit more capable than the 'full bloods' and you'd be able to live in a house and look after it. That was how they classed you.

The white people from the government and the missions called the Cottages 'Rainbow Town', because in their minds you had to be 'half-caste' or 'quarter-caste' or 'three-quarter-caste' to live there. The government managers decided what you were. We were classed as 'half-castes', even though my mum and dad were Aboriginal people and their parents were Aboriginal people. People would say to us, 'Oh, you're part Aboriginal.' And we'd say, 'Yeah, well which part?' That's what we'd say among ourselves anyway.

For a while I was trying to work out in my own mind what it all meant.

'Don't worry, don't take any notice,' Mum said to me one day. Then she said what she often said: 'You're as good as anybody else.'

That was what you'd call her motto for life. I don't know where she got that from – whether it was her parents, Papa Joe and Grandma Maisie. It might have even been from Barney Warrior or Aunty Glad. Anyway, after Mum said that, I just got on with playing with the other kids.

* * *

Mum met all the ladies who lived at the Cottages, and Josie and I met all the kids. Allan got an old ute and he used to run that as a part-time taxi. The adults and the kids all went off in our own different directions each day, us kids playing and going to school, the adults to work.

We became part of the Alice Springs mob. Not far away was St Mary's Hostel, near a big hill called Mount Blatherskite. Aboriginal kids who'd been stolen from their families were taken there, but it was also for Aboriginal kids from the cattle stations and communities a long way out of Alice. They'd come in so they could go to school. We made friends with them too, and we used to climb up that hill every now and then.

Our school was in the middle of town, and us kids would walk there from the Cottages, about three miles away. Some days in the summer the bitumen was melting, then in the winter the temperature would be below zero. The walk took us twenty minutes — well, it seemed like that's all it took. You'd be doing other things as you were tripping along. You'd go off into the acacia bushes to look at something or you'd check out something somewhere else. There were lots of those things taking your mind off where you were going.

Right in the centre of Todd Street — that's the main street — were two big gum trees. They didn't want to cut them down so they put the road around them. In the town itself there were two theatres: the Capitol and the Pioneer. The Capitol didn't have a roof, but it wasn't like a drive-in — it was a normal theatre, just without a roof. They had big deckchairs you could sit in to watch the movies and some big old chairs you could go to sleep on, which a lot of the kids did. Of course when it rained, you got wet. That was fun too. The people from the town camps used to come in on picture nights, climb into the trees next to the theatre and watch from there. On movie nights they were allowed to stay later than sunset. Both white people and Aboriginal people could go into the theatre, although they used to put the traditional people right down the front. At the Capitol there were no chairs down the front – you had to sit in the sand. With the Pioneer, they had a proper floor and chairs that went right down to the front.

The Capitol had boxing nights too, and they'd put on blind man's bluff for us kids. We'd be in the ring blindfolded and lashing out. The audience had a good laugh and we did too. Everyone loved the boxing and the pictures. Later, back at the Cottages, we'd act out the characters.

One day a group of women from the Cottages and a group of us kids went for a ride in a bloke's truck, all sitting in the back. Away we went through the Gap and down the back roads. All of a sudden a goanna ran across the road and the bloke stopped the truck. Even before he'd stopped, all the women were off and running around trying to catch the goanna. It went down a hole, and they got their digging sticks and dug him out. Then they clobbered him on the head with a waddy and that was it, he was dead. They cooked him there and then on the side of the road.

First they got a campfire going with some timber that was lying around under the trees, then they gutted the goanna and when the coals were hot enough they threw him on the fire. When it was cooked they gave me a bit of the back leg and it tasted like chicken.

That was another experience I now had of different foods and tools, and the different ways people lived. I'd seen the waddies that the people made in Point Pearce with the iron bedheads, but here I was seeing a different way to make them. A waddy's basically a throwing stick, and another way you can make them is with a branch of a tree that's got a knob on the end of it. You shape it into a long stem, and that will get you a good throw.

With a woomera, one of the other tools the people use a lot, they come in different shapes, but basically it's a piece of wood that's two or three feet long and wide in the middle and narrow at the ends. Some of the ones I've seen have string and beeswax at one end, which feels all stretchy and gives you a better grip. You put the end of your spear onto the beeswax and use the string to propel it, and that gives it extra power to go faster and straighter – it's like jet propulsion. A woomera has other functions too. You can use the pointy end as a digging stick, and in some cases they're carved like a shield. Some are wide enough in the middle that you can carry food in them. If you were at the shops and you bought a bag of tomatoes or carrots you could sit it in the woomera and carry it that way. It was a pretty good invention by the old people. I was starting to see they had some clever ways of doing things.

7

'That's when I came across the boys from St Francis House'

After a while my sister Maureen came up on the train to live with us, then Winnie came up too, with her baby, Freddie. When we went to the station to meet them, Mum had a little bit of hesitation. I ran into the carriage to pick Freddie up – I was going to carry him out and hold him up like he was a prize. But his nappy was wet and I quickly handed him back to Winnie. When Mum saw Freddie, that changed everything. He captured her heart and all the old problems were forgotten. There was Winnie, Maureen, Josie and me. We were a family again.

We were all growing up. Josie wasn't very tall and she had skin about as dark as mine. She was athletic and still a mad netball player. Maureen was gentle. She had dark skin like me too, and lovely hair and rosy cheeks, and she was chunky. I remember her cleaning the house sometimes. Winnie was lighter skinned, and she wasn't that tall either. For a while

Winnie lived with us and we helped look after Freddie. We thought he was really good.

Our first Christmas in Alice was coming up and it was school holidays. That's when I came across the boys from St Francis House. St Francis House was a boys' home in Adelaide especially for Aboriginal kids from the Northern Territory. An Anglican priest called Father Percy Smith and his wife Isabel ran it, and how it came about was that Father Smith used to be in charge of the Church of England parish in Alice Springs and he got to know a lot of the mothers with young boys. Often the fathers weren't around and the mothers wanted their boys to get a good education. That was hard for Aboriginal kids to do in Alice at the time, so Father Smith had the idea to set up the home for them in Adelaide where they could go to school. The mothers were right behind it. It was different from other places at the time, where kids were often being taken without their family's permission.

When I met the St Francis boys they'd been living there for a couple of years. Five were from the Cottages – David Woodford, Malcolm Cooper, Peter Tilmouth, Bill Espie and John Palmer – so it was easy to catch up with them and become mates with them, along with the other boys who lived near us that I'd already got to know, like Laurie and Richie Bray. They came from a big family and I used to go over to their place a lot.

All us boys would go to the movies together and if there was a boxing night on we'd be there. Anything that happened, we always seemed to be together. We all had little slug guns we'd been given as Christmas presents and we'd hunt small lizards. They'd be sitting there with their necks up, and you'd put the guns nearly to their necks and shoot. Sometimes you'd miss and they'd run away. That was all part of the game. We thought we were the ant's pants doing that sort of stuff.

Christmas time was monsoon time in the Territory, and when the floods came down from the north they'd run into the Todd River and through the town and out through the Gap. We'd all go to wherever there was a waterhole and have a swim, and we'd all be naked of course. Nobody had bathers. There was one near the Ghan railway line, and when the train came past it would be moving fairly slowly by then. The people on the train would be at the windows taking photos of these black kids swimming naked in a waterhole.

One day a group of us were walking along the Todd riverbed when it was dry – like it nearly always is – and someone said they were thirsty and how we didn't have any water to drink. One of the other kids said that wasn't true, that there was water here. They call it a soakage. He said you dig into the riverbed with your hand until you get down to the wet part. That day it was about a foot down. You could feel it and then you could see the water seeping through. It filled up and up, and then we drank it. It was really clear because it had been filtered through the sand. When the area around Alice Springs floods, the water's got to go somewhere, and a lot of it goes down into the ground. Had we done that when we were in that dry creek bed near Copley it would have saved Mum worrying about the baby not having any water. There we were, sitting on it.

That was another new thing for me to learn. I didn't know it when I was in Point Pearce, and I didn't know about it when I was in Leigh Creek, but here I was learning about it in Alice Springs.

Two of the other boys from the home lived in the old police station through the Gap. They were Charlie and Ernie Perkins. They lived with their mum, Hetti, who we all called Aunty Hetti. From the Cottages you'd walk through the Gap and veer to the right, and their place was nestled in under the MacDonnell Ranges. Charlie was a bit older than me, and Ernie was about the same age. That year I didn't see Charlie much because he had a girlfriend there and all his time was spent chasing her. I spent more time with Ernie, the other St Francis kids, and Laurie and Richie.

Right alongside where Aunty Hetti, Charlie and Ernie lived, close to the face of the ranges, was a young gum tree, and Aunty Hetti said to us to never go between that tree and the rock face, because if you did you'd die. She didn't give us any reason. Us being kids, we'd be standing there saying to each other, 'Go on, do it!' 'No, you do it!' 'You've got no guts!' 'You're scared!' Not one of us ever went through.

One day we were out riding our bikes and came to one of the town camps, Mount Nancy. They'd put a driveway in and we rode on it and a little way into the camp. We found a heap of spears and nobody was around, so we grabbed them and took off. When we got to Aunty Hetti's, she told us we'd better take them back. She said we shouldn't have taken them in the first place and we could get sung through them. We'd heard about being sung – we didn't really know what it meant, but we knew it was trouble. All sorts of things turned up in our minds about what it could be. We had to get those spears back. We talked about how we'd do it and how close we'd get. It ended up that when we got to about fifty yards away, we threw them back and took off. From then on there was no way we were going to take things that didn't belong to us.

We'd all heard a few of the stories that the old people told, and some of the beliefs they wanted us to believe. When us boys got together we'd all want to have a better story than the others, so some of us made some stories up that didn't actually exist. We thought we were being traditional people and that we knew everything about how traditional people lived. Now when I look back at it, it probably was just us big-noting ourselves with each other. One would say, 'Well I know this', and another would say, 'Well I know that'. It was the same with the languages around the town. You'd know some words of some of them, but you wouldn't know a lot. Everybody thought they knew more languages than the others. We knew nothing really, of what really happens.

I did a lot of things with the boys from the home and really enjoyed their company. I was starting to think there was something different about these boys. When they left, Laurie Bray went with them too, and one day I said to Mum, 'I wouldn't mind going down with the boys that were here from St Francis.'

Mum knew the other boys' mothers and she must have talked about it with them. They all knew Father Smith, because he'd been visiting the Cottages every week for a long time. The mothers all knew Mrs Smith too because she worked hard alongside Father Smith. The mothers would talk with them about their children and how they all knew that the local school wasn't too interested in educating Aboriginal kids. I worked out later that the Smiths were ahead of their time in some ways, and then not in others.

Mum said she'd get hold of Father Smith and see what he could do. In those days it wasn't something quick you could do on a computer – you had to write a letter and go through one channel then back through another before the approval came. Anyway, Father Smith and Mrs Smith must have agreed that I could go to St Francis House too, because next thing, Mum was packing my bag.

8

'Anything with a ball, I'd be playing it'

Instead of making the two-day trip to Adelaide on the train, Mum and I went on an old DC-3 plane, which only took a few hours. I don't know why we went by plane this time, but it might have been that Mum wanted to get down and back fairly quickly because she still had Maureen, Josie and Allan to look after.

We landed at Parafield Airport and went to Aunty Pearl's place at Port Adelaide, which wasn't far from Semaphore, where the boys' home was. Father Smith had told Mum how to get to the home, and the next morning we caught a bus along Hart Street and got off at Robin Road. We walked and walked and walked, and we were wondering if we were ever going to find it, then all of a sudden on our right was a strange and lovely big house with a tower and a turret. It looked like a castle. Mum found a street sign that told us we were on Park Avenue, so we'd found it.

We walked up to the front door and knocked. Mrs Smith opened it. She was a matronly-looking woman, fairly solid, with short wavy hair, and a big, lovely face. I knew from the other boys that everybody liked her. She took us through a long passage to the back of the house, past all these rooms, right down the end to the kitchen. We followed her through the kitchen and into the dining area, where the boys were all sitting around a big table eating, eight or nine of them.

Father Smith was with them. He got up and came over and said hello to Mum and me. I remember thinking that he didn't look very well. He was a tall thin man with a long thin face and that might have been what made him look a bit frail. But he'd worked hard to get this place for us boys, so maybe that's what it was.

This is St Francis House around the time I went there. It's in Semaphore South, not far from the beach on one side and the Port River on the other. *(Courtesy of the P. McD. Smith MBE and St Francis House Collection: www.stfrancishouse.com.au)*

Mum had done me up in flash clothes, and there I was: blue cap, grey suit, tie, long socks. When she'd got it all out for me that morning I'd said to her, 'They'll all laugh at me.'

'No they won't,' she'd said. 'You'll be right.'

Of course, as soon as I walked into the dining area they all burst out laughing.

'I told you,' I said to Mum.

She didn't say anything. It was water off a duck's back. She dressed me how she wanted me to be.

I was mickeying around with the boys while she was talking to Father Smith and Mrs Smith, then all of a sudden she was gone.

Oh, gawd, I thought, *I'm being a brave boy wanting to come down here and now she's gone home and I'm all alone and how do I get on?*

The first night was of course fairly horrendous. The home had two floors, and we slept and had our things on the top floor. Each of the rooms had three beds. The two boys I shared a room with in the beginning were Laurie Bray and Peter Tilmouth.

I was lying there in a strange environment not knowing what to expect. There were a few tears.

The next day I was up with the rest of the boys, off down to the bathroom, then eating breakfast, then getting ready for school.

For the first couple of months I was Laurie and Peter's slave. Every Saturday morning we all had to make the beds and mop and polish the lino. We were meant to take a turn doing the different jobs, but I ended up doing all the mopping and polishing while they sat on their beds and looked at me.

That was them showing me that I was a new kid and that they'd been there longer and were going to call the tune.

One morning, after a few weeks of mopping the floor and doing all the other jobs, I cracked and started swinging the mop around. If they were in the road, well, they copped it.

Laurie and Peter took off out of the room. They knew I wasn't going to put up with it any longer. Now they were thinking, *This bloke, well, he's got a bit of guts.* If you put up with it then it continues – once you do something about it, the whole picture changes. Now I was one of them. From then on I only had to do my share and they did theirs.

* * *

The first school I went to from St Francis was Ethelton Primary, which had girls and boys. When it came to recess and lunchtime, the girls would be on one side of the yard and the boys on the other. We St Francis boys were the only Aboriginal kids there.

I'd heard that when St Francis was first set up, the parents at Ethelton didn't want to have us there and they'd even had a protest at the gate. Father Smith had to do a fair bit of talking to the headmaster. If it's one or two Aboriginal kids, people think that's a novelty. But when you've got seven or eight, that to everybody spells trouble. Well, that was the thinking of people at that time. Father Smith had said to us that things weren't going to be easy.

When I first started at Ethelton, they put me into Grade Six with the other eleven-year-old kids. I probably should have been in Grade Two. Like I said before, I'd never had any trouble reading, and Aunty Doris had said I was pretty good at it. But I was hopeless at English and maths, and I couldn't draw. Whether that had anything to do with my broken arm and changing over from my right hand to my left I don't know.

Laurie was in the same class at Ethelton as me. He always used to wear a double-breasted coat to school, rather than a jumper or pullover. He was big for his age, and he was like a protector to me. When I was the new boy on the block, while he did his fair share of bossing me around, at the same time he was a good mate. I'd go everywhere with him. No one would want to pick a fight or call you names when he was around.

It was at Ethelton that I came across football, and it took my attention. My thoughts back then were that I'd rather be kicking a bag of air around than doing homework. At the home we had a couple of old footballs someone had given us, and when we'd get back from school a group of us would be in the paddocks kicking them round. It was a competition and it was really hard. Everybody wanted to be better than everybody else.

Sometimes I'd go out there by myself and I'd be thinking I was somebody else, a real footballer. I'd kick and chase the ball and give my own commentary on how I'd picked it up and how I'd done a back turn. I'd be saying things like, 'Copley just broke through the pack and took a beautiful mark, goes back to kick a goal!' Or, 'Copley has moved forward and the ball has landed in his arms!'

Anything with a ball, I'd be playing it. All the boys were probably the same. We didn't have much luck with schoolwork, but we could match most of the white kids at sport and often beat them. Playing with kids bigger than you, like us younger ones did with the older boys at the home, that made you quicker too. You got to see the strengths of the different boys. Like Charlie Perkins – he was a bit older than me, and when I was first at the home he was mixing more with boys like Malcolm Cooper and Peter Tilmouth. I was the next rung down the ladder.

One day Charlie and I were at the home playing cricket, just him and me, in the old coach-house that had been turned into a gym. We were using an old bat that was splintered and broken. I bowled the ball down to him, and he went to hit it and missed. A big splinter from the bat broke off and went into his calf. It frightened me and I burst out crying. He just stood there, calm as anything, trying to get the splinter out. Next thing he'd pulled it out. My first thought was, *Oh god!* and my second was, *This boy is different.* If that had happened to me I would have been whizzing around on the ground. But not him.

After he got it out I helped him go to the dispensary, and I think it was Mrs Smith who cleaned it up for him. I'd been having different thoughts about the different kids at the home and the way they handled things, and that was the first time I'd ever seen someone be like that. Charlie didn't scream or cry or anything. It took a lot of courage to do what he did. That's when I began to feel admiration for him.

* * *

We had jobs to do at St Francis. We'd take it in turns to make the school lunches, and you'd be on for a week at a time. You'd get up at five o'clock in the morning, go to the kitchen, spread all the bread, make the sandwiches, then wrap them up. They weren't very nice to look at, or taste.

One lunchtime at school some other kids wanted to change lunches with us. They had dainty little triangle-cut sandwiches with nice fillings all wrapped in nice paper and put in a nice brown paper bag. Ours were hunks of bread cut in the middle, sometimes with just a jam filling or beetroot, wrapped up in newspaper. We were scratching our heads about the fact that those kids wanted to swap lunches.

The other early morning job we had was to chop the wood for the stove. I didn't mind doing either of the jobs. That was how it was. You were on, you were off – no good moaning about it. I used to like doing the lunches because while you were doing it you'd cook toast and put heaps of butter on it and whatever else was around, like fritz. You'd have the best feed of your life while you were cutting everybody else's terrible lunches.

When we weren't at school or doing jobs, we were probably at church, because St Francis was a Church of England boys' home. Before I got there, Christianity to me was mostly an unknown thing, apart from seeing Papa Joe go off to church on Sundays at Point Pearce, and when Josie and I went to Sunday school at Leigh Creek for a while. But when you got to the home you had to conform. Every Sunday there'd be mass at St Paul's, the Anglican church in Port Adelaide, and sometimes in the evenings we'd end up at another little church in Ethelton called St Nicholas'. So it was mass in the morning and evensong at night.

You also had to get baptised in the Church of England faith. For a godmother, some of us had an Aboriginal lady who worked at the home, and a couple of the bigger boys became godfathers. Malcolm Cooper was mine – he was only a year and a half older than me but that's how it went. It welded us together.

After you went through baptism there was confirmation, which involved the bishop coming to the church and placing his hands on your head and inviting you into the fold. Before you could get confirmed the priest read a book to us all, and then they tested you on it. Then you had to go through a rehearsal so you'd know exactly what the bishop was going to do when he confirmed you. The service lasted an hour and a half, and there was a fair bit of a lead-up to it. You had to get yourself really organised. You could become an altar boy and a choirboy too. There were four or five of us who joined the St Paul's choir. I couldn't sing but I thought it was great dressing up in a collar and cassock.

We weren't allowed to eat before we went to mass because Anglicans had to fast before communion. Sometimes we'd get a ride to the church but most times we'd walk and it was a fairly long way. I still used to faint a bit, and I'd do it every time we went to church. Down I'd go, then I'd come round, and as I got up I'd bump my head on the pew and down I'd go again. The boys would be standing there laughing because I'd keep bashing my head. In the end they'd take me outside.

For a while any of the boys who didn't want to be in church did it as a trick – they'd make out they'd fainted then get up and go outside. But actually it was half real and half unreal, because we had to wait until the service was over before we could eat. As soon as it was, we'd run round to the hall behind the church, and the ladies from the district would serve us up bacon-and-egg pies they'd made and we'd scoff them all down. Later the Church of England changed its policy so that we were allowed to have a drink of milk and a biscuit before mass. I think it might have been because of us that they changed that.

Funny things used to happen at church. Sometimes we boys had a part to play in the music. The church had a pump organ and while the organist played the keys, one of the boys would sit on the floor next to the organ and pump on the bellows to push air into it to make the sound. One day the organist started to play the organ and all that came out were all these screeching sounds. The boy who was supposed to be doing it had gone to sleep.

Another time some of us carved our initials into the pews, and the next Saturday morning we had to cover them up with putty. Usually on a Saturday morning we'd be getting ready to go to sport, but that week we had to miss it. Charlie's initials weren't there, and he was meant to go off to play soccer, but the priest made him stay back with us because everybody had to. In Charlie's mind, he wasn't being treated fairly and that wasn't right. And of course he didn't want to miss sport. Even back then he was pretty sure that if something wasn't right it was wrong.

9

'There were tests you had to go through'

When Father Smith had started St Francis two years before, he brought six boys from Alice Springs. Then different boys started turning up, one or two at a time. One of the first to come was Gordon Briscoe. He was originally from Alice too. During the war he'd been evacuated from Alice and taken to a mission in New South Wales for a while. Then he ended up at the camp at Balaklava for nearly a year with his mum. She'd heard about the boys' home and wanted him to get an education.

By the time I got there, the boys already there had their own systems set up, including how things operated with new kids coming in. One time a big group came all together. They were from a Church of England home in Mulgoa in New South Wales, the same one Gordon had been in. It was a bit different to St Francis because a lot of those kids had been taken from their families without permission. Mostly they were from across the top of the Northern Territory – places like Roper River and Borroloola – and they'd been taken during the war when the Japanese were getting close to invading. A while after the war was over Mulgoa was closed, and about ten of the boys came over to Adelaide. What we heard at the time was that they were going to come to Adelaide, stay at St Francis overnight, then continue on to the Northern Territory the next day to go back to their families if they could find them. But that didn't happen.

That night continued for the next six or seven years. Some of the Mulgoa boys were younger than me, like John Moriarty, Wilf Huddleston and Tim Campbell. Then there were some really big kids like Wally McArthur, Jim Foster, Cyril Hampton and Harry Russell. They were on the verge of finishing school and getting out to work. When they all came it changed the structure of the home and the structure of the kids. There was no funny business with bullying, because the big kids would just step in and take care of anything like that.

Jim Foster used to give everybody nicknames. Wilf Huddleston's was Boofa. First of all he was Boofhead – it came from a comic – then he was Boofa. Richie Bray had a head like a fig, so first he was Fighead then Figgy, then it turned to Fig. John Moriarty was Morey. Peter Tilmouth was Truck. Malcolm Cooper was Coop. Bill Espie was Buckshot. Mine was Cop. Charlie for some reason stayed as Charlie.

During my first year, there were tests I had to go through. One was a boxing fight with one of the boys from the first group. We were in the gym and all the boys were there, mainly on other boy's side, because I was the new kid and I had to prove myself. I only had one 'second' – that was the name for the kid who was helping you. He was rubbing me down and giving me a bit of bravado, saying things like, 'You can do this!' I was a little bit stronger than the other boy, and by the end of the first round I was beating him. It turned out that he didn't want to come out for the second round, and in the end all his seconds and supporters threw him into the ring. I looked at him and said, 'I'm not gonna fight you anymore. That's it, right?' And I walked away. From then on I became one of the main boys.

That first year it was all just fitting in and finding my feet. I was working out where I was, and I was also thinking about the Christmas holidays and going back to Alice Springs – and whether I'd come back to St Francis the next year.

At the end of my first year at St Francis, I went home with the other boys on the train. It was good to see Freddie again, and Winnie had a new baby daughter by then too. I'd be mucking around with the boys during the days, then I'd be at home with Mum, Winnie, Maureen and Josie, and I'd hear them talking about what they'd been up to.

One thing was the curfew the town council had on Aboriginal people, where if they were caught on the streets of the town after sunset or before sunrise they'd be jailed. From what I heard, the women from the Cottages became a very strong movement and they weren't going to put up with that sort of rubbish. They marched in the town and did other things like that, and eventually the council overturned it.

At the end of the holidays I could have stayed there in Alice, but I went back to St Francis, because I'd got over the bumpy part of proving myself among the group and I enjoyed going to school. I wasn't learning anything, but I played football and soccer and rugby. Those things came before anything else, and I kept thinking that this game of Australian Rules football suited me.

Charlie was the same about coming back to the home. During the holidays he was in love with a girl from Alice again. All he had to say to his mum was, 'I'm not going back.' But he never ever said that. He was the type of kid who, as bad as a situation was, he wasn't going to let anything beat him. Every time we were there ready to get on the train, he was there too. Something was driving him to stick at it.

Father Smith's idea of bringing us kids together and then letting the Alice boys go home every Christmas was great. That was a key to the home being successful. Each of us boys had a separate life, but it all revolved around helping each other, and in later life that also showed. It created something that lasted for a lifetime.

* * *

In my second year at St Francis, 1949, we hadn't been long back when Mum came to Adelaide because Maureen was sick. She had TB, the same disease my dad had, and they brought her down to the Royal Adelaide Hospital. She died in March that year when she was seventeen and I was twelve. I don't know how long she'd had it for. All I remember now is her funeral, because it was in Adelaide and we left for it from my Aunty Edie's place, the same as we'd done for Colin's five years before. Maureen was buried in the same grave as Colin.

Each year when we boys got to St Francis we'd all have to go to the Royal Adelaide Hospital to be tested for TB.

We didn't understand what it was all about. We just enjoyed having the day off from school and walking from the railway station up to the Royal Adelaide and wandering the day away.

That same year Maureen died, there was a polio outbreak at St Francis. We had to stay home from school, and Father Smith taught our lessons to us in the common room, a nice big room with glass doors that led you out onto the front lawn. One day I was standing by the doors, and another boy came into the room and shoved me. I fell against one of the doors and smashed the window.

Father Smith came in and asked who broke it. Nobody owned up. One of the boys whispered to me to own up. 'I didn't do it, the boy who pushed me did,' I whispered back. I thought he should own up. It got to the stage where nobody was going to own up so everybody was to blame. We all had to put out our hand and get the cane.

After that sort of thing happened a few times, with nobody owning up and everybody getting the cane, one of the boys decided he'd had enough. Next time something went wrong and Father Smith came and asked who'd done it, he jumped up. 'I'll own up, Father, but I didn't do it,' he said.

Of course, that made it worse. *Whack! Whack! Whack! Whack!* We all got it. And of course soon after we'd all be sitting there laughing our heads off at just how funny it was. 'Oh, Father, I'll take the blame, but I didn't do it.' The cane soon got forgotten about.

Sometimes we'd change who we were sharing a room with. My first year I'd been with Peter and Laurie and then another year I was with Ernie and Laurie. That room was at the top of the stairs, and all the boys had to go through it to get to their own rooms. They'd run through holding their noses and when we asked them why they were doing that they'd say we were the three little pigs.

One night Laurie had been vomiting and he was lying on his bed with a bucket beside it. Charlie ran through the room and into the next room to talk to one of the other boys, and he slammed the door behind him. The door jammed and when it was time to go to bed Charlie was locked in. He climbed out the window and crawled along the roof to another window – but before he got there, we put Laurie's bucket under the window, and when Charlie climbed in he put his foot into the bucket. He pulled it out and his foot was wet and the lino was slippery, and over he went and hit the ground. We could hear him saying he was gonna kill us all. We were all lying in our beds laughing our heads off.

Charlie and Ernie were in the same room for a while. Ernie was a mad motorbike man and he'd read books on motorbikes. We'd all be standing out on the lawn and somebody would go past on a motorbike and Ernie would tell you what type it was and how many cylinders it had. He'd drive everybody crazy. Ernie was designing radiators to go in motorbikes long before Velocette did it – he was far in front of his time. One night we were all in bed and Ernie was reading his books. Charlie had to get up early and he asked Ernie to switch off the light. Ernie said he would in a minute and he kept reading. Charlie asked him again to switch it off. Ernie said okay but he kept reading. It got to the stage where Charlie got his boot, threw it at the light and busted the globe. Ernie bent down to his cupboard, pulled out a candle, lit it and kept reading.

* * *

All of us boys were in competition with each other. There'd be twenty kids all fighting to win. If you were running, it was who could run the fastest? If you were riding a bike, who could ride the fastest? You had to try and be first – that was the name of the game. Every time we all went out to play sport it was a competition. We made up rules that pushed it all harder too – for instance, with cricket. We had a wicket at the back of the home and cricket balls and an old cricket bat. The rule for that was that you couldn't block the ball – you had to swing at it as hard as you could every time, however fast it was coming. If you didn't then the bowler wouldn't bowl the next ball at you, they'd throw it and it would come twice as fast. If you missed, you were out.

If it was a soccer ball or a football, we'd get out on the paddock and kick it around, and it would be a mad competition between the lot of us. Being fast was probably one of my advantages. You had to be a little bit quicker, otherwise the other kids would get you. It made your eye better, and it made your reflexes better. Later in life all of those things came together.

While we were all competing hard to beat each other, if ever anything went pear-shaped, like bullying from other kids or being called names, we all welded together. That was just a great feeling. These kids were my best mates and my family. We'd do things together and go everywhere together. There were fights among us, but we'd get that out of the road and move on. We just looked after each other and we'd do things for each other, like the time Charlie got me to be his chaperone.

Charlie had a new girl he was seeing, and she lived at Taperoo, a bit of distance from the home. He was going to meet up with her somewhere near where she lived and walk her home. He said I'd better come too. I knew her brother pretty well, so I think Charlie thought I'd have an 'in' with her and I'd support him if any romance started to happen. We were walking down Victoria Road: he was twenty yards in front with this girl, and her brother and I were walking behind. When we got to her place, nothing had happened. He just said goodbye. On the way back to the home I said to him, 'What did you want me for? You didn't even kiss her. You made me come all this way for nothing!' We argued all the way back to the home.

I don't know whether in bigger schools and homes, nasty sorts of things happened. But at St Francis they didn't, at least not in the early years when we were there. All the boys had that same feeling about each other. It started at the home and it stayed all our lives.

10

'Sport was all I could think of'

Two years after I started at St Francis House, Father Smith had to take off. I remember him being there and the next thing he was gone. As far as we knew he'd done a good job. Back at the start we didn't really know what a priest's role was apart from wearing that long black gown at church and bobbing around up the front of the altar. But we found out that Father Smith, and Mrs Smith too, did all sorts of things, like helping us boys with homework and getting us gear to play sport in and keeping the home running by raising money.

After Father Smith left, Father Taylor became boss at St Francis. We called him Squizzy, after the Australian gangster Squizzy Taylor. We'd worked out Squizzy was a bit of a drinker because when we'd creep down the fire escape at night past the office, he'd be in there drinking the wine.

Mrs Taylor was trouble. We'd all be in the showers and she'd come straight in. 'Don't be worried about me,' she'd say as everyone would be screaming and hiding.

'*Well we* are *worried about you,*' we'd think. There were some hairy-legged kids there too, the older ones like Wally and Jim. They didn't want a woman walking around the wrong place. She was a peeping Tom, I suppose. She shouldn't have been in the boys' bathroom. That wasn't her job.

Laurie became known among us boys for his painting talent as well as for the double-breasted coat he always wore. Every morning before we went to school we had to line up along the passage, and either Father Taylor or his wife would inspect us to see if our clothes were right and we had our ties on. One morning we were all lined up and Mrs Taylor was inspecting us. First of all she looked at our shoes to see if they were clean. Then she looked at our knees to see if we'd had a wash. Then she looked to see if we had our ties on. Laurie hated wearing ties, and this day he'd got a piece of white paper and painted a tie on it, then stuck it on his shirt.

When Mrs Taylor got to him she said, 'Oh, Laurie, what a lovely tie.' She went to touch it and he took off down the passage laughing his head off. We all burst out laughing and ran out of the house.

It became a big joke. 'What a lovely tie you've got!'

I don't think the Taylors were there for very long. After them the boss was Wicky Wilson. We used to call his wife Turtle. Wicky wasn't a priest: he was a layman. He could be a preacher and he could hold evensong, but he couldn't give you communion. With Wicky, we seemed to have more evensong and other religious things than we did with Father Smith.

Then there was Gough Sherman, who we called Goughy. During the war he'd been an army minister in New Guinea, and he filled in at the home for a while. He did everything regimentally. We'd all be lined up ready to be inspected so we could get to school, and he'd take his time having his breakfast – you couldn't rush him. He wasn't very popular with us. He'd go swimming at the beach and you'd see him right out in the deep. Of course we were all praying there might be a shark around.

Sometimes the bosses whacked us if we played up. Father Smith had a cane and he'd give you a whack across the hands. Squizzy had a piece of rubber hose he belted you with. Wicky had a broomstick. Goughy didn't have anything to belt us with because after he'd served in New Guinea he thought he knew all about physical combat. One time he grabbed one boy's arms and said it was a jiujitsu lock. The boy just pulled his arm out of Goughy's hold, and we all thought how stupid it was. If Goughy had done that in New Guinea he would have got himself killed.

* * *

When I was thirteen I started high school at Le Fevre Boys Technical School. The headmaster there, Mr Vickery, had been really good right from the beginning. Back when the boys had first started going there, he stood up at assembly and said he wouldn't take any funny business from anyone who wanted to make rude or racist remarks about these St Francis House kids. If anyone did, he said, he'd lock them in the gym with us and let us sort it out. I think there were only one or two occasions when there was a fight between one of the boys and somebody else. Mr Vickery was a lovely man, and I think he had the respect of a lot of the teachers around the traps at that time.

I never wanted to miss school. I used to go all the time — well nearly anyway. But for me, school was about meeting up with your mates and playing sport. When I'd get home from school I'd throw my bag in my room and go out to the paddock and kick a ball around. Come the next morning I'd be rushing around trying to put together something the teachers would consider was homework, but they'd look at it and say it was rubbish.

Some of the boys did all right at schoolwork. For a few years Charlie won a prize at St Francis for getting the best marks at school, and later on John Moriarty won it a few times too. As far as I know none of the rest of us did that well at schoolwork, not the boys who were there when I was, anyway. More and more we were playing organised sports, and we were working out that that's where we could match the other kids and even beat them some of the time. On Friday afternoons we'd play Australian Rules football for the school, on Saturday mornings we'd play soccer for the school, and on Saturday afternoons some of the Mulgoa boys would play rugby league — Wally, Jim, Harry and Cyril had made a hit with the local league team because they were really good players. Later, when Malcolm Cooper left the home to work at a factory, he was in an Australian Rules football team the company had. They played on Sundays and we'd go and watch, and if they were short we'd get a game there too. That was our weekends.

Sport was all I could think of. In school classes I should have been listening to what the teacher was saying about Christopher Columbus or James Cook, and what we had to do for homework, but it never interested me. I'd be looking out of the window, thinking about how I could pick the

The Le Fevre Boys Technical School A-grade team when I was fifteen. I'm sitting in the second row, second from the right. *(Courtesy of the P. McD. Smith MBE and St Francis House Collection: www.stfrancishouse.com.au)*

ball up quick before anybody got close enough to tackle me. Then I'd be daydreaming: *I'm in front of the goals and there's not enough room to pick it up but I'll just flick it up to a certain height and swing my foot through and kick it into goal.* Then I'd be thinking, *I'm going to try that out in the paddock after school.* I'd say to myself, *Right, I'll get home quick and throw my books in the room and get my footy boots on and grab the ball and get out in the paddock and don't worry about those other things.* Sometimes what I tried worked and sometimes it didn't. At least I'd invented it, which made it more rewarding I suppose – that I could think of those things for myself and then do them. I'd be out there until dark, then come in and have tea.

Why couldn't I think about algebra or geometry like that? All I learned about geometry was the size of a football and how you can make it spin and how you can't. The dream was that I was going to be a professional footballer and I was going to get paid to do something I loved.

Charlie, John and Gordon took soccer as their game, although they kept on with other sports too. Charlie had started out playing Australian Rules in the school team and he'd had a go with Port Adelaide. Then a local soccer team called Port Thistle started up and they used one of our paddocks for practice. Charlie started playing for them, and he found a difference in the crowd that went along to the games. No one was calling out 'coon' or the n-word to him. The other players and their fans were mostly Scottish or English and they just appreciated his talent.

John was a good athlete too and he played for Port Thistle as well, and so did Gordon and Ernie and Gerry Hill, another one of the Mulgoa boys. When John was a bit older he and Charlie both played soccer in some of the big teams around Adelaide.

Wilf Huddleston was the same age as John and he was a good sportsman too, so that fitted the bill for us. He ended up having Australian Rules as his game. Everybody got on with Wilf – he was one of those blokes you meet who's just easy to talk to, always smiling and laughing and joking around.

Bill Espie was another one who was good at sport, good enough that he was invited to take part in a tennis clinic run by Ken Rosewall and Lew Hoad, the doubles champions in the world at that time.

We'd all go and watch each other play. That's how it was with us kids.

* * *

I was starting to hear more and more about the Port Adelaide Football Club. People at church would talk about them and I became wrapped up in it. There was a group of really good footballers in the Port Adelaide league side at the time and I was starting to imagine being at that level. When I was out in the paddock I wasn't being just one player: I was a whole lot of different ones, depending on if I was marking or kicking or handballing.

Sometimes, the Port Adelaide Football Club would send a couple of their coaches and top players to the school for what we called 'pasty night'. They'd bring a whole heap of pasties and Coke, and talk about the game and how to play it and what to do in different positions. They'd ask us if we thought we were able to be a hard player and get up if we got knocked over. The players were all tough men. I was a skinny kid and I didn't have a great physique at all, so I had to have a little bit of extra skill to be able to play without getting hurt. Some of the other players in my team at school thought I was going to be too light, so they'd try me out to see if I could take a bump. I soon seemed to be able to weave my body around and past them.

When I was in second year at Le Fevre, I was one of a group of boys invited to try out for the state schoolboys' team to play in Melbourne in the national carnival. Mr Vickery, the headmaster, was our coach and every Saturday morning we had to be at the Railways Oval in the city for practice. It was difficult for me to get there, because on Saturday mornings at the home we had jobs to do, and by the time I did that and caught a bus into the city, it would be too late. When I told Mr Vickery he said he'd pick me up and take me.

When the state team was selected, six of us boys from Le Fevre were chosen, and no one was more pleased than Mr Vickery that I was one of them. I couldn't repay him for everything by being a brainy person because I wasn't, but I could repay him every time I went on the football field. I'd be playing to win for him. I think he knew that.

Being an Aboriginal person, I had to get permission from the Aborigines Protection Board to travel interstate. They needed to see my birth certificate, but they couldn't find anything in the archives under the name of Vincent Copley, so everybody was wondering who the heck I was. The school and the education department people got all het up about it, and I was wondering if they were going to stop me from going. Finally they rushed into the Registry of Births, Deaths and Marriages and made a new birth certificate out for me under the name of Copley.

The day came when we were going to catch the overnight train to Melbourne. My school had played a game at Alberton that afternoon, and one of the other boys who was also going to Melbourne said to come home with him and then we could jump on the bus and go into the station together. So that's what I did. I thought Wicky the manager would be able to take my case to the station, but when I rang him he went off his head and said I was supposed to come home and get it myself. He said he wouldn't be bringing my clothes in. At the station I watched everybody putting their suitcases on the train and I just got on and thought I'd just have to work out what to do when I got to Melbourne. The train took off. When we got to Belair in the Adelaide Hills, the train stopped – and there was Wicky with my suitcase.

We ended up being over in Melbourne for eighteen days. We were billeted with families there and played footy at different grounds, like St Kilda and Footscray. There was no homework, just football, and I saw that all these kids from other states were as interested as I was, and playing as hard. This was all fitting in with my dream of being a professional footballer one day, so I kept dreaming.

11

'A different sort of family'

A lot of the local sport groups around Adelaide liked having us boys in their teams because we made a big difference. But the crunch for us would come after the matches. We didn't have our mums or dads there, of course, and nobody ever came up to you and put their arm around you and said, 'Good game, son.' With some games, if your mate who happened to be a white kid had done something good, he'd come off the ground and his mum and dad would be there and they'd put their arm across his shoulder and they'd be saying, 'It's a special meal tonight. You played a good game so we're going out for tea.' And you'd be scratching your head sometimes because he might have been pretty useless that day.

Some Saturdays if it looked like you couldn't get to the match, some of the team's supporters would go out of their way to pick you up in their car and take you. They'd get you there, but you had to get your own way home. Nobody ever invited you to dinner or anything like that.

It all came back to us boys being there for each other. One way we'd show our appreciation of each other, in a strange sort of way, was by saying stupid things to each other that other people didn't understand. Like when two of the older boys had been picked to play for Port Adelaide. Before they'd go out to play we'd shout to them, 'Don't walk on cement!' Everybody else would be saying, 'What are you talking about?' To us it meant, 'Don't get hurt' – it was our way of saying to each other, 'We all appreciate you and what you're doing.' It was similar to a hug, or similar to someone else saying, 'You played a good game', or, 'Good goal'. To us it had that meaning. Once you understood it, you knew you were getting praised.

When we were playing, if some of the spectators were giving us a hard time, saying words like 'boongs' and the n-word and telling us to go back to where we came from, we'd turn it into a joke. If someone yelled out to one of us to 'get back in your tree', days later we'd be walking along the road to school and one of the boys would say, 'Where's your tree?' and another one would say, 'What tree?' and the first one would say, 'That tree you're supposed to be in.' That was our way of overcoming that sort of racism. We were able to get on with our lives mainly because we were all together.

To us kids, in a sense it was the beginning of a different sort of family. Where do you go when you want to talk to somebody about something – something that's not worrying you but it's on your mind? You can't go to the manager of the home, you can't go to the priest. So you go to your mate and you talk it out with him. Then it would get around to the group that you've got this thing on your mind, and all of a sudden there'd be their little ways of wanting to help you. When we said to the blokes who were about to play football, 'Don't walk on cement', people didn't have a clue what we were talking about, but we knew. That's how we would manage to pass on our feelings to each other and overcome problems. We all knew and understood exactly what we were talking about.

* * *

If we weren't playing sport on Saturday mornings we'd go to the Black Diamond corner in Port Adelaide. It was the local shopping area, and a lot of people would be there. We'd stand on the corner, seven or eight of us, and we'd make jokes and do things like change the names of buildings to our own versions. Everybody would give us a wide berth, which was funny to us. Here we were just standing there doing nothing and laughing our heads off. They seemed to be frightened to come near us.

On Saturday afternoons we'd go to the pictures at the Odeon Theatre. Before he left, Father Smith had talked with the owner about letting us in cheap because we'd only get a little bit of pocket money. We'd have a shilling to spend, and it was sixpence to get in and we'd have sixpence to buy an ice-cream or lollies. As soon as I finished playing footy I'd be there.

That's where all the girls were on Saturday afternoons. They'd never want to be seen with you outside, but they'd meet you inside once the film started and the lights were off. At the beginning of the film all the boys from St Francis would be sitting together in a couple of rows, and as soon as the lights went out they'd all disappear. Next minute – *Doop! Doop! Doop!* – they'd pop up again alongside a girl. You weren't with the same girl every week: that was the code – you had to have a change and spread yourself around. The girls didn't want the same bloke all the time either. As you got a bit older you started to spend a bit more time with one girl.

After the movie, we boys would be walking home, and there'd be stories about who you ended up with and what you did. One day when we were all walking home after an action film, Gordon was dancing around sword-fighting and the rest of us were dodging him.

'You know that girl I was with?' I said.

'Yeess,' they all said.

'I got there late from footy and it took me all the first half just to put my arm around her. The second half I did the same, and I didn't know whether to kiss her or not.'

'Yeess, and then what happened?' one of the boys asked.

'I made up my mind at the last minute that I was going to try and kiss her.'

'Yeess, and what happened?' another one asked.

'I turned around and she turned around too and I kissed her on the nose.'

'So you kissed her on the nose, right. What happened then?'

'I was out of there as quick as I could. I didn't want her to see how embarrassed I was.' On the way home all these stories would come out.

There was a playground down in the sandhills in front of the beach, and on the weekends we'd be down there playing when all of a sudden the girls who were attracted to the boys at that time would just bob up. You'd take off with your girl and the others would do the same. We'd do normal little things. Have a bit of a cuddle and a bit of a kiss every now and again, once you'd got game enough to do those things. It never went any further than that.

With the upper-class girls, of course their mums didn't want you anywhere near their daughters. The girls would be in the theatre and they'd all want to be with us, and yet they couldn't be seen publicly with these black kids. It was strange, but it didn't worry us. We just had a good laugh.

The other kids, the lower social class people – the poor people, or whatever people call them – they didn't worry about us being black. We were mates with them and played sport with them, and they'd invite us to their birthday parties and their mums and dads would provide a good lunch. I remember one lady, Mrs McGee, who was the washerwoman at the boys' home. She had three or four boys, and we'd go to their place for their birthdays. The boards on the floor were all broken, and the family were really poor, yet she managed to cook lovely little cakes for everyone.

Guy Fawkes Day was always really good at the home because we had the tower on the corner of the main building and we could go up and watch the fireworks. One year I got talking with a girl who lived near us in the temporary migrant homes that had gone up after the war. We were sitting on the fence out the front of the home when I asked her if she wanted to have a look at the fireworks. She did, so I snuck her around the back of the home and in through the passageway and up the tower.

You could see all the bonfires around Adelaide. She really enjoyed it, and I enjoyed it too. I thought I'd see if we could have a cuddle, but she wasn't interested. Then next minute I heard somebody coming up the stairs. I grabbed her and pushed her into a little alcove.

It was Mal Bald, one of the assistants at the home. He said it was time to come down. I said I'd be there in a minute.

'No, now!' he said. 'Time to get down!'

I walked out and he locked the door and said for me to go first.

When I was halfway down the stairs I had visions of the girl being a skeleton later on if I left her there. 'Listen,' I said, 'there's a girl up there.'

'I thought so,' Mal said.

We went back up and he unlocked the door, and I told the girl she better come out. I was sheepish and she was sheepish, and when we got down to the bottom she raced back to her house.

Mal told me to go and find the other boys and tell them that Wicky wanted to have a talk with us all. So I went out in the paddocks and nearly stepped on one of the kids who was lying on the grass with a girl. 'Listen,' I said, 'get up and get inside, the boss wants to talk to us.'

A bit further away I could hear voices but couldn't see anybody. I yelled out, 'Where are you?' and a boy said, 'Up here!' I turned around and there he was with a girl up in the bough of a tree. 'Get down,' I said, 'you've got to get inside.'

Next thing we were all in the office with Wicky. He decided he was going to tell us all about the facts of life and what we should do and what we shouldn't do. What he said was pretty crude, and we were all shocked. He came out with the f-word. That was his opening line: 'You've all heard of the good old word ...' and then he said it. We looked at each other and nearly started laughing. Then it went on from there. He was fairly tongue-tied as he tried to explain it all.

As we all walked out after, one of the boys said, 'He got it wrong.'

'What do you mean?' someone said.

'Well, you don't do that, and you don't do this.'

'How do you know?' we all asked.

And it went on from there, all sorts of weird jokes and wonderful things. Most of us thought Wicky hadn't got it right, but nobody had ever told us about all that.

That's the way it was with us boys. Between us we'd eventually work things out, one way or another.

12

'You can have
the day off school'

Around 1950, Mum and Allan had moved back down from Alice Springs to live in South Australia, and Winnie must have moved back around that time too. She'd teamed up with a bloke she met in Alice Springs called David Branson, and they were living with their kids at Pine Point, a small port on the Yorke Peninsula on the opposite side from Point Pearce. David was working on different farms around the place, and Winnie was looking after the workers who came at harvest time. Over Christmas there'd be four or five men from Point Pearce there. I'd come and stay in the holidays, and there'd be about nine of us in the house. Mum's oldest brother, my uncle Cliff Edwards, lived in Pine Point too, a bit further up the road. He was a shearer and a labourer around the district, and we'd see a lot of him.

The old house was made up of two houses joined together. The rooms were fairly big and there were beds everywhere.

A local bloke called Ron Harvey, who had a farm at Pine Point, owned the house. His brother Clive ran the wheat and barley stacks at the port and hired the workers from Point Pearce. The Harveys owned the local shop too, and the Point Pearce people would go there and get cool drinks and ice-creams and book them up, then the boss would deduct what they owed from their pay. People ended up with not much money after working long hours.

Josie had moved from Alice Springs back to South Australia by then too. She worked for a while at the Franklin Hotel in Adelaide as a domestic, with about six or seven young ladies from Point Pearce who were all being employed as cleaners in hotels around the city at the time. Then for a while she worked for the Methodist Ladies College – whether she was a cleaner there I'm not sure. Sometimes she'd go over to Winnie's at Pine Point and work as a farmhand. Now and then she'd come down to the boys' home to see me, and when she had a little bit of money she'd give me some, so that was good. I think at the time she was sweet on David Woodward, one of the boys.

When Mum and Allan first came back they stayed with Winnie for a while, then Allan got a job working for a farmer at a place called Sandilands, not far inland from Pine Point, and they moved to the farm. In the school holidays I'd spend a bit of time at Winnie's and see Mum and Allan at Sandilands. I'd do odd jobs around the place, and sometimes we'd all go to the pictures at Ardrossan, north of Pine Point.

Mum used to come to Adelaide to see different people, and she'd stay at Aunty Pearl's in Port Adelaide, then she'd come and visit me at the home. One time she took me out of school for the day because she wanted me to do something with her. We caught the bus into the Adelaide railway station then jumped on the train to Moonta, which is a small town on the western side of Yorke Peninsula, a bit south of Wallaroo.

When we got there we walked three or four miles from the railway station, and I remember Mum was walking as good as anything. We got to a house, and Mum said she was going in. She told me to wait outside and that when she was finished we'd catch the train back. It seemed strange to me, going all that way up there and being left out in the street playing for a few hours. I don't remember seeing anyone else. I was running around the trees, and there was a playground. The old Moonta copper mines were out that way too, so there was plenty to see. I just amused myself.

When Mum came out she was really wobbly on her legs. It was a fair walk back to the Moonta railway station, and I was walking alongside her and she had her arm around me and she was leaning on me the whole way. When we got to the station she was tuckered out, and she sat down and had a bit of a spell.

On the train going back she was in pain, then when we got to the Adelaide railway station we had to catch a bus down to Port Adelaide. She got off near St Paul's church and went to Aunty Pearl's, and I stayed on the bus and went further on to the boys' home. I wasn't quite sure what was happening and she didn't say anything, and that was that.

Once I was back at the home I guess I got caught up in whatever was going on and I didn't give it much more thought, until sometime later.

* * *

During the summer holidays in January 1952, I'd just turned fifteen and I got a job working with Winnie's husband on the barley stacks, branding the bags as they went up the elevator to be stacked. One day at lunchtime we stopped for a feed, and suddenly I felt crook.

I went home to Winnie and told her I wasn't feeling too good. She told me to lie down for a while, but then I started to sweat and shake. Winnie raced up the hill to Uncle Cliff's place, and he filled up his old buckboard car with petrol and drove Winnie and me to the hospital in Ardrossan.

Because I was Aboriginal, they wouldn't take me, so we went across to Maitland, but they wouldn't take me either. So we headed for the government hospital at Wallaroo. When we got there, they came outside to the car and saw me in the back and didn't hesitate. They shoved me on a trolley and took me straight into the operating room and took my appendix out. I remember Mum came to see me there one day – she probably got Uncle Cliff to run her up in his car.

Later they told me that if my appendix had burst, I would have been history. At the time I just thought, *Well, at least they got it*. I didn't have any feeling of animosity against Ardrossan or Maitland. When you're fifteen years old you're really not thinking of blaming anybody, you're just sick and you're thinking you're lucky to get to a hospital.

It took me a while to think about what could have happened. Had we got a puncture or run out of petrol, well, you wouldn't be reading this story now. That sank in later, and my feeling towards those towns became a question of how could they let people die just because of the colour of their skin?

A little while later, when I was back at St Francis, Mum was ill again. She came down to Adelaide for some sort of treatment at the Royal Adelaide Hospital. For a little while she stayed in the boys' home because she had nowhere else to go. Wicky was in charge at the time and he made a room upstairs available for her. That was good because I could go up every day and see her. Then it got so bad that she had to go back into hospital and stay there. I'd visit her on Sundays, and I remember the ward she was in was an old wooden one.

On the long weekend in June I was staying with a schoolmate called Ronnie Frost and his family at Ferryden Park, and it was the first Sunday I'd missed going to see Mum. I was back at school on the Tuesday, and sometime during the day Mr Vickery found me and told me I better go home. 'You've got some news,' he said.

When I got home, Wicky Wilson was there. 'Your mother's dead, and you can have the day off school,' was all he said. And that was it. Which was fairly cruel.

It was the tenth of June 1952. I was fifteen and in the middle of my third year at high school. Mum was forty-four.

Everybody else was at school, and I was walking around the home all day feeling all odds and sods. Because the last time I'd seen Mum at the hospital I'd spent a bit of time with her, and I'd thought she was getting better.

When I went to school the next day, Mr Vickery was a lot more sympathetic than Wicky. He took me into his office and let me do messages for him all round Port Adelaide, rather than any schoolwork. That used to be his way of punishing me when I didn't do any homework: my class teacher would send me up to the office to get the cane, but Mr Vickery wouldn't give me the cane – he'd give me jobs instead. So I'd spend a pleasant day running around Port Adelaide doing little things for him. That was Mr Vickery.

The next day, two days after Mum died, we all gathered at Aunty Edie's place at Edwardstown. People changed into their good clothes and then some cars turned up. One of them was a black shiny car, with strange seats in it, that I went in with some of the others. We drove up to South Road to a funeral parlour, Partington's, and from there we went to the West Terrace Cemetery. Mum was buried in the same grave as Colin and Maureen. I'd had some grief when my brother and sister had died, but not as bad as this feeling when Mum died.

All I heard my relatives say was that the doctors couldn't stop the bleeding. I picked that up when people were talking to Allan. I don't know where I heard it, whether it was at Aunty Edie's or at the funeral or the cemetery. I picked up different things from people talking, and I was trying to put the pieces together, although I still can't place it all even now.

Winnie and Josie must have been at the funeral, and Aunty Pearl and Aunty Glad. Aunty Doris and Uncle Cecil Graham would have been there, and they took over looking after me a bit after Mum died. Papa Joe must have been at the funeral too, but I can't remember if I spoke to him there.

I'm surmising here now, but I think at that stage Mum wasn't really happy with Allan. She never said if she was pregnant or not, but I know she didn't want to be. What made me think she wasn't really happy with Allan was that if things were all right he would have gone with her to Moonta rather than me. Anyway, everything like that was hush-hush between adults. It was none of my business.

All these years later, I've pieced together what I can about what happened to Mum. Not long ago I found her death certificate, and it said she died of cancer of the cervix, which may or may not have been true. Josie told me one time that Mum had started haemorrhaging one day when she was at Pine Point, and Josie and Allan took her to the Wallaroo hospital. That could have been because of cancer or it could have been an abortion that went wrong. That's my thinking now. I might be well off the line.

13

'Everything pointed to us being tradesmen'

A few months after Mum died I won a medal for being the best schoolboy footballer in the technical schools in Adelaide. But it was all looking like it was time for me to finish up with school.

I said to Mr Vickery that I thought I was probably better off going to work. By this time I didn't have my mum or my dad. Colin and Maureen were gone, and Winnie and Josie were older than me and busy with their own lives. Aunty Doris and Uncle Cecil were looking out for me, but they were busy with their own big family too. As far as having anyone to point you to where you might go, it came from watching the other boys and what they did, and listening to the managers at the home.

In my early days at the home, some of the older boys were finishing up at high school and had to get themselves jobs. Father Smith mainly left it to them to find their own trade, and they could stay at the home for a while but then they had to find accommodation. I think the apprenticeship wage at that time was around three pounds ten shillings. You had to pay something like eighteen shillings per week for your accommodation, four bob to go on the bus to trade school twice a week, and then you had to eat. It was pretty tight. Again it was that situation of not having your own parents around and your own home where they could carry you for a while. The only family we had was us. That was probably a real battle for us all.

To their credit, those kids did a great job, because most of them got their own job and a trade. Once they left the home, though, they struck all the worst flophouses – that's what people called the boarding homes. They were like a normal house with a big yard, and the owner would put up little units in the yard and take in a few boarders. You'd be fed and your room tidied up and you did your own washing. We'd hear about them through word of mouth. They were the only places the boys could afford. When one boy went there then some of the others would end up there too. I was watching it all as a younger boy, and as I grew older I knew I'd have to become a part of it.

Peter Tilmouth had been in the first group of boys to come to the home, and he'd been one of the first to get a job. He'd applied for one in the city as a technician-in-training at the Electricity Trust, and he got it. On his first day he headed off to work with his tie done up like a real public servant. Then a couple of weeks later it was his first payday. We were all sitting in the dining room, and he walked in and he had a newspaper tucked under his arm – that was his sign to us that he was a working man. In the coin pocket of his trousers he had the tips of a five-pound note and a ten-pound note showing. He was showing us, in a way that he didn't want to show that he was showing us, that he'd been paid and he had money. When he sat down to eat, his dinner was already on the table, and he took a mouthful and he pushed the plate away and said, 'A working man can't come home to a hot tea that's cold.' Well, as soon as he said that, his tea was gone. The rest of us kids raced over and ate it.

For St Francis boys, everything pointed to us being tradesmen. No one ever said, 'Listen, why don't you work in a men's clothing store, or why don't you go to university, or why don't you go to college?' They told us to be a mechanic or an electrician or a fitter and turner. What they were saying to us was that this was all we could do.

I lined up a job as an apprentice boilermaker at the Harbors Board in Port Adelaide, and that was school over for me. I started at the beginning of 1953, and Ernie started there too as an apprentice blacksmith. We were both still living at the home, because they were still letting us do that until we got enough money to pay for our own accommodation outside. They wanted to make sure we were right, which was really good.

One of the older blokes at the Harbors Board was playing in the top side of the Port Adelaide Football Club. He was a boilermaker and he was showing me the ropes. We'd sit and talk about football. Everything revolved around football.

By then Malcolm Cooper was playing for Port Adelaide in the under 19s team, and he arranged for me to play in the under 17s. One day when I was playing in a match, a bloke from the club came down to the ground to watch. He was the coach of the under 19s, and after the game he came up to me. 'You're coming up here with me,' he said.

That's how I ended up with the older boys in the under 19s. They played me in positions where you needed that little bit of speed.

Every time the team played at the home oval at Alberton, Mr Vickery would come along. He'd sit with a group of his friends, and they'd take up a collection of money and give it to me at the end of the game. Sometimes I got five pounds, sometimes ten. They just enjoyed watching me. Here I was, a professional already, getting all this money.

I had a good year in the 1953 footy season. I won the H.W. Tomkins Memorial Medal for what they called the fairest and most brilliant player for the under 19s. I was still only sixteen. The day the medal count was on, all us boys at the home were in the common room listening to the radio through the loudspeaker. There were about twenty of us sitting on chairs and the floor and standing around under the speaker. When my name was called out as the winner, the boys broke out in a big cheer, and there were lots of hugs. Then the jokes came about what I should say at the presentation – silly things. They were all happy. That was a big lift to me, with not having Mum and the rest of my family around. The boys were my family, and they were really happy because of what I'd done.

I was disappointed that I wasn't able to show my mum the medal. At the next match after I won it, before the game started, the two teams were lined up either side as I ran out and onto the oval, and everyone was clapping. But as I ran I was thinking, *You're all alone. Right. The real mob you wanted to come and see you play just aren't here.* I was probably eighty per cent there and the other twenty per cent was just missing.

But life has got to go on. You're in a team and you do the best you can. That then becomes a reality. Later on I'd often think about what would have happened if I'd had my mum and my dad there.

* * *

Papa Joe had died too, a year after Mum did, when he was seventy-seven. Grandma Maisie had died a few years before. The last time I ever saw Papa Joe was one day in the city. I was coming out of trade school and on my way to the bus stop on the corner of Hindley and King William streets to head back to the Harbors Board, and I ran into him. We had a little bit of a yarn, and he told me he'd left Point Pearce and was living in a shed at the home of one of the old superintendents from the mission. Then my bus came and I had to go.

I wish I'd known more back then about why he was there. I found out later that the government wouldn't pay pensions to any of the old people who were living at Point Pearce. The only way they could get it was to leave. Mr Castine — he was the old superintendent — let Papa Joe stay at his place in exchange for doing some gardening. Papa Joe used to have his meals with the family, so he must have been looked after all right.

When Papa Joe passed away, nobody let me know. I think about that now, about why people didn't let me know. Whether they didn't know where I was, I don't know. Maybe it was because I'd left Point Pearce when I was young and we'd lost touch with some of my relatives. Although Aunty Doris knew where I was and Papa Joe was her dad, so I'm not sure.

14

'He's gone over the water'

More of the boys were working and getting their trades. Some had moved out of the home and were finding out it was hard to get a place to live when you're Aboriginal. They were also finding out they were getting paid less than the white blokes. Sport was what you could call a haven for a lot of us. We were recognised for our talent and some of the boys were seeing that they could earn a bit of money from it.

Charlie had started an apprenticeship as a fitter and turner at British Tube Mills on Churchill Road. To begin with he caught the bus to work, then he rode a bicycle. It was a long way, in all sorts of weather. He was getting more and more known for his soccer and he'd left Port Thistle and was playing for a club called International United, then in the summer he was playing cricket.

John was playing soccer for Port Thistle and Gordon was too. They were still going to school and so was Wilf. Malcolm was playing in the league team for Port Adelaide – he was their first Aboriginal player at senior level. He was still working at the chemicals factory, and he'd recently married Aileen Brumby. They had their own place not far from the home, and we boys would often meet up there. Aileen had been the cook and cleaner at the home for a long time, which is how Malcolm met her. She was like a big sister to me and a lot of the other boys.

Aileen was a Colebrook girl. There were Colebrook boys too. Colebrook was a place run by the mission people for children of Aboriginal mothers and white fathers that the welfare people had taken away. It started out in Oodnadatta in far north South Australia, then they shifted it south to Quorn, in the Flinders Ranges. Then they moved it to the Adelaide Hills in 1944 when the Quorn place closed. When Mulgoa had closed, some of the Mulgoa girls went to Colebrook the same time as the Mulgoa boys came to St Francis House. The Colebrook girls used to come and visit us at the home every few weeks, and there was a lot of social mixing between the two homes.

As we all got older, we'd be talking about what was happening with the government policies. One of those policies was an amendment to the South Australian *Summary Offences Act* that affected us boys and other Aboriginal people. One of the rules in it was about who you could 'consort' with. That was their legal word for who you could be friends with and muck around with. It was about more than that, of course. Different sorts of people couldn't consort together unless they had what the police said was a reasonable excuse. The amendment listed two new groups that couldn't consort: Aboriginal and non-Aboriginal people. That meant it was possible that if I was walking down the street with one of my white friends from Le Fevre or the Harbors Board, the police could arrest us and put us in jail. Or if one of the boys was out with their white girlfriend, now the police could come up to them and say they weren't allowed to be out together and to go home. Not many people knew what the government was doing, but we were living it.

The Aborigines Advancement League, the group my Aunty Glad had been involved with, decided to organise a big meeting at Adelaide Town Hall to protest about this new rule and all the other bad conditions Aboriginal people had to put up with. Peter Tilmouth became a bit famous for being one of five Aboriginal speakers at the meeting. On the night, he talked about things like not having proper citizenship and being treated badly when it came to housing. The newspaper reports the next day said there'd been a big crowd and it had been a great success.

Peter speaking at that meeting had an effect on a lot of the boys from the home and made us see that we could be part of changing things too. We were seeing that you could speak up about the way we were being treated and people were prepared to listen. That was good.

* * *

I was following all of this with the other boys, in between work and football. By 1954, I was a rising star with Port Adelaide. They took me out of the under 19s and let me play some trial games of the A and B grade players mixed in together. I played really well and was hoping to make the A grade, where I could earn a bit of money playing. If that couldn't happen, I wanted to go back to the under 19s and keep playing well there.

When the crunch came, I didn't make the A grade and I didn't go back to the under 19s. I was in the B grade. I didn't want to be there because that's where they put all the older blokes when they were on their last legs in the A grade. Not only that, with the under 19s you always had a good crowd and the eye of the selectors. In the B grade you were playing to about six people.

I played about seven games with the B grade and got less and less interested. My dreams of being a professional footballer and getting paid for it faded away. I was seventeen and I couldn't see myself existing on the money I was making as an apprentice, especially once I had to move out of the home. Ernie was in the same situation as me. The next crunch was coming. What were we going to do?

Winnie told me she had some spare beds at the Pine Point house, and I decided to head off there. I told Ernie he could come too if he wanted. As well as having accommodation, I said, we might be able to get jobs. Ernie decided to come.

Before we left I had one last thing to fix, which was to take my football guernsey back to the club. Wilf was playing for the Ports junior colts by then, and I asked him to do it.

Then Ernie and I took off on his little Bantam Beeza motorbike. He was driving with me on the pillion seat, and we were travelling pretty light.

Later I heard that when Wilf took my guernsey back to the club, the coaches asked him where I was. All he said was, 'He's gone over the water.' The news about me leaving

Port Adelaide and going across the water made it into the newspaper. That's how Mr Hayles found me.

* * *

Winnie's house in Pine Point being big was good, because her husband, David, and the kids and my Uncle Gilbert Williams were all living there too.

Pine Point was a seaside port and later in the year, at harvest time, things would get busy with ketches – little sailing boats – coming in and out to take the grain away. During that time of the year, four or five men would come across from Point Pearce for work at the port and they'd be lumping the wheat and barley as it came in from the farms. Lumping is where you put the grain into bags and then stack them up until they can be picked up by a boat or in some cases by a truck. It's how they did it before silos were built there. Some of the Point Pearce blokes were really good lumpers, so the bloke at the port used them all the time.

Ernie and I arrived in May, when it wasn't lumping time, which is why there was room for us. As well as Uncle Gilbert being around, Mum's brother Uncle Cliff was still living up the road and working on farms around the district.

One morning not long after we got there, I was in bed asleep and next minute I felt somebody shaking me. When I woke up it was still dark and Uncle Cliff was standing there holding a candle because the house didn't have electricity at the time. Standing next to him was a white man.

I was half-dopey and all I could think was, *Oh, gawd, it's too early for me to be waking up.*

They both started chattering at the same time, and at first I couldn't understand what they were talking about. I started to pick up that this white gentleman was a farmer and he was interested in football and he was talking about me playing for his team. That was the Curramulka team.

As he was talking I was trying to work out where Curramulka was. Those two hospitals that wouldn't take me when I was fifteen were on my mind, and I was hoping this football team wasn't in either of those areas – because if it was, I wasn't going to go there. I found out that Curramulka was closer to the bottom end of the Peninsula, so that was all right. The others had been more near the middle.

The man's name was Mr Hayles, and he mentioned giving me some work too. I thought, *Well, that's just what I need at present to get some money in my pocket.* He asked me if anyone else had come to talk to me about football. When I said no, he handed over a piece of paper he wanted me to sign. I scribbled my name on the bottom and he went away happy.

Uncle Cliff thought he was king of the country. He was all huff and puff because here's his nephew being signed up to play football at Curramulka by a bloke he was shearing for at the time. Me, I just felt tired from being woken up so early in the morning.

It turned out that a day or two after I'd arrived at Pine Point there'd been a piece in *The Advertiser* about how I'd left the Port Adelaide Football Club. The article didn't say I was at Pine Point, because all Wilf had said was, 'He's gone over the water.' He could have said, 'He's gone to Pine Point', but he let people guess. Uncle Cliff had been shearing sheep at Mr Hayles' farm, and Mr Hayles must have put two and two together and worked out that the water I'd come over was Gulf St Vincent.

You get one like Mr Hayles in every town. They played sport when they were young, and they love to give all their time to it. Sport's their life, so they look after the oval, they look after all the gear, they look after the players. He was that sort of bloke.

The day after Curramulka signed me up, Uncle Cliff took me to Mr Hayles' place and I became a shedhand, working with the shearers. My job was to pick the wool up and throw it on the table where the wool classer would check it, then I'd put it in a bale and close it up when it was full and set up another one. Another job I had was to sweep the wool away from the shearers' feet where they stood on what were called the boards, and I'd yard the sheep up for them too.

Two nights a week I'd go to footy training in town, and then we'd have the matches on Saturdays. Mr Hayles would drive me to training and the matches on Saturdays, and he'd drive me home again. His two boys played too.

The first weekend I played for Curramulka, there was an interzone carnival on where teams from different areas on the Peninsula competed against each other. It was at Moonta, nearly an hour away, and as we drove there I was telling Mr Hayles how I'd landed at Winnie's with very little stuff, just the clothes I'd had at the boys' home: a pair of grey trousers, my old school jumper and not much else. We came to one of the main towns on the Peninsula, and Mr Hayles stopped at a shop. He took me in and said to pick out a suit, and he bought me a lovely brown double-breasted suit and a tie and white shirt.

That was my first proper suit. I thought I was the ant's pants. At the boys' home all our clothes were second-hand. I used to hate them because you'd get them from the church and sometimes you'd have school shorts so tight that the lining would come down the bottom and people would think it was your underpants showing. When I left I said it was the end of second-hand clothes for me. The other boys probably said the same thing.

* * *

Out the back of the Hayleses' homestead were the shearers' quarters, which was where Uncle Cliff, Uncle Gilbert and I stayed. For lunches and dinners we'd go into the house, and Mrs Hayles would have a meal cooked for us. They had a big room with a big table that could fit eleven or twelve people, and there'd be Mr and Mrs Hayles, their sons Stan and Will, Uncle Cliff, Uncle Gilbert and me. Mrs Hayles also had a lady who used to come and help clean the house. The Hayleses had other kids too – some were at boarding school, and the older ones had grown up and moved away.

The shearers' quarters were in an old hut with a couple of rooms and a stone floor. One room had four beds and the other one had a big open fireplace where you could have a lovely fire. It had one of those old bathtubs too, which my uncles mainly used on Thursday nights before they went home for the weekend. They'd boil water over the fire and fill the bath up, then they'd take it in turns. When they were finished the three of us would cart the bath outside and tip the water out. Me, I'd have a shower at footy practice on

On the left is Mr Hayles's son Stan, who I worked and played footy with. On the right is Bruce Tucker, another friend. We were dressed up to celebrate our birthdays.

Tuesday and Thursday nights. If I wanted to have a shower on the other days, the Hayleses had one at the homestead I could use.

I hadn't spent much time with my uncles since I was a kid. At the start of the shearing week, on the Monday, they'd each shear fifty sheep a day, which wasn't bad but wasn't good. Then by the end of the Friday, they'd be shearing a hundred, sometimes a hundred and ten. They'd double it along the way, mainly because they weren't drinking. Then they'd go away for the weekend, and when they'd come back on the Monday they'd start again at fifty.

'Don't drink on the weekend,' I said to them one time, 'and you can start off shearing a hundred sheep straight away and you'll make more money.' But no, that wasn't their thinking. Their thinking was, once the shearing was done on Friday, the weekend was theirs to get a drink wherever they could. At the time, Aboriginal people still weren't allowed in hotels. Mr Hayles or another white person would go and get a few bottles of beer for them, and away they'd go. Once they started, they wouldn't stop.

I thought, *What a waste of talent.* They were good shearers, but it was stopping them from making double the money they could have had. It was something that, at the time, I couldn't understand, but in the end I did. When you want something and you can't have it, it makes you want it more. That was the way they were with the booze.

This was when Aboriginal people still weren't counted in the census as Australian citizens. You weren't really a person. So you had to rely on someone else to get booze for you, your friends or your workmates. Sometimes people would drink a concoction they called goom: methylated spirits mixed with water or lemonade. How horrible would it be drinking methylated spirits? But that's what they did. When I was with anyone drinking it and they lit a cigarette, I was always afraid they'd blow themselves up.

Once, I was in a car with some relatives. One was driving and the other two were in the back drinking. The two in the back started arguing. 'Stop the car, stop the car!' one of them shouted to the bloke who was driving. They wanted to get out and fight each other. I thought, *Over what? Two inches of methylated spirits? You've got to be joking.* But that was the way a lot of people went with the booze. A lot of the white men back then were pretty heavy drinkers too. They were hard workers and they'd let their hair down and drink on the weekends.

When the shearing season finished, Uncle Cliff and Uncle Gilbert went home. I stayed – there were plenty of odd jobs at the farm for me to do, like fixing things and getting on the tractor to plough the paddocks. The farm was made up of three farms altogether, and Mr Hayles's two sons each had their own, so I'd help them out too.

But staying in the shearers' quarters by myself at night was scary. The door didn't have a lock and I'd be there in a big room with four beds, forty yards away from the house. I went from having these two old blokes talking after tea, and feeling safe and secure, to living there with nobody around. Things in my mind would scare me, like those Kadaitcha men. What if they came looking for someone and they found me instead? In the end though I stayed for a while and was grateful for getting paid.

On the weekends I'd go to Winnie's and do things with Ernie. He wasn't a footballer, and because of that he couldn't get any work around Pine Point and Curramulka. With what he knew about motorbikes he was ahead of his time, but not with sport. At the time there wasn't any dole and I was giving him some of the money I was earning from Mr Hayles. But in the end Ernie didn't stay. He went home to Alice Springs where his mum was. All us boys were starting to go our own way and head off down different paths.

15

'We'll pick you up and drop you back home'

The first night I went to footy training, I was getting out of my work clothes and into my gear in the change rooms. They weren't very flash back then, just a tin shed with an open shower in the corner, a bench seat around the walls, and a hook where you'd hang your clothes. A bloke came over and sat down next to me and said hello. He said his name was Frank Joraslafsky. He was the first bloke in the team to come and have a yarn with me, and the second person in Curramulka to invite me out for tea.

I told Frank I didn't think I'd be able to make it to tea because I didn't have a car. 'That's all right,' he said, 'we'll pick you up and drop you back home.' Frank and his wife Pat hadn't been married that long, and they were living in a small stone house on Frank's parents' farm. Frank's family had come out from Poland a while back and Pat's family were from Brentwood, another little town on the Peninsula.

Peter Tilbrook, the coach, was the first person who invited me to tea at his house. He was a really good footballer who used to play for Norwood and had nearly made the state team. He was working on people's farms just out of Curramulka and then he bought his own. Whether he thought as the coach it was his responsibility to invite me out, I don't know. Anyway, I went and met his family and it was really good.

Not long after I had dinner with Frank and Pat, Pat's sister Margaret Short and her husband Geoff invited me for dinner too. From then on, other people would regularly invite me to dinner and I'd meet up with them all at the football on Saturdays. If there was anything on they'd all be wanting me to go. At the time I didn't have a great deal of money or clothes, but I still went to places, mainly to show that Aboriginal people can do those sorts of things too.

One day there was a dance on in one of the little towns north of Curramulka, and Frank and Pat said they were going to take me.

'I can't dance,' I told them.

'That doesn't matter,' Frank said. 'We'll teach you.'

Frank and Pat took me to balls and dances at all the different towns around the Peninsula. All the ladies would do themselves up in lovely dresses, and the hall would be done up and people would come from miles around. They'd have a local band playing and the dancing would go until one-thirty in the morning.

The first few times I went I just sat and watched because I still couldn't dance. Pat was a lovely dancer, and Frank was a big, tall bloke, six foot four or something, and he was a beautiful glider on the dance floor. They looked so good together, and that's when I started thinking maybe I could dance like that. Pat would get me up. 'Come on,' she'd say, 'you're going to at least try', and I'd stumble around and not know which foot to put where. They kept teaching me, and slowly I got more confident. Then, one day, I knew I could dance.

* * *

I still had a lot of relatives living in Point Pearce, on the other side of the Peninsula. Different uncles and cousins would get work on the farms around the district during the winter, and they'd stay in the shearers' quarters and play football for the local team. But in those days, once the football season finished, the work was gone too, and you'd have nothing to do for the next six months, unless you were a lumper. The locals expected you to go back to Point Pearce and wait until the next footy season. A lot of the work available to us over the winter was tied to football.

Currie – that's what everyone called Curramulka – was turning out okay for me because I had Winnie and her kids at Pine Point, and my uncles and cousins nearby, and I had work and sport and people I was getting to know, like the Hayles family, and Pat and Frank, and the footy players and the people at the dances. But not long after the football season finished there wasn't any more work. I was at a loose end, so I teamed up with two of my cousins, Bradley and Spencer. With not much of a plan and only a little bit of money, we headed for Adelaide.

We went from relation to relation, sleeping on their floors. Sometimes we'd have nowhere to stay and we'd sleep in big round cement water pipes we found alongside the river. Sometimes we'd break into clubrooms, especially if it was raining. The Ethelton swimming club was one place we stayed the night because I knew it had showers. We'd sleep, have a shower and be out the next day. That lasted about three months.

Being with my two cousins, we couldn't stay with any of the boys from St Francis House. One was married by now, some were doing their apprenticeships and living in flophouses, and some were still living at the home.

In Adelaide, there was more talk among the boys – and among other Aboriginal people and politicians and in the newspapers too – about the laws that affected us and how they needed to change. People like Aunty Glad and Charles and Phyllis Duguid were working hard to make sure Aboriginal people had more of a say in things and didn't just have white people speaking for us. All this was the talk of the town at the time, but meanwhile, Bradley, Spencer and I needed to get work and find somewhere to live.

In Port Adelaide there was a place called Fricker's Corner where out-of-work people – black and white – would go to try and get work. The bloke in charge would pick you out to do a job for the day, and once it was finished you'd get paid. When the three of us got work and we all had money, we could do things. But you weren't picked all the time, and some of the jobs were really bad. One was at a scrap-metal place where they were squashing motor cars into little blocks of iron. We had to pick the scraps up and stack them, but they didn't give us any gloves so our hands were bleeding by the end of the day.

We were eighteen and bumming around with nothing in mind. We'd work every second day, spend the money on stupid stuff, and go from relative to relative to sleep and eat. This was a different feeling for me, because up until then I'd always known where I was and what I was doing. When I was a little kid I'd wake up in the morning and Mum or Papa Joe would have breakfast for me and then there'd be lunch and tea, and then I'd go to bed and have a nice warm bed. The same when I got to the boys' home: you'd have breakfast, you'd be fed, you had your nice bed. Now I didn't know where I was. Was I going to sleep in a bed tonight or would I be sleeping in one of those big pipes on the side of the road? Would I be breaking into a club to get out of the rain? It was a big learning curve for me about what life can be like.

Sometimes I'd catch up with some of my other cousins who lived in Adelaide. For a while over the summer I was with a cousin at Semaphore Beach, where they had sideshows, and we'd go down there in the evenings. We got talking to some girls from Broken Hill who were on holiday with their parents. Their dads worked for BHP, the mining company there, and the company had a holiday house near the beach for their staff. For the next few nights my cousin and I made sure we met up with them and they were the same with us. My cousin was interested in one and I was interested in the other. She told me she was at the technical college there. I asked her about Broken Hill and she gave me a bit of an idea, and she seemed to hint that it would be good for me to go up there at some stage. They went back to Broken Hill and we left it at that.

Towards the end of January 1955, it was the start of grape-picking time in the Riverland. That's the same area where

Banks Long – the old traditional man at Point Pearce – was from, along the Murray River near the Victorian border. 'Why don't we go up there?' Bradley said.

But we had no money and didn't know how we were going to get there. Then I remembered a little office in Kintore Avenue in the city that Mum used to go to sometimes, so we went to the office and put our case to the bloke, and in the end he gave us three bus tickets to Barmera. When we got there, lots of our relations from all around the place were there already, living in pickers' huts where you could sleep and have a shower.

The next day we started picking grapes. I ate so many the first day that I had a bellyache all the next day. In those days the blockies – the people who owned the vineyards – didn't have whipper snippers, and grass grew up under the vines and there'd be spiders and snakes in it.

'I'm getting out of here,' I told my cousins after a week.

'Where're you going?' they asked.

'I don't know, but who's coming?'

Spencer said he'd come with me. Bradley said he'd stay, because his girlfriend had come up from Point Pearce.

We knew the grape trucks were filled at one or two o'clock in the morning, then they'd be driven to Nuriootpa to unload. So we hitched a ride with one of the trucks. Then we walked a little way along the road to Tanunda, found a tree and slept under it.

The next day we walked on to Lyndoch. Just as we got to the town, a ute came by, and the bloke pulled up and asked us where we were going.

'Adelaide,' we told him.

'Jump in,' he said, and an hour or so later he dropped us right in the city at the railway station.

We had a little bit of money that we'd earned from the pickings, so at the station we had a shower and a shave and bought new shirts. Now we had about ten shillings left.

'Where do we go from here?' Spencer asked.

I told him about the Broken Hill girls I'd met with my other cousin, and how they'd said it was a good place.

That night we were on the train to Broken Hill.

The next morning, when we got there, we asked the stationmaster if we could leave our bags with him while we went to a shop and had breakfast. After breakfast we went to the technical college in the main street to see if we could find the girl I'd met at Christmas time. I thought at least we might have somebody to talk to. She came out and I said hello, and she started to talk. I could see her starting to get a bit edgy and I thought, *Uh oh, what's going on here?* Then she told me she had another boyfriend. That was the end of that story.

So we headed back to the railway station. Then I remembered I knew somebody else who lived in Broken Hill – a footballer called Lew Roberts who used to play for Port Adelaide. He was working for Silverton Tramway, the company that ran the railway line to the mines.

We found Lew and told him we were looking for a football club to play for that could look after us. 'We're running out of money and haven't got anywhere to stay,' I said.

'Go away and come back later in the afternoon,' he said.

When we came back, Lew was there with the secretary of the West Broken Hill football club. They set us up with mattresses and blankets in the clubrooms. There were showers and toilets, so that suited us. We stayed there a couple of nights and did some training with the club.

The people in charge thought they might have a couple of good footballers here, so they found more permanent accommodation for us with a family called the Khans. They had two flats at the back of the yard, and each one had a single bed and a toilet and shower.

We couldn't get work at the mines in Broken Hill, because they were pretty particular about who they employed. I think you had to have been born there to work for them, which might have been the union rules, because it was big money and you were working underground. But we weren't in Broken Hill long before we got jobs at the Water Board. I was at a place, just on the edge of the town, where all the water from the Umberumberka Dam would be cleaned before it came into the city. Yabbies and other bits and pieces would get caught in the net as the water came in, and I'd clean that out. Once a week I had to put four or five bags of some cleaning gear in the water. Those were the hardest things I had to do – the rest of the time all I had to do was sweep and mop the floor.

I hadn't seen any other Aboriginal people around town. I knew there was a heap at Wilcannia, about two hundred kilometres away to the east, who all belonged to the Barkindji mob, but none of them seemed to come into Broken Hill. So Spencer and I teamed up with a group of boys around Railway Town who played in the B grade for West Broken Hill footy club. They all went to a police boys club and they played baseball on Sundays, so we did that with them too.

The brother of one of the blokes managed one of the clothes shops in the main street, and one day we asked him if we could buy some clothes and put it on the never-never, and pay him every week when we got paid. 'No problem,' he said, so we booked up a fair bit, because at the time we had very little, especially working clothes.

Back when Spencer and I had been grape-picking at Barmera, we'd gone to a dance one night at a place called Cobdogla. When we got there they'd all looked at us as if to say, 'What the hell are you blokes doing here?' It seemed to us that they were saying, 'How dare these two black kids come to a white dance!' We felt it as soon as we walked in, from both the men and the women. The women wouldn't dance with us because they thought they might catch something.

The main thing I worked out from this was that you don't let yourself get upset and curse and call them names. You just walk away. Though I felt a little bit like this was the way it was always going to be.

Spencer was a bit shy about going to the Broken Hill dances, but I said to him to just come and have a look. We went back to the clothes shop and bought some good clothes and dressed up and went to one. For a start we stood there watching everybody dance. The girls were looking at us as if to say, 'Don't come and ask me for a dance.' But I thought there must be one girl in the hall who would say yes – and there was. Her parents owned the fruit and veg shop in the main street, and we'd met them the day we arrived.

She and I had a good dance and a good conversation, and people saw then that I could dance and that I wasn't dirty or drunk, which they were expecting Aboriginal people to be. All of a sudden, everyone wanted to know who you were. From then on, we went to every dance that was on, and we'd dance every dance. People saw me playing footy too. The people in Broken Hill were a bit more friendly than the people in the Riverland. I don't think they were as discriminatory. Afghans and other nationalities had been living there a long time.

Spencer played one game in the A grade then he played most of his games with the B grade. I played for the As, and after seven or eight games I was leading in all the awards and there was a bit of a write-up about me in the *Barrier Times*. I was set. I wasn't going to leave.

Then one day at footy a bloke came up to me and said he had a letter from the Fitzroy Football Club. It said that one of their spotters had told the club about me, and they wanted to come up and look at me playing. Their recruiting officer flew up to Broken Hill and we had a talk after the match.

'How quickly can you come to Melbourne?' he asked me. In those days if you came from another state, you had to live in Melbourne for three months before they gave you a clearance.

'I'm ready,' I said. 'I might just have to fix up a couple of things first.'

'Like what?' he asked.

'Well, I've got a bill I'm paying off at the clothing shop.'

'Don't worry,' he said. 'We'll look after that.'

The next thing I was on a plane heading out of Broken Hill.

16

'The club found me a job in Carlton'

When we landed at Essendon Airport, Doug Nicholls was waiting to meet me. Doug had been one of Fitzroy's star players when he was younger, and now he was a pastor with the Churches of Christ Aborigines Mission. He was a short bloke like me and he had a nice round cheerful face. Billy Stephen, the captain-coach of the Fitzroy football team, was there too. I remember he had a black eye.

I went back to the clubrooms with Billy and Doug. They told me I'd be staying with Doug and he'd look after me for a start. The club would find me a job, and in the meantime they'd pay me a wage and cover my rent. The main thing they wanted me to do was get myself fit for next year's season.

Doug took me home to his place at Northcote, and I met Mrs Nicholls and two of their kids, Pam and Ralph. They lived next door to the Northcote oval and athletics track, and Doug was the curator there. Their house was a weatherboard, which was pretty common for houses in Victoria in those days because of the forests around the place. The lounge was their private abode and that's how we kept it. I didn't go past the kitchen and the sleep-out where my bedroom was.

For the first three months I didn't have a job and I got to know Melbourne and the inner-north suburbs like the back of my hand. As well as training a few days a week I'd go to the pictures every day, and I'd walk around town and find out where everything was. After a while the club found me a job in Carlton, working for some Chinese people Doug knew who owned a small factory that made goods for Holden. The factory was tucked away in the back streets near the Royal Exhibition Building. The owners were really good people to work for – they looked after me, and it was good pay.

A lot of Aboriginal people lived in Fitzroy, mainly in Gertrude Street and around the corner in Gore Street. Doug's church was just down the road and we all used to go there on Sunday nights.

Doug was one of the pioneers of Indigenous football. At that time there were very few others playing at that level, and he was good enough to represent Victoria. After he left football, he worked really hard to make things better for Aboriginal people. In 1951, a few years before I got there, he'd help set up the Council for Aboriginal Rights in Victoria. That had started with a meeting at the Melbourne Town Hall and it was all about getting justice for Aboriginal people.

Doug would often be a guest speaker at events around the state, and sometimes I'd go with him. One time we drove in Doug's little Ford Consul to Portland, about five hours' drive from Melbourne. On the way we called in at a convent at Ballarat to pick up a couple of young Aboriginal women who were singers and who were going to sing for the people while Doug took a break halfway through. When we got to the old picture theatre in Portland, the place was chock-a-block – you couldn't have fitted another person in.

People loved Doug. He was a thinker who commanded respect, and he was really good at getting his message across about the problems facing Aboriginal people in Victoria. He thought there were different ways to advance things for our people other than protest, at least in the way that a few of the younger blokes in Victoria had been doing at that time. Doug was very good friends with people in business, and he used his connections to get things done for his church and for Aboriginal people. He had an old saying: 'You can't play a piano without the black and the white keys. To get harmony you've got to play both. That's what life is.' It was his catchcry at every meeting he spoke at.

Coming home from Portland that night, Doug was driving. But after we stopped at Ballarat to drop the girls off, he asked me to take over. 'There's a four-gallon drum of petrol in the boot and here's the keys,' he said. 'Away you go.'

It was snowing in Ballarat and as I poured the petrol in the tank I spilled some over my hand, which made it even colder. When I put the drum back in and got in the car, there was Doug, wrapped in a rug and asleep. It was the first time I'd ever been out of Melbourne and I had to find my way from Ballarat back to Northcote.

Somehow I did, and we got back at about three o'clock in the morning.

From then on he did the same thing each time. We'd go to a place like Shepparton and on the way home we'd stop for a break and he'd hand over the keys and go to sleep.

Whenever Doug gave speeches the place would be full. He'd hold your attention. He was just that great. Everybody was searching for people to come together, black and white, and he was preaching that for a long time. He was like a magnet. I think he was on the right side of bringing people together. He'd point out simple little things that would just make the world better.

* * *

The first training night I had, it was wet and muddy, the ground was heavy, and I was a stone and a half overweight. By the end of the night, I was nearly dead. The training kept going like that for a while, until one day I realised I had to train harder. I'd been coming last in all the sprints, but I knew I could be much quicker and faster than most of the other players.

I trained hard four nights a week to get myself down to the right weight and show them I was ready and fit enough to be selected. Soon I wasn't last anymore. I think they all got a bit of a shock. When the time came for the start of the season, I played pretty well in the trial games and I looked like being in the first team. Josie came over from Adelaide to watch me play one time, and she stayed the weekend and that was really good. But when the full footy season started, I just missed out on making the first team.

Most teams go for five or six games before they make a change. The weeks went past, and Fitzroy had played nine games and I was still in the B grade. I came up against league players who'd been injured and were playing in the Bs until they were fit enough to go back to top. I was playing pretty good football, and I think I could have got into the A grade, had other things been out of the picture.

It was getting to be time to move on from Doug's place. When I'd first arrived in Melbourne I'd met a lady at his church and we'd started seeing each other. Now she and her family said I could live with them for a little bit of rent. They lived in Gertrude Street, not far from where I worked in Carlton and close to the oval for training. The tram went straight past their house and took you in one direction up to Northcote, where Doug lived, and in the other direction to the city.

The house was an old double-storey detached place with an outside shower added on as a lean-to. Another group of Aboriginal people lived around the corner, where there was a whole heap of flats. Some of the old-time fighters who'd been involved in the struggle for Aboriginal people for years lived there – people like Mrs Marg Tucker and her sister Geraldine Briggs and others from the Briggs family. They were all doing a lot for their people and campaigning and giving speeches to let white people know about the bad conditions Aboriginal people were living in. They were coming up with good ideas too, for what needed to change.

When they were younger, Doug and those ladies had all been inspired by William Cooper, who was well known for helping to set up the Aboriginal Day of Mourning and Protest in 1938. I was starting to see that the Victorian Aboriginal people were different to the South Australians at the time.

They seemed more vigorous in what they were doing in Aboriginal affairs, more organised and more vocal.

The family I was staying with were really nice and they looked after me, and so did the lady I was seeing. But soon she was talking marriage. I was only nineteen and I didn't want to do that. I could see where I was going to end up – living in a substandard house with seven or eight kids. That was how it was for a lot of people in Fitzroy at the time. While all the old ladies who lived around me were really nice people too, I couldn't see myself living in the same type of conditions this lady's family were living in. That wasn't their fault. They had to live somewhere. But I couldn't think about getting married, having kids, and finding a house – not at nineteen.

You didn't come here to get involved with a woman, you came here to play football, I said to myself one day. *This other thing is starting to take over your life. You've got to pull your head in a bit.*

Football was going well, and someday I probably would have got a game in the league. But the lady and I had gone from talking to each other to arguing and screaming at each other. I thought that if this was how life playing football in Melbourne was going to be, then it wasn't for me. I knew I had to get away.

Mum not being around anymore and not having any of my own family living there probably made it difficult too. I was making all the decisions about which way I should go and what I should do, and I didn't know whether I was making the right ones or the wrong ones. I didn't have anybody else there to talk to, so I had to work it out for myself.

Back then I didn't have a clear alternative in my mind – all I knew was I had to get out of Melbourne.

* * *

One day I told the lady I'd been seeing that I had to go to Adelaide. I told a lie about someone dying and that I needed to go home for a little while and then I'd be back. I'd just been paid, and I went into the railway station on Spencer Street and booked a train ticket to Adelaide for the next day. Then I went back to her family's place and packed my bag. I had very little gear except for my footy stuff and a new suit to replace the one Mr Hayles had bought me two years before. I'd worn that out from wearing it nearly every day.

That next afternoon I headed back to Spencer Street station to catch the overnight train. It was really crowded on the platform and so was the train when I got on. By then it was standing room only and I was glad I'd booked. I found my seat and I was sitting there ready for the train to leave when a woman with a baby got on. She couldn't find a seat and nobody else was getting up to give her theirs. I thought she was probably only travelling to Ballarat, so I got up and gave her mine. She didn't speak to me. Whether she thought I wouldn't have booked my seat because a black person wouldn't have got around to doing that, or whether she thought that a black person shouldn't be sitting in a seat, I don't know. At the time I just thought she was a lady with a baby and she needed a seat.

She travelled all the way to Adelaide, and I stood up all the way. The train stopped at stations and I'd get out and have a pasty or a drink, but I didn't get any sleep. It was a fairly horrendous night.

At eight in the morning the train pulled into Adelaide railway station. I got out and stood on the platform as people hurried past me towards the gates. What did I do now? I had to find something for the night.

I recognised a local league footballer I knew from schoolboy matches and when I'd played for Port Adelaide. He spotted me and came over, and we had a quick talk about what we were both doing. He knew who I was and that I had the talent to play league, but he took off without making any mention of it, so I let that go. If I was going to stay in Adelaide I'd need work and accommodation – and that situation hadn't changed since last time I'd lived here.

I had to make a decision. Should I go and stay with one of my sisters? But neither of them was living in Adelaide at the time. Should I go back to Port Adelaide footy club and say to them that I was available to play? Was there something else I could do?

By now the platform was nearly empty. As I walked to the gates, another thought came to me. The two nicest people I'd met at this stage in my life were the young couple living at Curramulka, Frank and Pat Joraslafsky. What if I rang them and asked if they could let me tread water with them for a while?

I came out onto the concourse. Across the other side, near the stone steps leading up to North Terrace, was a phone box. I took a punt.

Frank answered the phone. I put it to him and said I was hoping it would only be for a short time.

'Catch the bus tonight,' he said, 'and we'll be at Ardrossan to meet you.'

That was it. I walked down North Terrace to the bus station at the other end, booked a seat and dropped off my bag. Then I walked around Rundle Street for a while wasting time. I had a pie and a cup of tea, and I bought a ticket to a little ABC movie theatre where they showed the news. The show only lasted an hour or so, but that was enough time for me to sit down and close my eyes and have a rest.

The bus left Adelaide around seven that night. Two and a half hours later it pulled into Ardrossan. Sure enough, Frank was there waiting for me.

17

'They looked after me and made me part of the family'

As we drove out of Ardrossan and along the dirt backroads, Frank and I had our normal chitchat. We didn't stretch our minds too much. That's the way we were with each other.

Frank and Pat's place was tucked away in the scrub twenty miles out of town. They were still living in the little two-bedroom stone farmhouse with Frank's parents up in the homestead. And now they had Sandra too, their first baby.

When I'd first gone to Curramulka after the boys' home, Frank and I just seemed to click. He had a sister called Madge who lived at Currie and she was a lovely person too, but he always talked about wanting to have a brother, and I seemed to fit the bill. I used to call him 'The Man' and he called me 'The Man'. That's how we'd talk to each other: 'Yeah, Man.' 'No, Man.' When we'd played footy, Frank was a ruckman and I was a rover, and we used to be good at combining our play. That's how we got on so well, I think.

To cover my accommodation and board I did work around the farm, and Frank and I spent a lot of time together. When we'd bring the sheep or wool to Adelaide in the truck we'd probably say four words to each other, and three coming back. We didn't have to talk. That feeling was there.

I'd arrived in the winter of 1956, in the middle of the football season, but I couldn't start playing for Curramulka straight away because I had to wait for my clearance from Fitzroy. It was the same as when I'd left Broken Hill. You had to wait three months to get what they called your residential qualifications, to show you'd genuinely left the old place and were living in the new one. By the time I'd done my three months in Currie, the football season was over.

'Do you play cricket?' someone at Currie asked me one day.

I said yes pretty quickly, even though at the boys' home we'd mainly played different types of football. They said I should stay for the summer in that case, and that somebody would probably give me a job over the harvest period. That way, I'd still be around when the next football season started.

I was the only Aboriginal bloke playing cricket at the time. It was a bit of a saviour in the beginning, giving me an extra six months of employment and accommodation. Eventually it became more than that.

I was still staying mainly at Frank and Pat's, and I was doing work at other farms around the district. If it was shearing time and somebody wanted a shedhand, they'd give me the job. Then another farmer would need somebody for a week for some other job and I'd go and do that. I was starting to get some money.

In around October or November, a family who lived just out of Currie hired me and I stayed with them for a while. They had two girls and were fostering a little boy. They were sports-minded and church-minded, and I fitted into the picture pretty well with them. Then, over Christmas, it was harvest time and I went to another family's place, and when that finished I went to Geoff and Margaret Short's place. People around Currie got to know I was there to stay and I'd be ready for the next footy season.

When one job finished, somebody else would grab me. Everywhere I went, they were nice and kind, and they looked after me and made me part of the family. When I was in the main street of Currie, people would come up and talk to me and ask me what I was doing, and often they invited me out to their place for dinner. I'd say that I'd love to come but I couldn't get there, and they'd always say they'd run me there and home again after. It was a real first for me to be experiencing so much kindness from the whole community, and not just from one or two people.

I'd still go over to Frank and Pat's place for dinner and on weekends, and if I wasn't doing anything else, I'd stay with them. We got on really well. Sometimes if they needed to go somewhere, I'd look after Sandra. One time, when she was three or four, we were watching *Lassie* on the television and she had tears running down her cheeks because of the way Lassie was being treated. It got to a scary part and she jumped out of her chair and stood in front of the television. 'Don't look, Uncle Vin! Don't look!'

I nearly burst out crying. She was trying to protect me. It was one of the loveliest things that ever happened to me.

* * *

It was common practice in country football to change coaches each year, because usually local people did the coaching and they took it in turns. A lot of the blokes I'd played with last time were still in the team, including Peter Tilbrook, who'd been the coach. Peter was a very good coach, but there'd been what you'd call a 'country attitude' towards playing the game. It was a different type of play to what I was used to in Adelaide and Melbourne. The Currie blokes would do lovely big, beautiful drop kicks and high marks – that was the way they thought the game should be played.

I'd been coached by people who did things differently. At Port Adelaide there'd been Fos Williams, who just wanted everyone to 'run through a brick wall of people'. *Why does he want me to do that when I could end up in hospital for six months?* I thought. *Why don't I just step around the bloke? It does the same thing and it's much easier and at least I'm going to be here next week.* To Fos, none of that mattered. You just had to have the guts to stop the other players, right? Back then I was a skinny kid and I didn't want to run through any of those big men and try to stop them. It was always easier for me to duck around a big bloke. Fos told me once that he could see what I was saying, but when you were coaching the whole group you needed to get the best out of them and 'running through brick walls' was the sort of jargon he used. Not only that, Fos would do exactly what he asked you to do. He was as tough as an old lion.

After Fos, I'd come across a bloke called Len Smith who was the brother of Norm Smith, the famous Melbourne coach at Fitzroy. Len's attitude was entirely different, even in the way he spoke. He was a coach who didn't play, and the way he talked about how to do things was more technical. There are different ways to move the ball around the ground, and he was always thinking of better ways to do it and where to play different players to get the best out of them. That's not to say he was any better as a coach – he just had a different way to do it. I picked up on all those sorts of things.

Some of the Currie players had been keeping tabs on where I'd been playing. They knew I'd ended up with Fitzroy. That alone had to give you some status, whether you made a career there or you didn't. So before the 1957 season started, they asked me to be coach and captain.

Being a coach is a lot different to playing because you're supposed to be guiding the blokes. When you're talking to older people, as I was to some of the footballers, or when you're talking to millionaires, as some of the farmers were, and you are a different colour to them, those things that make you different as a coach are important.

At the beginning the Currie players were all wanting to know what I was going to do. Was I any good or wasn't I? That was the feeling I got from them. I thought, *Well, I can't talk rubbish to these blokes. I've got to know what I'm talking about and, when I get out on the ground, I've got to put it into practice.* So I did the best I could and led by example. I was grateful for my early football days, because all along the line I'd taken notice of how the coaches operated and how they got the best out of their players.

Curramulka had a different culture to what I'd been used to in league football. They didn't really have a purpose in playing — it was just a break from work. During the games you'd be standing by your mate, who was playing for the opposition, and you'd be talking about how much rain you'd had, whether you'd finished seeding, how the shearing was going, and how much wool you got. The change I made, I think, was to give them a purpose, and that purpose was to play for the town — to make Curramulka the mecca of sports on the Peninsula. I wanted them to all have the same attitude: that you're not playing for yourself, you're playing for Curramulka. It made a big difference.

My training regime was a lot harder than what they'd been used to. I think I frightened the hell out of them at first. I'd rant and rave a little bit, something they hadn't heard before. They hadn't heard a coach having an ongoing dialogue with players to try and lift their play, especially from one who was a black man and twenty years old. Can you imagine me with all these farmers standing around while I go off at them about what they need to do? But I had the feeling these blokes were interested in what I was saying and what I was trying to do. They'd get in as close as they could to hear me, and there was no noise from them. So I felt like I was halfway there.

Sometimes I'd get fired up and swear like billy-o at them. 'Listen,' I'd say, 'you need a bit of guts.' I'd tell them what they had to do and how they had to do it, and why they better not let the team and the town down, and when they got out on the ground, they'd be steaming.

Other times, I'd be serious with them about what we *didn't* want happening out there. At the end I'd say something or make a joke to get them relaxed and laughing. If we were getting beaten, they wanted to know what they had to do.

And they wanted to know whether I was clever enough to make the right changes in the field to alter the game, and whether I was saying enough things to lift each player to get them to give that little bit extra.

You know you're on the right track when you're winning games. I'd meet them in the town and they'd all want to stop and ask what was going to happen next week. They were relying on me to get the best out of them.

After a match one day, somebody told me that when I was giving the team the talk at three-quarter time they saw the opposition team moving over closer to us to hear what I had to say. That was funny. I didn't notice because I was focused on what I was saying to my team. Hearing that gave me a bit more confidence.

Another time during a game, a bloke in the opposition who was a big farmer on the Peninsula was standing three yards in front of me and kept turning around to watch me. Later, I saw him at a dance and he asked me what I reckoned about how he'd played me.

'Well,' I said, 'one thing – don't stand three yards in front of me and watch me, because by the time the ball comes and I run, I'm past you before you turn around.'

'Oh,' he said.

'That puts me three yards in front of you when the ball comes. So by doing it that way you're never gonna stop me.'

'What should I do instead?' he asked.

'You need to stand alongside me and watch the ball,' I said. 'Don't watch me. Watch the ball.'

He was a different player after that.

* * *

At some stage the Curramulka football club decided to knock down the old grandstand and build new change rooms. Everybody chipped in. That was their community spirit. We top-dressed the oval, and people brought their tip trucks and extra workers to do it. We remodelled the old grandstand and gave it new showers and toilets for both teams. It was a big job but all of the community were there to help. We paid for it by people doing things like dropping off ten or twenty bags of barley, or so many sheep, at the port and donating the money to the footy club. There were no grants in those days. It wasn't a big township, but it was really vibrant. People stuck together and helped out.

All the time I kept on doing farm work. I was in demand a bit too for my boiler-making skills from the Harbors Board, because I'd learned how to weld. One of the farmers had bought an oxygen welding set, but at that stage no one in the district had clocked up much experience with them. I remember the farmer's eyes and his sons' eyes when I showed them how to use it – they were delighted. That made others want me to work for them. If things got broken they knew I could fix them.

Most of the work I did was manual, and I was young and fit and not frightened to work hard. If I started at a job I just kept at it. Sometimes we'd start at five in the morning, and I'd be up and out on the tractor doing the seeding, and we wouldn't knock off until nine o'clock at night.

I kept up. They probably thought I wouldn't, not being used to it. But I was determined I was going to keep up.

It was the same in the shearing sheds. I decided I was going to become the best rouseabout and board boy they'd ever seen. They called you the board boy because the shearers stood on a special wooden board when they sheared the sheep and your job was to keep the board as clean as you could. I wasn't going to let any loose wool be around on the floor, and I made sure I picked the fleeces up right. And I knew the shearers and the boss appreciated it.

I tried to make it part of my life that I was consistent and didn't let anybody down. I wanted people to think, *This bloke always turns up for everything and never lets you down. He's gonna be there when he says he's gonna be there.* I wasn't going to let them think that I was a drunk, because I wasn't. If I was living in their house I wanted to show them that I was a good clean person and a good dresser. I was trying to show white people that Aboriginal people can do those things. Sometimes, instead of getting on a soapbox, I think the best thing to do is to show people that Aboriginal people are the same as them.

Back then, if you did what I was doing, some Aboriginal people thought you were being a 'whitey'. But at that time, there were no Aboriginal businesses and no Aboriginal organisations for us to work for. Where did you have to work? You had to work with white people. They were the bosses and the owners of the companies you worked for. Where else were you going to go?

A lot of people reckoned people like me could have gone back on the mission, to Point Pearce. But what for? I watched my cousins die early because they were bad drinkers. They just had nothing in life. They'd go as far as Maitland, about ten miles away, and spend the afternoon there then go back to Point Pearce. They'd go to football, then straight back to Point Pearce.

When you were gathered as a group on a community like Point Pearce, or other communities where the government put Aboriginal people, there was very little work and very little money. You had to work on the mission but the wages were lower than white people got, and on top of that the government took out some of your earnings to cover your rations. The government controlled what you did and where

SOUTH   AUSTRALIA.   **N.º 195**

UNCONDITIONAL EXEMPTION FROM THE PROVISIONS OF THE ABORIGINES ACT, 1934-1939.

In pursuance of the powers conferred by Section 11a of the Aborigines Act, 1934-1939, the Aborigines Protection Board, being of opinion that *Kathleen Winifred Copley* of *Point Pearce* , by reason of his character and standard of intelligence and development, should be exempted from the provisions of the Aborigines Act, 1934-1939, does hereby unconditionally declare that the said *Kathleen Winifred Copley* shall cease to be an aborigine for the purposes of the said Act.

The seal of the Aborigines Protection Board was hereunto affixed on the *first* day of *May* 194 *6,* in the presence of

W R Penhall
Secretary.

10b50—6.41 1280

J.B.C. Deputy Chairman.
J.T.C. B Member.

This shows you the sort of control the government had over us. This is the exemption Mum had to get before we went to Leigh Creek in 1946. Back when we first moved to Adelaide, she might have had what they called a limited exemption. *(State Records of South Australia, GRG52/19/0/4/195 Kathleen Winifred Copley)* you went and whether you could get an exemption certificate. In those days too, there was no dole money going around.

People had to make the best with what they had. The government welfare people would let you have meat and milk from the mission farm, and the baker would come in from the local town with the bread. But the rations were pretty basic. A lot of the time they didn't include fruit and vegetables and people didn't have much money of their own to buy good food. You'd add to the rations by going fishing if you were by the sea, or catching rabbits or kangaroos. You were all there in that one place, and you all had the same problems. The only little bit of money you could earn was as a shearer or lumper or bag sewer, or, if you were a woman, as a cleaner, like my mum did. You could earn a little bit of money on the farms doing seasonal work like I'd done before, and like my uncles did. But very few farmers would keep you on once that was done. You'd come back home to the community.

These were some of the situations that our people were in. If you had no money you couldn't buy decent clothes. What clothes people could afford to buy they did, and sometimes Point Pearce held dances at the hall and some of the people had a suit or a good dress they'd wear for it. But often they just couldn't afford it. The families were usually big, and often they only had a two-roomed house to live in.

Sure, there were lots of people – like my grandparents and my mum's family and my dad's family – who still had the dignity they'd learned from their own fathers and mothers. But a major problem for people in my time – apart from being under the government's control – was to want something they couldn't have. For most people, no matter who you are, if there's something you can't have, you want it. And for a lot of the men that was to have a drink.

For a long time, Aboriginal people had been prohibited from drinking. All you had to do was be caught with a bottle and you'd be jailed. That happened lots of times. Some white people were booze runners – they'd buy it at one price and sell it at double the price to Aboriginal people.

As for myself, I didn't have a drink of alcohol until I was twenty-seven. I'd tasted it and I didn't like it. Then, one weekend I was playing cricket in Adelaide. After the game finished, we went to a hotel. It was stinking hot and a bloke bought me a schooner of beer. I drank it quickly and it tasted so nice I thought, *Oh well, I'll have another one of those.*

But I wasn't a heavy drinker. It never got to the stage where I was dying for a drink and I'd give everything for a drink. If we went out somewhere I'd have a beer with the rest of the blokes after cricket or after footy, but that was it. Sometimes I wouldn't even have a beer.

One year when I was captain-coach of the Currie team, after the football season had finished we went to Booborowie for a weekend away and to play a game. There was only one pub and we were all sitting in the lounge. The owner came straight over to me and said, 'Sorry, I can't serve you.' I just said to the owner, 'That's okay, mate. I don't drink anyway.' He didn't know what to say. All the other players were up in arms and wanted to go somewhere else. But the next closest pub was in Burra, miles away. Plus we were going to be playing football in Booborowie the next day. 'No, we'll ride it out,' I said to them. It was just one incident. I knew there were other places doing the same, where they wouldn't serve

Aboriginal people in the bar. Some pubs back then had a little hole in the wall at the back of the place where Aboriginal people had to go to collect their drinks. This was how things were across the country before the 1967 referendum, when Aboriginal people could finally be counted in the census and seen as proper citizens.

There might be Aboriginal people who wonder why I put in the story earlier about my relatives drinking goom, because it's a bit degrading to my people. I've put it in because it happened, it was life at that time, and I was part of it. The point is, when you've got nothing else, and very little control over your life, what do you do?

18

'I went to every dance and never felt out of place'

Dances were still a big part of life in Currie. Frank, Pat and I would go whenever and wherever a dance was on. Sometimes they'd be in really small places like a church hall out in the scrub. Everybody from around would come, and the place would be full and rocking. The band would be made up of locals playing different instruments – piano, saxophone, guitar, drums. It was real country-style. They'd have a really good supper too.

I went to every dance and never felt out of place. I was getting a bit of money in my pocket and could buy decent clothes. I was always dressed as well as anybody else, and I'd dance all night. Some of the dances we did were the quickstep, foxtrot, modern waltz and progressive Canadian barn dance. That last one was good because you'd go into two big circles, the women on the inside and the men on the outside, and the women would move one way and the men the other, and as you moved around you'd dance with different girls. You'd speak to lots of girls that you probably otherwise wouldn't have had a dance with at all.

It gave me an opportunity to say hello and get their feelings about dancing with an Aboriginal person. A lot of the time they'd seen me play footy and they knew who I was – that helped. And they could see I was a modern dresser, especially compared to some of the old farmers who stuck with one suit. I didn't have the same old, same old: I had five or six different suits. Things like that made you stick out. I think people looked at me and appreciated it.

As well as those dances on Saturday nights all around the Peninsula, they'd have a big ball once or twice a year, like the RSL or the Catholic ball. For those you'd dress up that little bit more. At the time, I thought I was showing people that Aboriginal people can do these things too. But in reality I was enjoying myself so much that perhaps I didn't care about that. I just danced my legs off!

How I came to have good suits was that one day I was in Adelaide and came across a little shop called Scott's Menswear. I went in and the bloke working there asked me what sort of suit I was after. His name was Ollie and he was a dapper dresser. He was a migrant and I found out he'd played soccer with Charlie. By then Charlie had become one of Adelaide's star players and had been recruited to play soccer in England. When Ollie heard I knew Charlie, our relationship grew. In the end I could go in and buy a couple of suits and say, 'Put that on my bill and I'll fix it up,' and he'd say, 'No worries.' He'd always get paid.

Ollie really looked after me. I'd have the latest city styles, which usually took a couple of years to get to the country towns. First there were the ones with one vent at the back. Then, rather than blue or black pinstripe, you could get all sorts of colours, like green. Then came the suits with two vents at the back. Then things like single-breasted rather than double-breasted. You could have a three-piece suit too, although I didn't go for them much. The size of your ties changed from long thin ones to big wide ones. Your shirt collars changed from pointed ends to rounded ends, then for a while they had a gold trim going through the collar to pull it together. And cufflinks for your shirts – I had a whole variety of them.

For all those years I was in Currie, and all the balls that I went to, from Kadina to Wallaroo, down to Yorketown, Warooka, Edithburgh, the whole of the Peninsula, there was only one time I remember that anyone refused to dance with me. Not a bad percentage.

The dance happened to be in Maitland, which in the early days had been classified as a racist place. The people from Point Pearce used to do their shopping there and they'd often be treated pretty rudely.

They were two girls who were toffee-nosed and thought they were better than anyone else. It was funny. Everybody else I'd asked for a dance said yes, but when I asked each of them they both said no.

The next dance was the progressive Canadian barn dance, the one where you're in two circles, with the blokes on the outside and the girls on the inside. When I came to those two girls, instead of dancing with them I walked along as though they weren't there.

Well, they were very embarrassed. You could see it on their faces. Because everybody was looking at them and must have been wondering why I didn't dance with them. It didn't worry me, but it certainly worried them. I'd decided that if they didn't want to dance with me when I asked them, they weren't going to dance with me in this one.

I didn't want to be swearing and calling people names. I thought there were better and more dignified ways to do things.

* * *

Near the end of 1957, I took a job with Mr and Mrs Thomas, who I knew from football. I'd had my first year as captain-coach with Currie and we'd won the premiership, and sometimes I'd meet Mrs Thomas in the street and she always wanted to stop and talk. She was a red-hot fan of the team.

Mr Thomas's name was Watkin Holmes Thomas, a Welsh name, but they all called him Ken, and Mrs Thomas's name was Alice. They had four kids. Pat was twenty, about the same age as me. Marlene was seventeen, Brenda fifteen and Robert nine.

Mr Thomas said they were looking for someone to help with the harvest but he couldn't pay me much, and I said that was okay. I wasn't interested in what they could pay me – all I was concerned about was having somewhere to stay and three meals a day. Next thing it was all decided, and I was in the car going home with them.

The Thomases' farm was about ten miles from Currie, at a small place called Port Julia, and it was just under a thousand acres. It was hilly and sandy, and it had a bit of scrub on it, which was good because when the sheep were shorn they had somewhere for cover if it was rough weather.

Their land ran right down to the beach, so when I was driving the tractor I could watch what was going on at sea. I'd see dolphins jumping and sometimes a whale. If it was hot you could go down and have a swim. It was a good place to train for footy too – when I wanted to get really fit I'd run down to the beach every morning.

The farm was probably a bit marginal, in terms of growth and yield. If you wanted the rain you had to be on the other side of the Peninsula. But they kept their heads above water, although sometimes it was difficult.

The house was a lovely big old place with a veranda right around. Inside there were three or four bedrooms, and on the veranda there was a long sleep-out, which was where I stayed.

The Thomases' place became home. I called Mrs Thomas 'Mum', which she liked, and I called Mr Thomas 'the boss'. They called me Vin or Vince. As well as the farm work I helped him out with different jobs around the house. One time we put in a tennis court because the three girls were playing that a lot. Another time we put in a shower and dug a pit for a septic tank.

When other farmers were shearing, or putting in seed for the crops, or harvesting or lumping, Mr Thomas would let me go off to work with them. One job I had was driving a truck in the quarry. In between, I'd just do little jobs for him at the farm.

If I had to go to footy practice and I couldn't get a lift, I'd take the farm ute. After a while Mr Thomas thought he'd help me get a car of my own, to give me a little bit of independence. We went up to Maitland to the used caryard and bought a little black-and-silver rag hood Vauxhall. You'd fold the hood back so it went from being a covered car to a sports car. With the hood down and the wind blowing, I thought I was Stirling Moss – although the Vauxhall would have been battling to go sixty or seventy miles per hour. Mr Thomas paid for it – I think it was about a hundred pounds – and I paid him back. Later I traded the Vauxhall in for a grey Austin A40, then a green-and-white Holden and later a Valiant. I was earning money so I was able to do it.

When the lumping was on I'd earn big money. They paid per bag, and sometimes there'd be days where you were working from seven in the morning to eight at night without a let-up, apart from lunch. The farmers wanted to get their crops off and

Here's my first car. That's the Thomases' house behind it, with the sleep-out on the right, where I had my room.

in the bags and out of the farm and down to the port as quickly as they could. Then they could clean up and go for a holiday.

I mentioned 'lumping' before. I'll tell you a bit more about it, because a lot of people don't realise what's involved and how much skill there is in it. Once the wheat or barley has grown, it's reaped with a combine harvester and header. Someone drives it through the paddock and the header cuts the top off the plant and collects it in the harvester. The header's set up so that when it reaps the crop it strips all the rubbish from the head of the grain. Back in those days the grain would either go into a box or come straight out of a pipe, and a worker would be on a little platform filling up big jute bags. Once a bag was filled you sewed the top up tight enough that the grain wouldn't come out, then you put it onto what they called the elevator, which had a moving belt that took the bags up onto the farmer's truck and trailer. Once it was there another bloke would sling it onto his shoulder, then swing round and stack it. That's lumping the grain.

When the truck was full we'd drive it down to the port and the same thing would happen in reverse. You'd have other lumpers working at the port too, building the stacks properly – there was a certain way to do it, otherwise the whole thing would fall over. You'd start off with rows of wood to keep the bags off the ground in case it got wet. You had to be careful about mice plagues too, and so you'd build a tin boundary about two and a half feet high around the stacks. Once you had the base set, you had to know how to tie them all in, one by one, until you were three or four storeys high.

Sometimes you'd build the stacks in a big shed, but if there wasn't enough room in the shed to do it, once the stacks were finished you'd build a cover with corrugated-iron roofing that you sat on the top of the bags then covered with jute or hessian. You'd have boards down each side of the stack that you nailed the cloth onto. It was like a makeshift shed.

The work was hard. You'd be really busy and some of the bags would be very heavy. Each one had stitched seams on either side and if you had the seam running on your neck as you carried them it would cut you. One time we had a couple of blokes working with us who said they were good lumpers, but by the end of the day they had blood running out of their necks because they'd been carrying the bags wrong. The stacking wasn't so easy either. Sometimes the farmers who were less experienced than us would try to help, and you'd end up with the stack all out of kilter. Next minute it would all fall over and you'd have to start again.

There were lumpers everywhere on the Peninsula, mainly where they could get the bags to transport. Some of the loads went out by boat and some went out on trains, so there'd be lumpers at the port and by the train lines. In the early days there were ketches that ran across the gulf from Port Adelaide to all the little towns like Pine Point, Ardrossan and Port Julia. They were good days working at the port.

It all came to an end when silos were built. Everything shifted to bulk handling and they switched from sea and rail to trucking the grain out. At the farms, as the grain came off the harvester, we'd still put it into bags and we'd still put the bag on the elevator up to the truck, but the trucks had big bins, and as the bag came up someone would be standing on a plank with a knife and they'd grab the bag and cut it open and tip the grain into the bin. They'd throw the bag on the ground, and someone else down there would stack the empty bags up. When the bin was full, the grain would be taken to the silo. Most of the trucks by then were tip trucks, and they'd drive into the unloading bay and tip the grain into a grid and it would go onto belts and into the silo system.

With bulk handling coming in, Mr Thomas decided he needed a new grain elevator. The way they worked was by moving all the grain from the header straight into a holding bin, instead of into bags. From the holding bin you'd empty it into trucks that would take it to the silos at Ardrossan – no more bags, no more sewing. The new grain elevators were a fairly heavy piece of machinery that sat on two wheels. They had a motor, a long chute and a mechanised shovel to scoop the barley or wheat up with. Nobody had to handle anything – you just started up the motor and that did all the work.

One day the boss saw an advertisement for a grain elevator up in Wee Waa in New South Wales. Some people there who used to live at Maitland were selling it. Wilf Huddleston and Tim Campbell, who'd been another one of the younger Mulgoa boys, were staying with me at the farm, and I suggested to the boss that we could go up and get it, because I had a tow bar on my car.

It was a long trip and we had to stop at a motel for a night. When we got into Wee Waa the next day, we went into the post office to get directions. But the people in the post office ignored us as if we weren't there. Out on the street we asked some other people and they just brushed us aside. We spent half the morning trying to find out where to go.

'Come on, let's get out of here,' I said to the others after a while. 'This is a racist mob.'

'But what about the elevator?' Wilf said.

I rang the boss to tell him what had happened, and he said to come home. He was quite prepared to think we'd get an elevator some other way.

We took off and were driving along when I saw a sign — it was the place we'd been looking for. We went in and the two Maitland people were ready for us. I asked them what the matter with the people in Wee Waa was, and they said they were a bit touchy because, to them, Aboriginal people were what they called 'chippers' — people who weeded the cotton crops by hand. As far as I could gather, they treated them like African slaves. All of this was good learning for me. I'd never learned it in school, but I certainly learned it out in the open world.

Towing the elevator back to Currie was hard on my car and it cracked one of the pistons in the motor. The boss had a pit with pulleys in the shed that we used for taking tractors to pieces and putting them back together again. Doing the car was a piece of cake. And the elevator was really what the boss wanted on the farm, so it was worth the trip.

* * *

When the boss bought me the car, I went to see Josie the first chance I had. She'd married Freddie Agius in 1956 and they'd moved to Port MacDonnell, which is a few hundred kilometres south of Adelaide, straight down from Mount Gambier. You can't go any further south — it's right at the bottom of the coast and from there you're looking to Tasmania. It was a nice little town and they fitted in well. Freddie was working on the cray boats and coaching the local football team. He'd played league football for West Adelaide, so he was pretty good. Josie being a mad netballer, the town liked having her there too. That's what towns like that were always looking for – netball and football players.

It was a fair trip from Currie. I left early one morning and stopped the night with Winnie and her family, who by then were living in Taperoo, a suburb near the boys' home and Port Adelaide. Then I got up at about four in the morning and headed down the coast road through Meningie and past Raukkan.

I spent a fortnight with Josie and Freddie, and I could feel all the time that Josie wanted to go back to Adelaide for a week or two to catch up with Winnie and the kids. Freddie was working long days on the cray boats, away for a week or more sometimes, and she was home looking after their sons, young Fred and Raymond. I think she probably felt a bit lonely there. So when it was time for me to go home, Josie and the boys came with me.

We took the inland road this time, and on the way we stopped in at Penola to see Aunty Doris and Uncle Cecil Graham and their kids. The government had moved them from Point Pearce to Penola, along with another Point Pearce family, the Wilsons, who were my cousins too. This was the assimilation time, when the government was trying to blend Aboriginal people in with white people, rather than have us living on missions and reserves. Aunty Doris's kids were talented sportspeople and so were the Wilsons. I think that's one of the reasons why they were among the first lot to be moved from Point Pearce. Places like Penola were football mad, and I think the government thought they'd fit into those communities all right. The kids went to school and the older ones got jobs, and they all played sport.

They copped a bit of prejudice – the kids being called names, people calling them and other Aboriginal people 'you people' and not in a nice way – that sort of thing. Aunty Doris soon took care of that and set them right.

Not everyone there was like that, but enough were, at least in the early days. After I'd been to Penola a couple of times I could see the difference between how they reacted to my uncle and cousins, and how Currie people were with me and people like Uncle Cliff. When I'd first gone to Currie I'd expected it to be like Penola, but it just wasn't. You were quickly part of the town. They treated me just like anyone else. That was Currie for you.

19

'In England he could walk down the street with whoever he liked'

All up I lived with the Thomases' for thirteen or fourteen years. I was nearly twenty-one when I first went there and I left when I was thirty-four.

When I first moved in, the three girls, Pat, Marlene and Brenda, didn't see me as being an Aboriginal person from Point Pearce. They saw me as a working man helping their dad and mum on the farm, and they saw that I played football for Currie. Like their mum, they were mad football followers.

I don't know how long I'd been living there when the youngest sister, Brenda, and I had our first kiss. She reckons it was only a few months. It was impulse. We were in the lounge room and Brenda was sitting on the lounge, and I think I was trying to fit in between her and her sister. All of a sudden we were entangled, and her lips were there so I kissed them.

'Aw, gee!' she said, jumping up.

We both looked at each other in amazement. I don't remember whether it was Brenda or me who said, 'What did we do that for?'

I don't know what colour I turned, but she'd turned red. Anyway, it was over and done with. We thought it was just something that happened and it wasn't going to happen again. But I don't think Brenda minded that it had happened, because from then on she didn't want anybody else.

We were a bit sneaky for a while, trying not to let anybody know we were making contact. They all worked it out, though. Brenda and I used to sit out on the front veranda and talk, and her sisters would poke their heads out of the window or come outside quickly and try to catch us at whatever they thought we were doing. Which we weren't.

There was something going on, though. At the farm I did a lot of fencing. I'd be in the tractor with the post-hole borer hooked on, going along and putting all the holes into the ground at the right distances apart. When you're putting the post holes in you've got to make sure you're in a straight line from start to finish. If you turn even just a small distance from the line you want, you could be three or four feet out by the end. Having a crooked line wasn't what fencing was all about. Papa Joe had taught me that. So I'd have someone at the other end watching me in the tractor and letting me know whether I was straight or off line. One particular time I was putting a fence in down a slope to the beach. Brenda was watching me to help me make sure I got it straight, but mostly she was watching me.

Brenda's parents must have realised at some stage that Brenda and I were becoming what you could call friendly. I'm not sure Brenda's mum appreciated it at first. One day I was walking through the kitchen and I said something to her, and when she answered me she called me 'Mr Copley'. She'd never done that before. I thought, *Hello, she's twigged here.* I think it was a short way of saying she wasn't okay with what was going on. Brenda was six years younger than me and I was a bit of a football star, so I suppose she was impressionable.

There were different girls around the district, especially once I'd learned to dance, who enjoyed dancing with me and striking up a conversation. But with any of them it never got to more than that. There was just something about Brenda that was different to other girls. Her dad and mum were strong people, and she was too. Before too long, she was saying to her parents that we were going to get married, whether they approved or not.

But I still had no intention of getting married young. I was looking at other young blokes around the district who were married – and some, I could see, their wives weren't happy if their husbands spent too much time at footy or away on footy trips. I wanted to keep playing and coaching football really well, and I said to Brenda that I didn't want to get married until I'd finished. She fitted in with that for a long while.

Brenda was pretty smart. She topped the class at her school, and the teacher wanted her to study to be a teacher, but she wasn't allowed to. Her mum wanted the kids to stay there in the district. At the time I think a lot of farm kids only went up to Grade Seven, but Brenda did an extra year of school by correspondence. The education people in Adelaide would send her things to read and write about, and she'd send them back and be marked on them, and she did well. When she finished school she started selling Avon beauty products and she'd deliver them around the district and bring in her own money. She had jobs cleaning people's houses too.

I was getting to know Brenda's life pretty well because I was living there. I saw her two older sisters get married and leave and start to have their families.

Brenda and I did lots of things together, and she was getting to know all about the other parts of my life. Winnie and Josie used to come and see me at the farm with their husbands and kids. Brenda would look after the kids and she'd take them everywhere. We'd go to Adelaide pretty regularly too and catch up with Winnie and Josie and their families there. We'd go and see the St Francis boys too, and different ones of them would come for weekends, or a fortnight in the school holidays.

Whenever any of the boys visited, Brenda would set up extra beds in my room in the sleep-out, and we'd spend the weekend down by the beach or looking for rabbits. Charlie, John, Gordon, Wilf, Tim, Gerry and some of the other boys used to come over and stay for a weekend or over their holidays.

Brenda loved cooking for the boys. The boss usually would have killed a sheep for us all, and Brenda would make roasts and big plates of sandwiches. Then she'd send them home with a leg of lamb. She really wanted to look after them all. One time Charlie came and stayed on his way driving to Alice Springs and she spent half the day making sandwiches for him so he wouldn't starve on the trip.

'You don't have to do that,' I said.

'Yes I do,' she said. She just loved them.

* * *

Curramulka ended up being the best team in the Southern Yorke Peninsula League for a few years running. We won the premiership in 1957, 1958 and 1959, and I was the coach for those years. That alone gives you a little feather in your cap, I suppose. All the ladies of the district loved watching the footy too, and they loved that Currie was winning. Whenever they saw me in the street in town they'd want to talk to me. 'You better come out to tea,' they'd say. That was the feeling of Curramulka.

Playing for the Curramulka Magpies. You can see the blur of the ball just to my right, and all the cars lined up around the oval.

On the Peninsula there were a few different football leagues, and every year each one would pick a combination team to play in a carnival. Our league had six teams in the competition. A few players would be picked from each team and then they'd pick a coach.

One year when I was coaching Currie, and we hadn't lost a game all season, I thought I'd probably be the coach of the combined team. But the selectors picked an old bloke who'd retired three years before. I had a shot at them about it and reminded them that we hadn't been beaten. In response they said they'd make me the captain of the team, then they walked away as if to tell me it was nothing to do with me. I thought, *Okay, that's their decision, that's fine*, and I kept going to training with the other players.

At the last training night before we played, the selectors came up to me. 'When you're out there, don't you make any moves and don't say anything to the other players,' one of them said. 'Leave that to the coach.'

I was upset. I was going to be out there as the captain of the team and they were saying I wouldn't be allowed to talk to players or move them around. 'Listen,' I said, 'I'm the captain. What you're saying isn't how I learned to play football.' I said to them that I thought that apart from it being racist, it was also rubbish. Then I told them to make somebody else the captain. I said I'd still play because I was part of the team and I wasn't that chicken-hearted – you'd have to be a pretty small man to want to spit the dummy over it, and that wasn't in my makeup. I kicked four or five goals that match. I gave it the best I could. I wanted them to remember who I was.

Apart from that time in the combination team, I think there was only one bloke who had a racist attitude in all the years that I played football on the Peninsula. That was at Minlaton. He was a big-noter in the community, and he had a big mouth. He couldn't catch me and he called me a 'black bastard'. So I stopped and I punched him. I hurt him and I intended to hurt him. Not that I'm like that usually – it was just in the heat of the moment. The rest of the Currie team didn't appreciate what he said to me either.

You'd hear those stories about blokes who couldn't play as well as you, and the first thing that would come out of their mouth was the colour of your skin. People would be calling you names and wanting to hurt you if they got the opportunity. I thought it was a waste of their energy and it made them a lesser player.

Years before, I'd been playing football at Adelaide Oval and I did something good in the play that annoyed a bloke in the opposition. I don't know what it was, but he started chasing me and calling me racist names. I ran from one end of the ground to the other, and he finally caught me down the River Torrens end. I fell over and he jumped on me and started punching the hell out of me. And I was laughing. There was no anger. I knew that unless he really wanted to harm me he probably wouldn't. When I started laughing I felt his attitude change, as if he was thinking, *What's the use? Here I am trying my hardest to hurt him and he's laughing.* He jumped up and went on with the game.

Most of the blokes that carry on like that are frustrated because you're three yards quicker than they are and they can't catch you. Sometimes anger comes out in their voice or they try to do all sorts of stupid things to stop you playing the way you are. But Mum's words would always be in my head: 'Whatever happens, you've got to show them you're as good as anybody else.'

* * *

I broke my leg during a match in the 1960 season and had to have it pinned. It laid me up for a few months. When I went back to playing footy it was taking a while to come good, especially on the hard ground of the country ovals.

I'd kept in touch with my old Port Adelaide coaches and I knew that Fos Williams was coaching South Adelaide. I decided to see if training on the softer grounds in Adelaide might be better for a while, so I drove to Adelaide and trained for a couple of nights. Realistically, I thought I had no hope of making the team. I was just there so I could train on the soft grounds.

I ended up playing eleven games with them. I'd drive there every Tuesday and Thursday for training then stay at Winnie's place, and I'd head back to Currie the next morning. On Saturdays I'd go back for the match.

Mostly I held my own in terms of talent, except for one day. I was battling a bit with my leg and Fos ripped into me. He wanted me to come back to Adelaide to live and work. If I'd wanted to be fair dinkum about playing football I could have done that. But my own thinking was that I'd proved to myself I could make it if I wanted to. It had been the same at Fitzroy. I thought I was probably good enough to play top football, but each time other things had become too hard to cope with. I was comfortable at Currie. I liked the people and the work, and I liked living at the Thomases' and being around Brenda. I didn't want to move, so I said no to Fos.

* * *

Around the same time I was playing football in Currie, Charlie had been playing professional soccer with some really good teams in Adelaide, first United International and then Budapest. One day he was spotted by a talent scout from England, and they offered to pay half his fare for him to go over and try out with them. So in 1957 he'd gone over by boat. He had a look around parts of Europe and played soccer in different cities in England. One match was at Oxford University and that gave him some ideas about going to university himself.

Charlie noticed how in Europe and England he could walk down the street with whoever he liked, whereas in South Australia he hadn't been able to because of the consorting law. And then there was the South Australian *Aborigines Act*. It had been in for a long time and it gave the protectors control over us, like being able to take kids away from their parents and having the exemption certificates.

Before Charlie went to England, and then while he was away, some of the Colebrook girls and the St Francis boys had been meeting up regularly to talk about the problems with the laws. They decided to get in touch with a local politician called Don Dunstan, who was in the state Labor opposition. Dunstan had been to Point Pearce in 1956 and been shocked by how bad conditions were for the people there, and he was starting to stir things up. Being a lawyer, he thought getting some of the laws changed was a good place to begin. A group of people decided to start off trying to get the consorting part of the *Summary Offences Act* repealed.

People in the Aborigines Advancement League were all part of it too, including Aunty Glad. They ran some good campaigns to let the public know the bad effects that law was having. There were public meetings and people wrote letters to the editors of the newspapers. They'd point out silly situations, like one where an Aboriginal bloke and his white workmate used to drive together to work every day, then one day they got pulled over by a policeman who told them they could be charged with committing an offence. That's how ridiculous it was.

Charlie was part of the campaign before he went away, and he started to give speeches. The league organised a petition against the law and something like 7000 people signed it. Gradually the politicians got the message and in 1958 the state government repealed that section of the act.

Getting that change to the law taught us a lot and got everyone fired up to do more about the *Aborigines Act*. Parts of it weren't always being enforced anymore, but the threat of it was always there. The league and other groups started going round the traps telling people about it and getting them to sign a petition. That time they got something like 14,000 signatures. The politicians argued about it for a while and then, in 1962, they brought in a new act of parliament which overturned the old laws that for years and years had controlled us. It was another big turning point for us.

As well as work and politics, we boys were still playing sport. Charlie had been away for nearly two years when

Adelaide Croatia brought him back to South Australia to be their captain-coach in 1959. John had still been playing for Port Thistle and Charlie brought him over to play for Croatia too. They were both really popular players. Gordon at that stage had been playing Australian Rules football with Exeter Football Club – that's a suburb next to where the boys' home was – and so had Wilf Huddleston, Richie Bray and Harry Russell. Then Charlie got Gordon to switch to soccer and play for Croatia too. Wilf and Richie ended up following in Malcolm Cooper's footsteps and playing league for Port Adelaide.

I'd come to Adelaide regularly to see the boys, and Brenda would sometimes come too. We'd have St Francis House reunions, and Father Smith and Mrs Smith would be there when they could. We'd get together at somebody's house and have dinner and talk about old times, and about all the changes. A lot was happening.

* * *

In early 1961, Charlie met Eileen Munchenberg at a soccer dance. She was from a big German family in Adelaide. In September that year they got married, and soon after they moved to Sydney so Charlie could go to university there. But before he could go to uni he had to go to college to get the right entry qualifications. He'd been made captain of the Pan Hellenic soccer team in Sydney, and he was getting paid to do it, but it wasn't very much in those days. Not like now. He had some cleaning jobs in the holidays, but mostly Eileen was supporting them, working as a bookkeeper and typist.

One time John, Gerry and I went over and spent a weekend with them. They were living in a rathole in Glebe, just across the road from Sydney University, and they were both working hard. But they still managed to look after us and feed us really well.

Lots of times Charlie was nearly ready to give it up, but he kept going. At university he was doing an arts degree and studying politics, and he was working more and more with a church minister called Ted Noffs and a group of people who wanted to set up a centre where Aboriginal people could come to get help with jobs and education and finding somewhere to live. Around the country more and more of the people who'd been living in missions were drifting away from them and into cities, because of assimilation, which was the go then. In 1964, Charlie, Ted and the others they were working with bought a building in George Street in Sydney, where they started up the Foundation for Aboriginal Affairs. That's where Charlie really started to become vocal, and he never really stopped.

20

'Winnie met with the prime minister'

Not long after Charlie and Eileen got married, Gordon had gone to England to play soccer, and he'd stayed there a while. That's where he met Norma, the lady he married. When he came back in 1964, Charlie helped him find work and accommodation in Sydney.

In 1959, a couple of years before Gordon went overseas, his uncle, a bloke called Maxwell Stuart who was from Alice Springs too, had been blamed for the rape and murder of a young girl and sentenced to death. This girl, Mary Hattam, had been murdered in Ceduna, on the west coast of South Australia, the year before. A lot of people were saying Stuart hadn't done it and that justice hadn't been done – both white people and Aboriginal people were saying that. The local Catholic priest set up a fund to get Stuart good legal advice and try to get him freed. *The News*, a South Australian afternoon newspaper, got behind the campaign, and then some politicians got involved and they had a royal commission into it. For Gordon, it must have been hard – really hard – seeing his uncle being treated like that. That case was big news and it showed how unfair it was that people who weren't even counted as citizens could still be tried and sentenced to death. There was a lot of doubt about the evidence, and Stuart ended up not being executed.

One of the people who donated money to help get legal advice for Maxwell Stuart was a bloke called Sparkes Harris, who owned the big grocery store in Yorketown, further down the Peninsula from Currie. He gave them something like a thousand pounds, a lot of money at that time.

Currie used to play against the Yorketown footy team, and this bloke's son – he was called Sparkes Harris too – was one of their players. The younger Sparkes became a good friend of mine and he still is, sixty years later. His first name's actually Joseph – Sparkes is a family name, and all the blokes in his family are called that.

One day after a game, Sparkes invited me to his place. I met his two sisters and his mum and dad. Sparkes and his family were very kind people. They were good Catholics, not that that made a difference to me. From then on we'd meet up at football in the winter and cricket in the summer – he was a mad cricketer – and we'd meet up at the dances too.

Then, in the middle of 1965, Sparkes rang me out of the blue. 'Do you want to go on a holiday to Hayman Island?' he asked. That was the first time anybody had ever asked me to go on a holiday with them. I'd been making big money lumping wheat, so it wasn't a problem.

We headed off and met up with a couple of other people who were coming too. Sparkes and I were in the same unit sleeping and we were eating together. Later on, after the trip, I realised we'd broken the law. 'Do you realise we could have been jailed?' I said to Sparkes.

While South Australia had got rid of the law that said Aboriginal people couldn't mix with white people and white people couldn't mix with Aboriginal people unless you had a good reason, Queensland still had their version of it going. Here we'd been, sitting in a plane together, on the bus, on the boat from Proserpine to Hayman Island, and then in the same cabin. *Jeepers*, I thought, *could they really have jailed us?* Things were changing, but each state was tackling their different laws about us in their own time.

I didn't find out about the Queensland law until after I got back home, so it didn't stop me enjoying my holiday. But something else nearly did. Each day on Hayman Island, Sparkes and I would pick up the newspapers. One day, there was Charlie on the front page. The police had him by the scruff of the neck and were dragging him off somewhere. He'd lost so much weight since I'd last seen him – he looked like a greyhound dog.

Charlie and Eileen had been living in Sydney for a few years by now, and he was still at university. In one of the photographs you could see he was at the airport and he was holding a young girl. *Oh gawd*, I thought, *what's he up to now?*

The little girl was a five-year-old Fijian-Indian girl called Nancy Prasad. The government had been deporting her to Fiji as part of the White Australia policy, and some Sydney University students wanted to do something to show the rest

Charlie in 1965 with Nancy Prasad, the little girl who was about to be deported because of the White Australia policy. *(Ted Golding/ The Sydney Morning Herald)*

of the country what was going on. So they decided to stage a kidnapping at the airport. Nancy's family knew all about it and were okay with it. And who did the actual kidnapping? Charlie, of course. The authorities were about to put the little girl on the plane when Charlie grabbed her and took off. Another student was waiting out the front in a car, a Volkswagen Beetle. Charlie jumped in with the girl, and they took her to a hiding place for two hours and kept her safe. Her family knew where she was the whole time.

What Charlie and the other students did that day was show people just how stupid the White Australia policy was. It had been brought in by the Australian government in 1901, and it said that anyone wanting to migrate to Australia who wasn't British or Irish would have to pass a dictation test to be allowed in. Back then they were mainly aiming it at Asian people, and Aboriginal people got caught up in the prejudice around it because they weren't white either. When Charlie kidnapped Nancy, it finally started to twig in people's heads.

The White Australia policy probably hampered the advancement of Aboriginal people, even though it couldn't ever get to the point where they could deport us. When we were playing footy there were lots of times people would say, 'Why don't you go back to where you come from.' I'd think, *How stupid are people? They're the ones who came here, not us.*

In the newspaper stories about Charlie kidnapping Nancy Prasad, they talked about the Freedom Ride too. That'd been in February 1965, six months before Nancy's kidnapping. Charlie's famous for the Freedom Ride: a fifteen-day bus trip he and some other students from Sydney University did through parts of New South Wales. They protested about swimming pools where Aboriginal kids weren't allowed to go, and RSL clubs where Aboriginal people who'd fought in the war couldn't be – places like that. They let the media know what they were doing, and the Freedom Ride got a lot of publicity. So Charlie was getting known.

Sometime after all the kerfuffle in 1965 with the Freedom Ride and Nancy Prasad, Charlie was in Adelaide for a visit, and Brenda and I came across from Currie and caught up with him. We were driving down Grand Junction Road on our way to Port Adelaide, and he was telling us about the Freedom Ride and how people had tried to run the bus they were in off the road. He was saying he'd wondered what the hell had struck them because it nearly killed them all. That wasn't him exaggerating.

But his story about kidnapping Nancy Prasad – well, all I knew was that Charlie's version of that story was a great exaggeration on the story that had been in the newspaper. He told us that the students had it all planned about what they were going to do. He said they took a Kombi van to the airport – in his mind it wasn't even just a car anymore – and Charlie was going to snatch her from the cops and slide the Kombi door open and jump in, and then the person driving the Kombi would take off.

'I grabbed her and ran for the Kombi,' Charlie said, as we were driving along. 'There were bullets flying all around us. Then I jumped in the Kombi and the bloody thing wouldn't start.'

Brenda's eyes were sticking out of her head – she was thinking that somebody could have shot him. But of course there were no bullets. He was making it all up. 'Don't listen to that,' I said to Brenda. 'He's telling lies.' That's how he used to stretch the stories for us. Brenda said he was the best storyteller she'd ever come across.

If there hadn't been people like Charlie doing things like the Freedom Ride and the Nancy Prasad kidnapping, those laws would have gone on for another twenty years. A lot of Aboriginal people, and white people too, realised we needed to come up with different ways to make people see how racist a lot of the laws were and that they'd been there for a long time and had been having really bad effects on Aboriginal people and other people too. They were also holding back any chance of there being good relations between black and white people in this country.

At the same time as Charlie was starting to make his mark in Sydney, a big push was on to change the Constitution so that Aboriginal people would finally be counted in the census and be recognised as citizens. Talk about it had been going on for years, at least since the 1938 Day of Mourning and Protest, when a group of Aboriginal people met in Sydney on the anniversary of 150 years of British rule and made a public call to the Australian people for full citizenship and equality.

Twenty years later, the people fighting for change were getting more and more organised, and a group from the different states got together and started up a national group. Its name ended up being the Federal Council for the Advancement of Aborigines and Torres Strait Islanders, or FCAATSI for short, which sounded like 'ferkatsi' when you said it. Charles Duguid organised the first meeting in Adelaide and people like Doug Nicholls were there too.

It wasn't long before Aboriginal people were directing FCAATSI more and more, which was really good. We knew the problems for our people first-hand. Like in Adelaide at the time where, not far from Taperoo where Malcolm and Aileen lived, and Winnie too, a lot of Aboriginal people were living in tents and existing on very little money because they couldn't get work, or if they did they were paid less than white people. That was all happening to people we knew really well. It fired us up to try and fix it.

* * *

In South Australia, John and Malcolm had a big part in starting up another group called the Aboriginal Progress Association of South Australia. That got going in 1964 and it was different from the Aborigines Advancement League in being mainly run by Aboriginal people. Some of the other St Francis boys were involved at different times, and Winnie was there too. Aunty Glad was a part of it for a while as well. Ever since I'd known her, from when I was a little kid, she'd been working hard to make things better for Aboriginal people in South Australia.

Malcolm was the first president, and to start with, the association used to meet at his and Aileen's home. One of the things they focused on was supporting Aboriginal people with their education – that was the beginning of Aboriginal people in South Australia being able to do college entrance studies and go to university.

A lovely old couple called the Masons from Gerard mission in the Riverland used to come to the meetings, and Marj Tripp was always around. She was an Aboriginal lady from Victor Harbor, south of Adelaide, who'd joined the navy and was involved in everything happening, like marches and national meetings. George and Maude Tongerie came along too. They were a few years older than us and we knew them from the boys' home, because they used to invite five or six of us to their place in Prospect for dinner every now and again. They were both from around Oodnadatta and they'd been Colebrook kids too. George had been in the air force during the war and fought overseas.

Don Dunstan came a few times to the meetings because he wanted things to change too. He'd invite us to Labor Party get-togethers, and sometimes Charlie would come over for those.

A little while after the progress association got going, Aunty Glad started to get different ideas about how to do things. She wanted Aboriginal women more involved in taking care of the problems our people had, and in 1966 she set up the Council of Aboriginal Women of South Australia, with Maude Tongerie and some of the other Colebrook girls like Lowitja O'Donoghue and Faith Coulthard. The state government gave them some money and they worked out of an office in Pirie Street. They did a lot of work to support women, especially mums with little kids, and they ran programs like the *Sunday Mail* Blanket Drive and a special Christmas tree every year at Bonython Park for the kids. Ruby Hammond, a lady from near the Coorong, further south of Victor Harbor, worked for them too. She was younger than Aunty Glad, and as well as being a field officer supporting people, she went out to talk to groups of mainly white people and let them know about the difficulties Aboriginal people had. She was a really good talker and people listened to her. Ruby and some of the other council women did a lot of talks in the lead-up to the 1967 referendum about why it was important to vote yes.

At the progress association we also had the idea to bring our people together through sport and family athletics days, and other social catch-ups. John and Winnie started up an Australian Rules football team we called the Nunga Football Club – Nunga's our word for ourselves as South Australian Aboriginal people, like Koori is in Victoria. Our team was the first Aboriginal team to play in an Adelaide association, and we'd play teams from the police and places like the Minda Home for people with disabilities as well. The boys from the home made up half the team and the other half was made up of boys and blokes from Point Pearce and Raukkan. That's how it worked for a while.

We had dances too so Aboriginal people could get together. In the beginning there was very little outside help, so one or two of the boys would be MC or on the door collecting the money, and their wives would do the cooking.

On Saturdays I'd play football for Currie and then on Sundays I'd jump in the car and drive over to Adelaide and play for the Nungas. I'd go along to the progress association meetings when I could, then I'd head back to Currie that night or the next morning.

Because I was making money working on the Thomases' farm I was able to upgrade my cars, and I ended up with reasonably good ones that wouldn't let me down. I'd feel confident jumping in and driving to Adelaide and back. John had a Volkswagen that broke down all the time and Malcolm had a car for his family, and we'd all join up and go on picnics. We'd go up to Port Gawler, Humbug Scrub, places like that around the city, or down the beach. If it was hot we'd go for a swim.

Every Easter, Aboriginal people would travel from around the country to Canberra, and sometimes other cities, to meet up at the big FCAATSI meeting. Each state and territory had an official delegate who was called the state secretary. Over the years the people who did that job for South Australia were Aunty Glad, Malcolm, John, Winnie and, later, me. There ended up being something like 360 resolutions on the FCAATSI books. Housing, health, jobs, wages, land rights, art and culture – all of those things were being discussed at those FCAATSI conferences.

One year Malcolm had been part of a delegation that met with Robert Menzies, the prime minister at the time, to let him know about the bad conditions Aboriginal people were living under. Another time, in the lead-up to the 1967 referendum, Winnie was part of a group of FCAATSI delegates that met with Harold Holt, another prime minister. Doug Nicholls was in that group too.

The FCAATSI group with Prime Minister Harold Holt in 1967. My sister Winnie is second from right. The others are Gordon Bryant, Faith Bandler, the PM, Doug Nicholls, Harry Penrith and, to the right of Winnie, William Wentworth. *(National Archives of Australia: A1200, L62232)*

* * *

After the 1966 football season finished, Sparkes asked me if I'd coach Yorketown the next year. I said yes. I was still part of the Currie community, and in a country place like the Peninsula I thought there might be a bad feeling when the two teams played each other, but there wasn't. One or two people probably had a thing about it, but overall everything continued along the same lines as before.

I was at the Thomases' and working around the district and going down to Yorketown three times a week for coaching and the matches on Saturdays. It was the lead-up to the referendum, which finally happened on the twenty-seventh of May 1967. That was when Australians voted to say Aboriginal people should be counted in the census and be seen as proper citizens. More than 90 per cent of Australians voted yes and every state supported it. That showed a pretty big change of heart by Australians.

Lots of Aboriginal people had worked really hard for it, and white people too. It's a pretty significant date and lots of people remember it. I was on the Peninsula driving back and forth to Yorketown for football and getting the seeds ready for the crops.

Yorketown made it into the finals that year, and they hadn't done that for a while. But the next year it fell to pieces. The players didn't have the same heart that the Currie players had. It was a bigger town and different situations. After two years coaching Yorketown, I came back and played again with Currie.

21

'Things were starting to change'

Brenda was adamant we were going to get married.

Her dad had said that we had to think about our kids and that they might cop some rubbish.

'Well, our children will be brought up to be very proud of their Aboriginal heritage as well as their Welsh heritage,' Brenda said. She told him he could give us his blessing, but that we were going to get married with or without it.

She'd wanted us to get married for a long time. I'd said I wasn't going to get married until I was thirty and finished with football. I was in my last year of footy and a bit older than that when Brenda picked the date. It was good she did that, because I'm the worst maker-upper of my mind.

By that time, we'd been seen together all around the district, at the balls and footy and everywhere. Everybody knew we were going to get married one day. By then, too, I knew that her parents had accepted me. On Saturdays in summer her dad played bowls and I played cricket, and we'd meet up after at the hotel for a drink then come home and have tea together. And her mum had stopped calling me Mr Copley a long time ago.

Brenda put the wheels in motion. She set the time and the date, and she was ready to roll. But there was one thing I was still supposed to do, and that was to ask her dad for her hand in marriage. I didn't have a clue how to do that or even where to start. I was putting it off as long as I could.

'Go on, ask Dad about marrying me,' Brenda would say to me.

'I will, I will,' I'd say back. This went on for a few weeks.

Brenda's dad and I used to go over to the shed, and we'd do some work then have a yarn about different things. One morning, he was sitting there on some equipment and I could tell he wanted me to ask him.

'Now what about this wedding?' he said eventually.

What am I going to say? I was thinking. I started to say that the best thing to do was to ask Brenda. Then somebody called out to him from the house, and he got up and took off, so I didn't have a chance to answer. *Oh, phew, gee that's good,* I thought.

That was the end of the conversation. Until the next time. And the next time.

Later on Brenda told me that she and her dad and her brother, Robert, had been winding me up. Apparently each time he said to me, 'Now what about this wedding?' I'd jump up, walk around and look outside the shed, then come in and sit down again, and then be about to say something. Robert would be watching, and that would be the signal to call the boss away and leave me there. They'd all be laughing about it after.

This is at Point Pearce when I was a little kid. I'm in the middle row on the left. At the back is Aunty Doris. Wearing the jockey cap is my brother Colin, and next to him is our sister Maureen. The others are some of my cousins.

I'm here with Mum and my sister Josie. We're not sure where it is, but it's probably me dressed up for school when we lived at Mile End. I liked wearing smart jackets even back then.

By the time I was living at Point Pearce mission in the 1930s, it had a few more buildings on it than when this historic photograph was taken in 1890. *(State Library of South Australia, B 9804)*

These are Mum's parents, Joe and Maisie May Edwards. Grandma Maisie was an Adams and was descended from Kudnarto and Tom Adams. Papa Joe looked after me a lot when I was little. *(South Australian Museum)*

On the right is my grandfather Barney Warrior as a young man. On the left is his brother, whose name was Fred Warrior. The gentleman in the middle is Fred McGrath Barney had a son he called Fred, and that was my dad. *(South Australian Museum)*

A group of the St Francis boys in 1950, on our way to school. The tall one on the left is Laurie Bray, then there's Desi Price, Kenny Hampton, Richie Bray, Malcolm Cooper, Gordon Briscoe, Ron Tilmouth, me, Gerry Hill and Wilf Huddleston. *(Courtesy of the P McD Smith MBE and St Francis House Collection: www.stfrancishouse.com.au)*

In 1950, four St Francis boys were in the choir of St Paul's Anglican Church in Port Adelaide. I'm in the middle of the front row, David Woodford is second from left, Bill Espie is behind my left shoulder and Charlie Perkins is at the front on the far right.

I was one of six Le Fevr Technical School boys selected for the South Australian schoolboys' football team in 1951. The headmaster, Mr Vickery, was really proud of me. We played in a national carnival in Melbourne

You can tell how happy I was to be wearing the Fitzroy Football Club guernsey. This was the 1956 season. My kids remember that we had a small framed copy of this photo on top of the television for years. Kara always thought my hair looked funny.

Curramulka Team

A Grade Premiers 1958

I guess you can spot me here, in the middle holding the ball. This was my second year as captain-coach of Curramulka, when I was twenty-one. We'd won the premiership and we all look pretty happy. Frank Joraslafsky is standing behind my left shoulder. *(Courtesy of Curramulka Community Club)*

Curramulka Districts Assn.
COUNTRY CARNIVAL — 1960

Here's me in my Currie cricket whites. At the back, third from the left, is Rex Watters, and in the front row, sitting on my left, is Norm Agnew. In November 2021, I went to Currie to see all my old friends and I caught up with Rex and Norm. *(Courtesy of Norm Agnew)*

This was lumping time at the Thomas farm, around 1960. You can see how big the bags of wheat were. Lifting them onto the Bedford truck and stacking them kept me pretty fit and strong.

Three of the Short brothers and me taking a break from shearing. That's Keith on the left, Geoff in the middle and Gordon next to me. We're at their Uncle Lyn Short's farm at Curramulka sometime in the 1960s.

Here's Charlie Perkins, fourth from the left, on the Freedom Ride in 1965 with other students from the University of Sydney. Ted Noffs at the Wayside Chapel coordinated the publicity. The ride got lots of attention and so did Charlie. *(State Library of NSW)*

Doug Nicholls was a big part of my life. He and Mrs Nicholls looked after me when I first went to Melbourne. I learned a lot from Doug about football and about how to make things better for our people. This is at Sydney Town Hall in 1970. *(Mitchell Library, State Library of NSW, courtesy of SEARCH Foundation)*

Our wedding day in 1971. After the ceremony at the Curramulka Anglican Church, we went to Brenda's aunty and uncle's place for the official photographs. Next to me are Josie and Winnie and next to Brenda are her mum, Alice, and her dad, Ken.

Brenda and me on holiday at Kings Canyon in the Northern Territory, in the early 1970s. I was working when we first got married and we couldn't have a honeymoon, so we had this holiday a bit later instead.

Our first national NAIDOC Ball, in 1974, also became known as the NACC Ball, because we were celebrating the new National Aboriginal Consultative Committee being set up. Gough Whitlam was the prime minister and he came along and gave a speech about how important the NACC was. *(Courtesy of AIATSIS, item IDENTITY.003.BW-N05716_18A)*

n 1976 the National Aboriginal Sports Foundation carnivals were in full swing. This is Charlie and me, at centre and right, at the opening of the weekend carnival n Adelaide, with a representative from the South Australian state government. Courtesy of AIATSIS, item JACKOMOS A04 BW-N03781 06)

Over the years we had lots of reunions with Father and Mrs Smith and the St Francis boys. This was for my son Vincent's baptism in 1976. From left to right are Desi Price, John Moriarty, Charlie Perkins, me, Mrs Smith, Father Smith, Les Nayda and Gordon Briscoe. *(Courtesy of the P. McD. Smith MBE and St Francis House Collection: www.stfrancishouse.com.au)*

Here's Brenda with Kara and Vincent in the garden of our home in Manningham, Adelaide, in the late 1970s. Vincent has always loved music and he remembers nights we'd be playing The Seekers and Marty Robbins, and he wouldn't want to go to bed

Brenda was really good at keeping photos of me, but we don't seem to have many of me at work. It was a different world then, as far as people having cameras in their pockets. Here I am with Lowitja O'Donoghue, a former Colebrook girl who headed up ATSIC in the 1990s.

In 2005, I went to Lord's Cricket Ground in London to meet with the English Cricket Board and find out more about the 1868 Aboriginal cricket team tour of England. They showed me the original Ashes trophy and I was surprised by how small it is – just four inches high.

Some of my large extended family at a family gathering at our home at Hillcrest, around 2010. My daughter, Kara, and her husband, Callum McEwen, fourth and fifth from the left at the back, were living in London at the time and they'd returned for a short visit.

This was taken in 2014 and it's Kara and her husband, Callum McEwen, on the left, and Vincent and his partner, Andrea Bishop, on the right. Andrea is now deceased, which was of course very sad for Vincent and all of us

This was at Riverton in 2000, when a group of us met up to talk about the Ngadjuri book for schoolkids we were compiling. From left to right there's Adele Pring, my sister Josie, me, my cousin Irene Agius, my nephew Fred Warrior, Sue Anderson and Fran Knight. *(Robert Hannaford)*

The day the sculpture of a Ngadjuri woman and child was unveiled at Riverton in 2016. In the red jacket is Lowitja O'Donoghue and next to her is Vera Hannaford. Vera's son is artist Robert Hannaford, who created the sculpture. The Riverton community raised the funds for it. *(Lea McInerney)*

The young lady here is Emily Strawbridge, my great-niece, when she was four. With her is my niece Kathy Sutton, who is Emily's aunty. We'd popped over to Curramulka for the day to catch up with family. Kathy's been a great help to me as my co-driver and assistant on my Ngadjuri projects. *(Shendelle Strawbridge)*

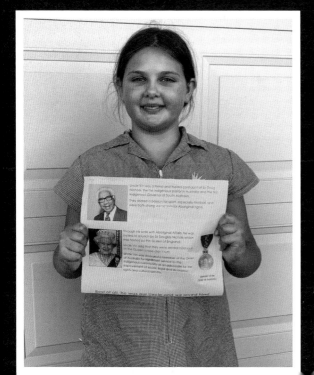

My lovely great-niece Emily Strawbridge, aged ten, with a recent project she did about her Uncle Vin for her school in Brisbane. *(Shendelle Strawbridge)*

This engraved stone is at the entrance to the Jesuit church at Sevenhill, near Clare. It acknowledges Ngadjuri people as the traditional custodians of the land, and it's been there since 2018. My niece Pat Waria-Read, who's Winnie's daughter, wrote the words in partnership with one of the Jesuits. I was there in 2019 with historian Skye Krichauff and Helen Macdonald from the Clare and Gilbert Valleys Council. *(Lea McInerney)*

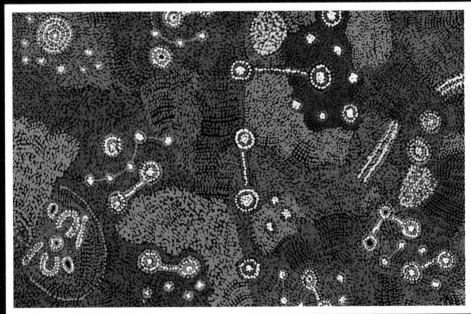

The painting on the cover of this book is *Minyma Kutjara* by Venita Woods. Born in the community of Docker River in the Northern Territory, Venita Woods is the granddaughter of acclaimed artist Maringka Baker. Now living in Kanpi on the Anangu Pitjantjatjara Yankunytjatjara Lands in South Australia, Venita paints Dreaming stories passed down to her from her grandmother. *Minyma Kutjara (Two Women)* tells the story of two sisters as they travel home across Country. *(© Venita Woods/Copyright Agency, 2022; courtesy of Japingka Gallery, Fremantle)*

* * *

Brenda was fairly strong in her own beliefs about racism. That showed when she chose her bridesmaid. Colleen Tschuna was an Aboriginal lady from Yalata on the west coast, near Ceduna. She'd been working at the Yorketown hospital for a while, and she used to come over and stay at the farm. When I first got to Currie, people said, 'Oh, there's a lovely young Aboriginal nurse at Yorketown, why don't you tee up with her?' I said, 'Why?' And they said, 'Well she's Aboriginal.' And I said, 'Well so what? Love's not colour.' Colleen knew some of the boys from the home too, and we'd all do things together. She and Brenda were the best of mates. Colleen would come and stay with us, and Brenda would look after her and run her everywhere because she didn't have a car.

One day Colleen needed to do some grocery shopping, and she and Brenda went to the general store in Maitland. Brenda walked around with her as she got things off the shelves. When Colleen went to the counter to pay, Brenda was waiting behind her. The lady at the counter looked around past Colleen to Brenda and said, 'Can I help you?'

That was like waving a red flag at a bull, of course. 'Leave it, Colleen, leave it,' Brenda said. 'We're getting out of this racist place.'

Colleen got all embarrassed. 'No, it's all right,' she said to Brenda. She would have just hung her head and waited.

'No, don't say any more,' Brenda said. 'Come on, we're getting out of this shop.'

That was the way it still was in parts of the Peninsula. Our mob had got used to standing back and waiting for everybody else to be served first. I'd first experienced it as a little kid, when I'd be with my older cousins near Port Victoria at harvest time. The barley and wheat would go into jute bags and my cousins would sew them up. I'd be watching them and I saw that they were really good at it. At lunchtime we'd all get in the horse and cart and go into the town to buy a slice of fritz and a roll. I'd be with them and we'd walk up to the counter thinking it was our turn, and there'd be a white lady or a white man behind us and they'd get served first. It was noticeable. At the time it became clear to me that this is how Aboriginal people are treated. I was five or six at most. That's probably what Brenda's dad and mum were worried about when they thought she was being pig-headed about getting married to me. 'You have kids,' they said, 'and they're going to suffer, and people are going to be calling you and them names.'

That didn't stop Brenda. When we were planning to get married, Brenda could have had her sisters as bridesmaids, but she chose Colleen.

* * *

Charlie and I had been keeping tabs on each other and catching up whenever we could. Around the time of the Freedom Ride and the Nancy Prasad kidnapping, he got the job as manager of the Foundation for Aboriginal Affairs in Sydney and finished university. He'd kept speaking out and in 1969 the government in Canberra hired him to work for them in a new set-up called the Office for Aboriginal Affairs.

Brenda and I would go to Canberra with some of the boys to see him. There'd be four or five of us: John, Wilf sometimes, Tim and Gerry. We'd catch up with Charlie and Eileen, and Gordon and Norma, who'd moved to Canberra too because Gordon was going to university there.

Sometime around then, Charlie came over to stay at the farm for a few days. During that visit we talked differently about what was happening with Aboriginal people – that lots of changes were coming, and white people in power were starting to listen more to what Aboriginal people were asking for.

Don Dunstan had become the Premier of South Australia, and Gough Whitlam, another Labor bloke, was leading the federal opposition party. Whitlam was talking a lot about how Australia needed to improve things for Aboriginal people and bring in land rights too. The government in Canberra looked like it was going to change at the next election. People were talking about self-determination for Aboriginal people, and even the government that was in was starting to make it part of their policy.

In between all the talk of politics, we'd be sitting round telling stories about the old days. Like the time about ten years before, when Charlie came to see me at the farm on his way to Alice Springs to visit his old mum, Hetti. Back then he had an old beat-up car and I wasn't too sure it would make it. He was getting ready to head off, and we were looking at the car. It didn't have a spare tyre or a jack.

'Where's your spare, Charlie?' I said.

'What do I want a spare for?'

'You're travelling to Alice over some of the worst roads. If you get a puncture, you're done.'

'Oh,' he said. 'Cop, can you get me one?' By then he knew he had Brenda as his ally.

'Brenda, do you think Cop and your dad can find a spare wheel?'

Brenda was wielding the whip to make sure we found him one. Of course he'd always do the same for others.

* * *

A few days after this latest visit of Charlie's, I was sitting on the tractor thinking, *Here I am, I've been in a utopia for all these years and I just couldn't find a better place.* I remembered how, when I first came to Currie from Melbourne, one night at footy training I'd fallen over and hit my head. The oval back then didn't have grass like the city ovals did – it was dirt with bits and pieces of gyprock sticking up out of it. I remembered how I lay there thinking to myself, *Don't worry, you're only here for a short time.*

Fourteen years later, I was still there. What Currie gave me, well, I don't have words for it. It was something that had never existed in my life before. Right from the very beginning there, all these firsts happened for me. The first time anyone asked me to tea at their home, and having people taking me to dances and teaching me how to dance. Soon enough, it wasn't just one or two people in the district, it was eighty per cent of people who appreciated me being there to talk about things with them, and they'd always listen to my point of view.

White people being interested in what I had to say – that was something that had never happened before I went to

Currie. Walking along the street in Ardrossan or Maitland I could feel the difference – people would try to avoid me. They'd think I was 'just a black from Point Pearce'. In Curramulka at the beginning, it was a strange feeling to *not* have people look at me that way.

Currie showed me that not all the world finds it difficult to deal with people of different colours. I'd found a group of people who didn't see that. What they saw was a human being who had something to offer. Often I'd think, what would I have done if Pat and Frank had said, 'No, we're sorry, we can't take you.' Where would I have gone and what would have happened to me?

But that day after Charlie's visit, as I was going round and round the paddock on the tractor I thought, *There must be something more for me to be doing than driving tractors.*

22

'The women of Currie outdid themselves'

John came over to Currie to visit. He'd been studying at Flinders University and he'd just become the first Aboriginal student there to get a degree. He was still involved with the Aboriginal Progress Association and he told me they'd been given some government money to start up an organisation that would be a centre for Aboriginal people to come to for all sorts of services and support. It was going to be called the Aboriginal Cultural Centre, and they were looking to employ Aboriginal people. John said a job to set it up was coming up, and he suggested I apply for it.

I applied and had an interview. I got the job but they wanted me to start straight away. I was lined up to coach Currie again when the season started, and Brenda and I were still talking about when we'd get married. 'You better pack your bags,' I said to her.

I left the farm work and started in the new job. That was in March 1971. During the week I'd stay with Malcolm and Aileen, and on weekends I'd go back to Currie for football and to see Brenda. A couple of times she came over to Adelaide on the bus. Then, when it was getting closer to the wedding, I looked for a place in the city for us to live.

The day Brenda and I got married, I played footy until half-time then said goodbye and headed off to get ready. Frank left then too because he was my best man.

The wedding was in Currie's Anglican church, and Father Smith from the boys' home married us. Brenda loved that he was there because she thought he was wonderful. She'd been to the St Francis reunions with Father Smith and Mrs Smith and the boys over the years. She did lots of the cooking for them, and she'd be there enjoying the same old jokes from us. Father Smith came to know her and that made them really close. She loved his quiet manner. Before the wedding he told her a few stories about me in the early days which she'd never heard. Father Smith and Mrs Smith were both pleased to be there too.

Brenda had made her wedding dress and Colleen's bridesmaid dress. Winnie and Josie were there and a few of Mum's sisters – Aunty Mary, I think, and Aunty Doris, and her husband Uncle Cecil – and all of Brenda's family. A few of the boys came: Malcolm and Aileen and their family, Gerry and Des Price. Charlie couldn't come – he was in Canberra and he hadn't been well. John was travelling overseas on a Churchill Fellowship, and I can't remember where Gordon was at the time – they were all travelling a fair bit in those days.

Our wedding day, on 26 June 1971, in Curramulka. Brenda's dress that she made herself was really good. Everyone looked great that night.

When we came out of the church the footy team were standing there in a guard of honour for us.

We had about a hundred and fifty people at the reception, which we held in the main hall in town. The women of Currie outdid themselves with the spread they put on. There was a group of ladies who looked after all the functions, like weddings or when the town celebrated winning the grand final. They'd all bring a plate of homemade food: mornay, sausage rolls, cakes, things like that. As I wandered around the room that night I was thinking, *You've been in some big shows here in this hall, but this is a big show.* Everybody was up and being merry.

Brenda's dad and mum had been through five years of drought on the farm and couldn't really afford to pay for a wedding, so we said we'd pay for it ourselves. In the end, though, they paid for the reception and I paid for the alcohol. As well as a keg, I bought a dozen bottles of champagne. Brenda's dad drank a little bit too much that night. He wasn't a big drinker but he liked a beer. Brenda remembers seeing him at the end of the night dancing and holding on to a champagne bottle. He seemed happy.

* * *

I'd found a two-bedroom unit in St Peters in Adelaide, and that's where Brenda and I had our honeymoon and started our married life, because I had to go back to work. We weren't on our own for long – a few months after the wedding, Gerry broke his leg and came to live with us for a few months. Brenda was always pretty good about things like that. She loved the boys, but she wasn't scared to let any of them know if something annoyed her. She'd get to the point sometimes where she'd say, 'Listen, pull your head in and don't do this and don't do that.' She played a really important part in our lives.

When Brenda met me I'd turned everything in her life on its head. She and her sisters were brought up on a farm, and they only really knew the people within the district. She was probably going to marry another farmer's son and live on a farm and raise sheep and cattle and kids. That was the expectation. They all went to one-teacher schools. When they finished Grade Seven, all that was available were courses you had to write away for. It was a very limited life as far as meeting and knowing other people. About the furthest they'd ever travelled was they had an aunty at Whyalla they used to go and see on her birthdays and at Christmas. Once I think they went for a holiday at Portland or Mount Gambier. That was the extent of their travel. Their life revolved around the farm and Currie and the towns and little jobs they could get cleaning houses and selling Avon and things like that.

Then along came a bloke who tipped all her thinking over, to where she was uncertain and unsure, at least for a start. But once that very small stolen kiss happened, her mind was set. That was the end of it. Nothing was going to stop her, not even me.

Those first years in Adelaide, Brenda and I rented a few different places. We were starting to get some experience of the different attitudes people had. Sometimes when we'd visit real estate agents they'd say, 'You're not going to have any wild parties, are you? You don't drink, do you? And have you got enough money to pay the rent?' All those sorts of questions they wouldn't ask a white couple. Brenda was getting used to that attitude, and it probably made her much stronger in her views. Eventually we'd get something, but she had to go through those embarrassing situations.

One time we were looking to rent a house, and we went in and talked to the real estate people, then Brenda filled in the application form. When we came out she looked back, and when we got in the car she said to me, 'Did you see that?'

'What?' I said.

'As soon as we walked out, he threw the application in the bin.'

There were so many places we went to where things like that happened. Brenda would be in tears sometimes. In the end she'd say, 'Right, you stay in the car.'

'Oh, right, okay then.' I'd sit in the car and look at the trees and the birds, and I'd think, *It's a lovely day, the sun's shining, I'm glad to be alive.*

Brenda had to experience it for herself. To me it was like water off a duck's back. In my mind these people were ignorant. I'd grown up with it and I was used to it. I felt more for Brenda. I thought, *Oh, you have to cop this every time you go somewhere – people looking at you and making comments.* This was in the early days of us living together, and it was probably the sort of thing her mum and dad had tried to tell her might be difficult. She had to work out how she'd handle it, which she did.

I thought that Brenda needed to see the world and see how people lived. She'd met the boys, so she knew what to expect in that department once we got married. She'd become a big part of the reunions we'd have. She'd become part of the boys' family, and if they got sick and we had room to look after them, we'd look after them. If we had parties, they'd be coming round. We'd go places and we'd have a car-load of them, all talking stupid things about life and making jokes. Brenda could joke the same sort of way. I'd been with a few girls previously, and when they met the rest of the boys I'd get a feeling about them along the lines of, *I don't think I can put up with these blokes.* That didn't happen with Brenda. She met the boys' girlfriends and wives and made friends with them. She got to know Charlie's wife, Eileen, and Gordon's wife,

Norma, and the three of them got on like a house on fire. They all had one thing in common, and the rest of the world could please themselves.

I started to see a real lot of strength in her. We'd go out for a meal, and if the waitress looked past me to serve her, she'd pick that up very quickly and she'd say something. She soon let people know. I'm the opposite – I'd sooner walk away than argue.

I think the attraction with Brenda was her stubbornness, and seeing her grow, and knowing in my own mind that she would be able to cope. I didn't want to put anyone under stress. There were lots of lovely girls that I met along the way and became friendly with, but they just didn't seem to fit in with what I was thinking. I knew there'd be times when it was going to be really hard. Brenda fitted the bill pretty well on that. She didn't take any funny business and she just got stronger as she went.

It was good to see the way she changed to become very, very strong. She didn't take any rubbish. One day we went to a bank to borrow money for a mortgage. I was in front, and the clerk looked around me. 'Can I help you?' he said to Brenda.

Well that was the end of that. She gave him a mouthful. 'We're getting out of here. We don't want your money that bad.'

When she was younger and something like that happened, she'd shudder and wait for me to say something. Of course I'd just say, 'Oh okay, that's fine.' I'd put up with that rubbish plenty of times before. I'd just be thinking, *All right mate, you're a dope.* But as time went on, Brenda wouldn't let people get away with it. That was really good. I think her mum and dad realised that about her too, and they were happy to see it.

My way of dealing with the rubbish we copped was to get on with doing what I wanted to do as much as I could. What my mum said was always there for me: 'You're as good as anybody else.' I wasn't frightened of going anywhere or doing anything. I'd just go. If people wanted to move away from me, that was fine. I didn't waste my time and energy being frightened of those people. There were plenty of good people around who didn't do that.

Sometimes I'd meet up with Aboriginal people I knew and take them to one of the best restaurants. 'Oh we can't go here,' they'd say.

'Why?' I'd say.

'Well it's too flash. They don't allow Aboriginals.'

'This is where I booked us in, this is where we're going to eat,' I'd say.

They were only little things, but that was probably the beginning for some of them of thinking differently. They started to realise they didn't have to be scared of going here and going there. In my own little way I suppose that was a contribution I made to a different type of thinking.

I could see that times were starting to change. Charlie and other Aboriginal people were becoming more and more prominent in the media, and the government was setting up different bodies for Aboriginal people nationally, and gradually more Aboriginal organisations were being set up in the states. The feeling I had back then was that gradually this racism would probably simmer down a little.

* * *

The first thing the Aboriginal Progress Association did with the new funding was set up an office at 264 North Terrace, opposite the Royal Adelaide Hospital. The next thing we had to do was find a building for the services we wanted to bring together. The idea was that instead of people having to go to different places for health, employment, housing and other support, it could all happen from one place. We had a look at similar set-ups in smaller places in Swan Hill and Ceduna, and then we started looking around Adelaide for a building. We had enough money to pay for a secretary as well, and we hired a middle-aged white lady called Mrs White. She did a really good job and we worked together well.

A few of the local people didn't like it that some of the old St Francis boys were involved in the progress association, because they were classed as being from the Northern Territory. A lot of the South Australian mob classed me as a Northern Territorian too, but Aunty Glad knew who I was, so that wasn't a problem. Our group and Aunty Glad's Council of Aboriginal Women had been talking about bringing the two offices together for a while, and before too long we moved the association from North Terrace to Aunty Glad's office at 129 Pirie Street.

I appreciated what Aunty Glad was doing with the women, and I was trying to keep her informed about what we were doing so there were no grey areas. Every time a building came up that we might be able to use for a centre I'd take Aunty Glad and Ruby Hammond, who was still working with her, to see what they thought of it. Aunty Glad was getting to know the boys better too, and after a while she got different ones to play Father Christmas at the Christmas parties she put on. Little things like that were happening to close that gap between Aunty Glad and the St Francis boys.

Other St Francis boys were making their own contributions. Harold Thomas had come to the boys' home after I was there, but all us St Francis boys always had that connection. When Harold finished school, he got a scholarship to the art school in Adelaide, then after he got his degree in fine arts in 1969, he got a job at the South Australian Museum as a curator of Aboriginal art.

The museum was just across the road from my first office on North Terrace, and one day he dropped in. 'I'm designing a flag for the march,' he said, and away he went. Next thing, he had the flag designed. The march he was talking about was for National Aborigines Day in Adelaide in July 1971, and the flag was the one we have now. It was the first time it had ever been flown.

That flag turned everything on its head. For the group marching down King William Street that day, it gave them a big lift to have this flag flying at the front of the march.

Brenda made them for a while. She made really good ones that didn't tear. They were the proper flagpole size, the same as the Australian flag. People were ordering them by the hundreds – Aboriginal people and government departments. She made a hundred for the Adelaide city council. That kept her busy, and she enjoyed it and got paid for it. She would have made a thousand flags, easy.

After the July 1971 march, wherever you went all around Australia among Aboriginal people, that design and those colours would be there. All the kids were wearing them. It brought people together and made a big difference.

23

'I began to wonder more about Dad's family, the Warriors'

Charlie had been having bad kidney problems for a few years, and they made his life pretty hard sometimes. He'd only been working at the Office of Aboriginal Affairs for a while when his kidneys failed. When Brenda and I visited, we saw some of the hard things he had to go through.

He was put on dialysis to clean the poison out of his blood, but it was still the early days of those machines. The Canberra hospital didn't have kidney specialists at the time, so Charlie had to go to Sydney. Then the doctors taught Eileen how to do the dialysis at home. It was a lot of work and they had to be really careful. If anything went wrong they'd have to call the Sydney doctors. By then too, they had young kids.

All through it, Charlie kept going to his job and working for change for his people. That was the courage of the man.

Not long after Brenda and I got married, Charlie and Eileen were back living in Adelaide. Charlie was having more problems with his kidneys, and I think they'd come back to

Adelaide to be near Eileen's family for support. He and Eileen were living in a house at Woodville that they'd fixed up with all the equipment for his dialysis.

I remember him wanting to go everywhere in between the dialysis sessions. We did a trip to Port Lincoln, and then not long after he rang and we were off to Alice. He didn't tell me at the time, but he was waiting for a kidney transplant. I think he might have thought he was going to die before he got one, and he wanted to die at home in Alice.

We were staying at a hotel and things were playing on his mind. 'You'd better go. Take a walk or do something,' he said to me.

'I'm not going,' I said. I never said anything like, *I know what you're up to.* I just said, 'You're not sending me away.'

The next morning I said, 'Charlie, what were you going to do?'

'Jump out the window,' he said.

We left the motel and as we walked along the street past it, I looked up. 'Were you going to jump out of that window there, Charlie?'

'Yeah,' he said.

'It's on the first floor, you would have only broken your leg.'

I burst out laughing. Then he burst out laughing. That was the funny thing about Charlie and me. I could look at him and he could look at me and we'd just laugh.

It wasn't long after that when the Queen Elizabeth Hospital in Adelaide rang him to say they had a kidney ready for him. After he had the transplant he went back to Canberra.

'Why don't you move into the house in Woodville?' he said to me. And we did.

* * *

In the winter of 1972, we heard that Winnie was in hospital in Port Augusta. We went up to see her, but she died not long after. Things had been fairly hard for her sometimes, like they were for a lot of Aboriginal people trying to get work and look after their families and battle the system at the same time. She'd been moving between Taperoo and Port Augusta, a small city a few hours north of Adelaide. I'm not sure why she went back and forth. It might have been connected to what she was doing with the progress association and Nunga footy, because she was really involved in them both. Brenda and I would go and see her when we could.

One of the last times we saw her had been when we were on the verge of getting married. We were all together in Taperoo having a meal and a singalong, like we always did. Winnie sang a country-and-western song, one that would make you cry. When she finished the song, she came up to me. She had tears running down her face. 'Don't forget you have another side to your family.' That was all she said. I knew she meant the Warriors, our dad Fred's family. I cried myself.

Sometimes over the years, I'd see my aunties – Dad's sisters – at football matches, or I'd catch up with them unexpectedly in different towns on the Peninsula. But those catch-ups were very short. I wasn't taking that extra time with them. My aunties had no way of coming to see me – they had no cars and couldn't easily get away from Point Pearce. They didn't have phones in their homes and had to go up to the mission office to make a call. It was up to me to take advantage of being able to go to them, and find out more about them and my dad and their family. I was old enough and close enough to be able to do that, and I didn't do it.

Winnie's words had stuck in my brain, and after she died I began to wonder more about Dad's family, the Warriors. It would be a long while, though, before I found out more.

* * *

In December 1972, a new Labor federal government led by Gough Whitlam came in and started to make big changes. Their motto leading up to the election was 'It's Time', and that was the mood for a lot of things, not just Aboriginal advancement. The government turned the Office for Aboriginal Affairs into the first ever federal Department of Aboriginal Affairs – that gave it a lot more clout. The minister they put in charge was Gordon Bryant, who'd been working with us on FCAATSI for a long time. He'd once heard Doug give a talk in Melbourne and from then on he wanted to do everything he could to make things better for Aboriginal people. He'd helped Doug set up the Victorian Aboriginal Advancement League, and he was pretty well known for supporting land rights for Aboriginal people.

One of the first things the new department did was set up what they called the National Aboriginal Consultative Committee. The first step was to get Aboriginal and Torres Strait Islander people registered on a special electoral roll so they could vote in elections to choose Indigenous people from around the country to represent their views to the government.

Charlie was responsible for running it across Australia, and the government's policy was for Aboriginal people to do the work as much as possible. So the department employed John to work with Charlie on it nationally and he moved to Canberra too. In South Australia our up-and-coming centre was picked to run things, so I had a fair bit to do with it there. We hired people locally to enrol people and then get them to vote, and we hired cars for them to visit places all over the state, like Ceduna on the west coast, the APY Lands in the desert up north, the Riverland and south from there along the Murray.

My nephew Freddie, Winnie's son, was one of the people doing the visits to the communities, and I sent him to Yalata on the west coast. He drove over in a hire car, a Valiant Charger like the ones racing-car drivers drove at the time, and he thought he was king. After Yalata, he had to go to a place they called 20 Mile Camp, about three hundred kilometres north. It's in the Maralinga Tjarutja Lands and is known as Oak Valley now. The people there were all traditional people living in humpies. They were a part of the Pitjantjatjara mob, but they spoke their language with a slightly different dialect to the Pitjantjatjara people who lived further north. That was because they'd been moved off their traditional Country when the British government was testing atom bombs there in the 1950s and 60s. Once they'd done that it was too contaminated with radiation for the people to go back, so they stayed at 20 Mile Camp.

We eventually got the rolls and the voting finished, and the people who'd won seats went to meetings in Canberra to talk about what their communities needed. That was the start of the National Aboriginal Consultative Committee. People's attitudes about what could happen were changing.

24

'You're having a girl'

Brenda had taken the call. I was at work. It was a lady who wanted to know if we could look after David Gulpilil, who was going to be in town to appear in an opera called *The Young Kabbarli*.

I'm not sure where she got my name, but it might have been through the Aboriginal Cultural Centre. They'd heard something about there being a hostel in Adelaide, and my name was the contact they had. They thought I was running one at my place, but it was just a mistake someone made.

Brenda didn't let that stop her – she said he could come and stay with us. Next minute he lobbed on the doorstep with his brother. Brenda was well prepared. We had the room, and we looked after them.

Gulpilil was young and full of enthusiasm. One day out of the blue he said to Brenda, 'You're having a girl.' He touched her on the tummy, then he pulled his hand away and on his finger he had a bit of string that had blood on it. It frightened the hell out of Brenda. She looked at her belly and saw there was no blood there, but there he was with that string. He mesmerised her. When later she found out she was pregnant – well, as far as she was concerned, David was God.

Some of those things you've got to experience to get a clear understanding. What he said wasn't rubbish. A few years later I caught up with him a couple of times on his Country at Ramingining, and he was living his culture.

So many people stayed with us over the years. Wherever Brenda and I lived we always had room for people. Sometimes it would be one of the boys while they were in town for a few days, and other times we'd have traditional people come from the Top End or from the Central Desert. People like Wandjuk Marika, the artist from Yirrkala, and Harry Jakamarra, the boss of Yuendumu, who was ahead of everyone in his presentation, and his Aboriginal and English languages. He dressed really dapper. He'd come down to Adelaide because the dental people wanted to take a study of his teeth and try and work out why they were so good. Another bloke who stayed was Helmut Pareroultja from Hermannsburg. He was religious, which suited me. Having been in the boys' home for seven years I had a knowledge and a feeling about religion, so I wasn't out of place with people like Helmut.

* * *

Nine months after Gulpilil said what he said to Brenda, she was about to have the baby. In the meantime, Charlie had lobbed into town on work business. What I had to do was get Brenda to hospital, leave her there, pick him up, take him to the conference, and then carry on as things happened. He'd want to see the boys or other people. Strange as it may sound, Charlie was the first priority, and away we went. Brenda's mum had come over from Currie, so she was there to help.

Next minute, I was the dad of a baby girl. Gulpilil was right about that too. I saw her when she was a day old. This lovely little baby. We called her Kara.

I had a big L plate on me – I didn't know where to start and what my role was going to be. It wasn't that I didn't know how to change nappies and things like that, because I did. Back when I was in Currie and working for Frank and Pat, if they had business to do in town they'd just take off and say, 'Look after Sandra.' And Brenda's sister Marlene and her husband, Don, lived just up the road, and they had Kathy and later Shendelle. They'd be at work at the Currie deli, and I'd drop in and Marlene would bring Kathy out, and I'd carry her around and when she was old enough I'd take her for walks. I loved those little kids. At Currie people knew me and their kids did too. Everywhere I went I'd hear, 'Hello, Uncle Vin. Hello, Uncle Vin. Uncle Vin, do this. Uncle Vin, do that.'

So I was prepared for Kara, in that if she needed to get in the pusher and go for a walk, I'd take her. If Brenda wanted a spell, I'd look after her. When she was little I used to blow on her bum and she used to giggle. But a lot of the time I was away and Brenda had to battle on by herself. And she was getting extra grief because of her being light skinned and Kara being darker. She'd get a bit edgy at shopping centres because sometimes people would come up to her and say, 'What a lovely girl! When did you adopt her?' That would nearly straighten Brenda's hair out.

Most women would have left me. That you can't be around to see your kid born. Anyway, whatever happened, Brenda handled it. If work meant me going away, it meant me going away. You just have to carry on. There wasn't much I could do about it. Back then if it had happened with anybody else but Charlie, it would have been unacceptable to Brenda. She loved Charlie, and she loved sitting down and listening to him tell his stories. Brenda and Eileen were really good mates too. She reckoned Eileen was the toughest woman she'd ever met.

We wanted to get Kara baptised, and the boys had to be there. Father Smith did the ceremony at the Church of England in Glenelg. Kara was about six months old and she was just so lovely. We had about twenty people there that day, and lots of kids as well.

* * *

All through 1973, I was travelling back and forth to Canberra on business for the consultative committee. By then, the Aboriginal Tent Embassy was in full swing outside Parliament House. It had been set up on Australia Day in 1972, after Billy McMahon, the prime minster at the time, said on the radio that he was going to give a speech on land rights, which we'd been talking about for years. Then he said his government wouldn't even be considering it. That was it. Full stop. There'd be some short-term leases, but no land rights. And there was very little talk of how to help Aboriginal people who lived in terrible housing or didn't have enough food or paid work. What he said didn't go down too well.

This was at the beginning of the Aboriginal Embassy in Canberra in January 1972. These blokes are Billy Craigie, Bert Williams, Michael Anderson and Tony Coorey. *(Wikimedia Commons)*

Charlie was in Adelaide and crook with his kidneys, but he was still in touch with everyone in Sydney and Canberra. He had this idea he told a couple of his mates, and that was to set up an Aboriginal Embassy in front of Parliament House. Chicka Dixon, one of his mates from the foundation in Sydney, came up with some money to cover petrol for a few of the blokes to go to Canberra. When they got there they put up a beach umbrella and a sign saying 'Aboriginal Embassy', and some other signs about land rights, and that was the beginning of the Tent Embassy. It's still there.

Charlie moved back to Canberra not long after his transplant and one day I went to the embassy with him and a few others who were working with him. There'd been lots of protests right from when it first went up, and the police were trying to get people to move on. Things would get pretty heated. Charlie had his new kidney and couldn't afford to get involved in any of the rough stuff, so he had to be kept aside — otherwise he would have been thinking he could fight alongside everybody else who was getting their heads kicked off. What he did instead, when there weren't so many people around, was mow the lawn around the tent and take the Sunday roast meals from home and give them to the protesters. Eileen told me they had fried eggs on toast those nights. He helped them out with money too.

Around the same time, some of us were involved in the National Aborigines and Islanders Day Observance Committee — what's now called NAIDOC. That had been the next step on from the National Aborigines Day in 1971, when Harold had flown his flag for the first time. But the history leading up to NAIDOC goes back a long way. People around the country were doing different things to recognise Aboriginal people, and ideas were coming from everywhere for something to happen nationally. Doug was still looking after the Victorian Aboriginal Advancement League in Melbourne, and he wanted a day of prayer. Some people wanted a sports day. Neville Bonner, who became the first Aboriginal person to be a senator in parliament, was in Brisbane at the time, working for the One People of Australia League, and they had their own ideas too.

Two church ministers at Tranby College in Sydney had been running an event there for a few years — I think it was a type of prayer meeting too. They were white and they'd agreed that white people shouldn't be leading the event anymore.

They wanted to work with Aboriginal people to change it into something we wanted. John and I went to Sydney to meet with them and talk about ways we could have something nationwide that would be run by us. Charlie was involved in that too.

The next year, John was elected the first chairperson of a national organisation that would be run by us. That first national committee came up with the idea of having a march and a ball in a different city each year. One year it might be Darwin, the next Sydney. For the first year, we decided to have it in Adelaide, because most of the committee were from there. As well as the march and the ball, the committee had specially designed a poster and awards for the best students and the best sportsmen and -women in the country. The awards were a way of letting the broader public understand that if they wouldn't recognise us, we'd recognise ourselves.

We had about ten awards all up, and we had the first NAIDOC Ball at the Wayville Showgrounds Auditorium. Gough and Margaret Whitlam turned up and Gough talked about the National Aboriginal Consultative Committee and how important it was. We had a belle and a beau of the ball. My cousin Maude Wilson was the belle and I was the beau. We stood out. She had a lovely blue gown on, and I wore a black dinner suit I'd had specially made. All the women and men were dressed up. It really was a celebration.

* * *

When John and I had been in Sydney talking to the Tranby church ministers about a national day, we'd heard that some people there had set up the first Aboriginal legal aid service in the country. Charlie and Chicka Dixon were part of that too, and a legal bloke by the name of Hal Wootten from the University of New South Wales. We thought we should start up something similar in Adelaide, because Aboriginal people there had no way of getting legal support and a lot of the time were being jailed for no reason.

Back in Adelaide we set up a meeting and hired a local bloke, Charlie Agius, to go around the community and let everybody know about it. About seventy people turned up: Aboriginal people and a lot of people from law firms too. I chaired that first meeting and we elected a board.

A top gun lawyer called Elliott Johnston became the chairman. He was a QC, and for a start the legal service worked out of his office. The official name we gave to it was the Aboriginal Legal Rights Movement. Elliott said there were two things we needed to do first. One was to get cards printed with details of the service that we could give to Aboriginal people, so they could get legal advice if they were picked up by the police. The idea was that they'd give the card to the officer and get them to call one of the lawyers – although what happened in the early days was the police just tore up the card.

The other thing we did was appoint bail officers so that Aboriginal people would have someone to go to court with them and help them understand what was going on, and speak on their behalf if they needed it. Ruby Hammond and I were the first ones. At the start we were wondering what bail officers were.

The first time I did the job, I attended court at Port Adelaide with an Aboriginal bloke who'd been in and out of trouble.

He told me all about the court process and I got all excited. 'Gee whiz,' I said, 'what do you do now? Anything I can say?'

He knew more about the law than I did, and of course it was him, not me, who said everything that needed to be said to the judge. 'Good job,' he said to me as we walked out of court.

Ruby ended up being pretty interested in the legal stuff, and she worked a lot with Elliott. I had my role already in place to get the cultural centre set up and that's where I was putting all of my efforts. I kept my ear to the ground on what was happening, so that as soon as we could we'd move an officer from the legal service to the cultural centre.

Around the time we'd set up the legal service, we came across a building for sale that we thought could work for the centre. John was the chair of the Aboriginal Progress Association at the time, and he wrote a letter to Gordon Bryant, the bloke who was now Whitlam's Minister for Aboriginal Affairs, saying we'd found a building at 128 Wakefield Street and wanted to buy it to set up the centre. The cost was $126,000.

John mentioned in the letter to Gordon Bryant that we'd be at a conference that was coming up in Brisbane, and we'd catch up with him there. John couldn't go, so I went on my own. Luck had it that as I was walking up the stairway of the Trades Hall office, I ran into Gordon Bryant. I stopped him and asked if he'd got our letter with the application for the money. He said he'd read it.

'How much is that building going to cost?' he asked.

'A hundred and twenty-six thousand dollars,' I told him.

'Meet me here tomorrow at the same time, same place.'

So there I was the next day. Down Gordon came with his entourage, and he handed me a cheque for $126,000. My hand was shaking. *Cor blimey!* I thought as I put it in my pocket. I couldn't find any words.

When I got back to Adelaide I went to the bank to put it in, but the bank said I couldn't deposit it because we didn't have a bank account in the name of the organisation. It was going to take a fortnight to open one up.

The cheque for $126,000 sat on our mantelpiece for a fortnight. When the fortnight was up I deposited it and we got another cheque from the bank to pay for the building. We walked in and we were the owners.

That was the beginning of the Aboriginal Cultural Centre. Later it became known as the Aboriginal Community Centre of South Australia, then the Aboriginal Community Recreation and Health Services Centre of South Australia. Now it's Nunkuwarrin Yunti, and it's in a different building further up the street.

That first building was good. It had three storeys, a big hall for functions, and small halls for meetings. On the bottom floor was another large enclosed area that was air-conditioned and a few other smaller offices, and there was parking at the back. It suited the things we wanted to start with. The health people from Norwood sent their Aboriginal workers to work out of it. The Commonwealth Employment Service sent one of their blokes to work out of it, and there was Aunty Glad's group and our group, the progress association, and then there was a sports group. Once we got started, the Aboriginal Sobriety Group, which a church organisation ran, started to meet there too. The building was becoming as we wanted it: a place to hold all the groups and where Aboriginal people could come to get services.

25

'Mandawuy Yunupingu showed us around the school'

When Kara was a few months old, we moved to Canberra. The Whitlam government had kept going with its policy of employing Aboriginal people in the Department of Aboriginal Affairs and Charlie had been made assistant secretary.

After we'd had the elections for the consultative committee, Charlie brought the people who'd organised the voting in the different places – like I'd done in South Australia – to work in Canberra as project officers. He was moving people around and fitting them in where he needed their different abilities.

I started out working on one of the new national programs to set up hostels for Aboriginal people around the country. Right from the early days of the FCAATSI conferences, short-term accommodation in hostels had been a big discussion for a whole heap of reasons: for young people in remote areas to be able to get an education in bigger towns, for people looking for jobs where there wasn't enough housing, for older people and single parents who needed help until something more permanent could be sorted out. As soon as Charlie got into his first Canberra job, he'd helped with setting up a company called Aboriginal Hostels Ltd. Then, in 1973, he became the first chair of its new board. The policy at the time was that most of the hostel staff had to be Aboriginal people. They pretty well stuck to that with both the hostel staff and the staff in administration jobs.

Charlie wanted to go around to the communities to talk about what they needed, and he took me with him. Our trip out to the communities in the Top End was a big learning experience for me in the differences in the ways people lived, especially in remote areas. I also saw that the places they lived in were really beautiful.

First, Charlie and I went to Kakadu to find a place for a hostel for the rangers. We went to Jabiru in a helicopter and flew all over the escarpment, then we landed near the border store at Oenpelli and looked around there at possible sites.

The next place we went to was Maningrida, a big community of a thousand people or more from different language groups. It was right on the Arafura Sea, with plenty of fish. I remember talking to two Aboriginal lads there who told us how they were training as pilots.

From Maningrida we went to Elcho Island. They were islander people. Then we went to Nhulunbuy, where a big mining company was based. From Nhulunbuy we travelled a little way south to a place out in the middle of the scrub called Dhupuma College. The headmaster at that time was Mandawuy Yunupingu, and he showed us around the school and talked about what the college meant to them. He later became the lead singer of Yothu Yindi, although at the time he never said anything about his music.

Then we went to Yirrkala, where the trees had a particular bark, and as we were driving in, I could see that the huts were made out of the same material. Yirrkala is famous for its bark paintings, and the bark petition that sits in Parliament House. That was a petition the Yolngu people made to the government in 1963 against a new mining development that would mean they'd lose their land, sources of food and sacred sites. They'd written it out in two languages, English and one of the Yolngu dialects, and pasted it onto a piece of bark with traditional paintings on it, then they sent it to Canberra to the politicians. That got caught up in the battle for land rights that went on for a long time.

While we were there we met with a bloke called Roy Marika, who ran the town's council, and he showed us round. Roy was a really important person in the land rights movement in the Territory.

The town had good facilities, and another thing I noticed was that everybody's houses had flags made out of a piece of cloth or a sheet, to mark that somebody had passed away and to indicate they were grieving. All the community brought presents to the house of the family of a person who had died – suitcases filled with food and other gifts. That was more learning for me. While you'd think most communities are the same, every one had something that was a bit different to the others.

After Yirrkala we flew to Groote Eylandt and met up with Wilf from the boys' home, who'd gone back to the Northern Territory by then. His traditional Country was further south, at Roper River. Wilf was working at a mining site, and he told us a story about how somebody from the mining company got lost and the company got hold of him to be the tracker to find the man. Away they went, Wilf at the front of the pack. He was leading them round and round, and all of a sudden he came over his own tracks. He didn't want to make a fool of himself, so he quickly turned around and went and got somebody from the community to track the person down. The company had asked Wilf because he was Aboriginal – they thought he knew the area, but that wasn't his Country so of course he didn't know it. He just went along with it.

Just across the water from Groote Eylandt was a place called Rose River. That was a lovely place too. Its traditional name is Numbulwar, and it had been a church mission. From there we went to Ngukurr, which used to be the Roper River mission. That was another big community, and it was where all Wilf's family were from. A Catholic priest from the mission days was still there and picked us up, and we stayed with him. The actual Roper River was smack bang close to the community, and they had fish and crocodiles in it. Some people were catching buffalo too. It was a good meat to eat and a few people were involved in exporting them.

One night while we were at Ngukurr, we went to see a movie at the basketball court. The backboard was the screen and they were showing *Cleopatra*. Everybody was watching it and trying to understand what the movie was all about, with these blokes Julius Caesar and Mark Antony. They were all quiet until one part of the movie where Mark Antony slapped Cleopatra and Cleopatra slapped him. They all thought that was a hell of a joke. Laughing and cheering broke out on the basketball court.

From Ngukurr we went back inland to Katherine. At the time the town had a little house they were using as a hostel for the people that came in from the communities for health reasons. Later on, Aboriginal Hostels bought an old motel called the Corroboree and turned it into a big hostel for kids coming in for school. For them it meant that rather than having to go so far away to Darwin for college, they could go to Katherine.

We flew everywhere. Mostly we were in a little light aircraft. It was usually pretty good except when you were flying in the late afternoon and hitting the storms – then it was as bumpy as hell, and sometimes I'd wonder whether the thing was going to make it. All the time we were hearing what people needed, and then we took that back with us to Charlie's office to work out what sort of hostels were needed where.

I did some other trips in the Top End without Charlie. One place I visited was Milingimbi, an island close to the coast, part way between Maningrida and Nhulunbuy. Going back a long time, the Milingimbi had trading connections with the Macassan people from Indonesia. In the community they had a lot of tamarind trees and people were walking around in sarongs, so you could see the influence of Macassan culture straight away. I can remember looking across the sea and thinking about how the Macassans got here and how they must have had good sailing vessels to come across that particular sea. Most of the communities have something different about them, and that was Milingimbi's story. It was right in front of your eyes – those two communities wanting to exchange things with each other and that giving them a connection, and how friendship must have been a part of the deal. Milingimbi was also where David Gulpilil's mum lived.

Over in Queensland, we had hostels in Cairns, Brisbane and Mackay. West of Darwin there was a place called Timber Creek, one of the loveliest places I'd seen in terms of scenery. Then there were communities in Western Australia like Kununurra and Wyndham.

Up in the Torres Strait we set up a hostel on Thursday Island for the kids coming in from the different islands to go to school. For that one we found an old house and renovated it.

Another time I was on Thursday Island with the bloke who became the manager of Hostels for the northern region: his name was Joe McGinness and I'd known him for years. He was born in Darwin, and he was a great footballer. In the early days of FCAATSI he was one of the major drivers in trying to get things moving for Aboriginal people and he was the president for about ten years. Joe was a real big man and he always used to walk along whistling. His wife Amy was from the Torres Strait – she was a Thursday Islander. We called them Uncle Joe and Aunty Amy, and they used to stay with me and Brenda sometimes. One time when Kara was a baby, Aunty Amy and her niece came around, and they were singing her a lullaby in their language. Kara loved it.

One night the Thursday Island dancers put on a big show, and we had a feed of fish and turtle down on the beach that the ladies had prepared. That was the first time I'd tasted turtle. It was really rich, and you wanted to be close to toilets if you had too much – it was just straight in and out. After that we went back to the community tennis courts, and the dancers were dressed up in traditional outfits. During the dancing, if the women and children liked the dancers, they'd run over and tip Johnson's Baby Powder over them – that was their way of saying they appreciated that person and that he was a good dancer.

We looked at setting up a hostel on the Tiwi Islands, although we didn't do anything there at the time. Down the south-eastern parts of Australia, we had them in Sydney, Dubbo, Canberra and Melbourne. In South Australia, where I was mostly involved, we had them in Adelaide, and we put one at Point Pearce too.

In Alice Springs, the Hostels people built a new one for the old people that they called the Hetti Perkins Hostel, after Charlie's mum. We built other hostels in Alice Springs, then had more over in the west, in Perth and Broome, where we worked with a bloke who was one of the Mowanjum people, who are a pretty large traditional group from around Derby.

We looked at setting up one in Hobart too. So that pretty well covered hostels around Australia at that time.

In the end there were a fair few, around seventy or eighty I think in those first few years. Some weren't full to capacity, and others were losing money. Some cost more to run, like the Hetti Perkins Hostel, because the people there were old and needed a certain amount of care. We found out some of the hostels couldn't be sustained – not at the time, anyway. But we were learning and it was all part of the beginnings of Aboriginal people having more control over the services we needed.

I was also learning a lot about people and places, and the different food people ate and how they cooked it, and the sorts of ceremonies they had. It really opened my mind to who we all were, and it got me thinking about the way I lived and how it was the same and how it was different, and whether that mattered.

26

'Did you get the photos?'

I worked on the hostels in Canberra for about eighteen months, then they decided to put regional managers in each state and I came back to Adelaide and did that for a while. It was 1975 – Kara was nearly two and Brenda was pregnant again. One day, the phone rang. It was Charlie. He'd just published a book about his life and about trying to make things better for Aboriginal people. It was called *A Bastard Like Me*.

'We're off to Kuala Lumpur,' he said.

I asked him what we were going there for, and he said we were going to try to see Muhammad Ali and bring him to Australia. Ali was going to be fighting Joe Bugner in a big international match.

We let a few people around Adelaide know to see if we could get some help to put on an event. One who was interested was Alan Hickinbotham, a businessman and the president of the South Adelaide Football Club, which is how I knew him. He invited us for tea to his home, just down from Unley Road, where all the millionaires were. He said if we could get Ali over he'd hire a big hall and we could charge people $100 a head for a meal and to hear Ali talk.

We flew out of Adelaide. At Sydney Airport a bloke came over and asked us where we were going. His name was Keith Butler and he was a sportswriter for one of the Adelaide newspapers. He knew about Charlie from his soccer days and the Freedom Ride.

We told him we were off to Malaysia to try and see Muhammad Ali, and he said he was going there to cover the fight. We told him we didn't know whether we'd be going to the fight or not, because our main aim was to see if we could get in to have a talk with Ali. Keith said he'd try to get us a couple of seats.

'That'd be good,' we said.

We got to Kuala Lumpur and were waiting to get in a taxi, and Keith bobbed up again. We were all heading to the same place and he jumped in. Ali was staying at the Hilton so that's where we stayed. He was in the penthouse and we were in the basement.

The next day Charlie dropped his book off at the door to Ali's penthouse, along with a couple of boomerangs. We thought we'd probably hear from him at some stage. We wandered around Kuala Lumpur for a few days while we waited, and one day we ran into an old mate of Charlie's who he'd gone to Sydney University with. This bloke was a local, and he invited us out to tea with his family. That broke the monotony. It was a fairly big meal – about eight courses – and lovely food. We started with soup and ended with soup. I'd never done that before.

When we got back to our room, there was a message that we had to be at the penthouse at six o'clock the next morning.

'It's a bit early, but never mind,' Charlie said to me.

When we got up there, the lounge room of the penthouse was chock-a-block with people. Ali had just finished training and was lying naked on the massage table getting a rub-down, and all his flunkies were scattered around the room. As we came in, he half-lifted his shoulder, looked around at us and started screaming. 'Get the chequebook! Get the chequebook!'

Charlie looked at him. 'Hey, listen, you! We didn't come here for your money. We came here to see you. You can shove your chequebook where the sun don't shine!'

Charlie grabbed me and turned me around. 'Come on, Cop. We're getting out of here.' He was pushing me back towards the door, then all of a sudden Ali was sitting up. It must have twigged that here were some blokes who weren't wanting his money. 'Stop them! Stop them!' he yelled.

Charlie was still pushing me to the door.

'Listen, Charlie,' I said, 'this bloke can fight a bit, you know.'

'I don't care!' Charlie said. 'Nobody's going to insult you and me like that.'

Ali's blokes blocked off the door. We turned around and went back in, and Ali asked us to sit down.

'Look,' he said. 'We're sorry about that. What are you boys doing here?'

'We want you to come to Australia to meet the Aboriginal people and give them a bit of a lift,' Charlie said.

'I need to finish here and get showered,' Ali said. 'But anytime you want to, you just come up and we'll sit down and have a talk.'

We went up again the next afternoon and it was different from the first time. This time it was just the three of us, and we sat in the dining room at a great big table. I remember there was a bowl of fruit on it.

Ali was saying how he didn't like flying, then he wanted to know what the people in Australia were like. We gave him a run-down on it all. He'd read Charlie's book and was talking to him about the things he'd done. It was good that he read it – he showed that he was wanting to know about Aboriginal people, as well as this man, Charlie, who was sitting beside him.

We had a lot of discussion about how we lived and what was happening. Just as we were telling him how we'd like to take him out to communities and show him how some of the traditional people live, in came the press. They were jumping over the table, grabbing the fruit from the bowl, and pushing in with their cameras to try and get a photo of Ali.

One of them pushed me so hard my head was nearly on the table. 'Let's get out of here,' I said to Charlie.

Of course Ali was a different man when the press was there. He was the old brash confident person again, spouting things about the boxing match and when Bugner was going to drop, and all of that. So we got out.

We ended up visiting him four or five times. We'd just knock on the door and usually we'd catch him by himself. One time we were there, Ali had to have a photo shoot, and a professional photographer was there with an apprentice. The apprentice was putting up big lights with big globes, and you could see he was shaking. All of a sudden, he tripped and knocked one over. The globe hit the ground and went off like a gun.

Next minute, all of Ali's bodyguards were in there with their guns drawn, thinking we'd shot him. We were ducking for cover! Then it all settled down, and the bloke took his photos and headed off.

We said to Ali that we were heading home to Australia.

'No, no, you're not going. You're gonna stay and see the fight,' he said. He called a bloke into the room. 'You go down and fix up these two gentlemen's bills, right? Put it on my account and get them two seats to the fight.'

So Charlie and I extended our time there. We found out that Lionel Rose, an Aboriginal boxer from Victoria, was fighting the preliminary bout before Ali came on, and so we went around to where he was training. He burst out crying as soon as he saw us. He was really homesick because he'd been in Kuala Lumpur for three months and hadn't seen any Kooris since he'd left Melbourne.

Every morning we were there we'd catch up with Keith Butler somewhere in the hotel. 'I'm nearly there with the seats,' he'd say.

'Good on you, Keith,' we'd say.

The fight was at a soccer ground, and around the ground was a bicycle track and then a fence, then another gap and then the grandstand. Right on top of the grandstand were little boxes five hundred yards away. That's where the press was – they were commentating on the fight from there with binoculars – and there was me and Charlie ringside! We were like kings.

Ali won his fight: it was a draw, but he won on points. Ali was a big man, but Bugner towered over him.

After the whole thing ended, we headed back to Australia. There'd been a fair few photos taken of us – some with Ali with his arms around the two of us – and the bloke who took them told us he'd leave them at the counter at reception for us to pick up.

'Did you get the photos?' Charlie asked when we got home.

'No, I thought you did,' I said.

So we never got them. Anyway, we know we were with him – that's the main thing. Ali was just really good to be with, and when we were with him by ourselves he was so humble.

From then on, when we saw his fights on television, we'd recognise his bodyguards. 'Well we know them too,' we'd say.

'Why didn't I get his boots or his dressing-gown or his shorts or something?' I said to Charlie once.

'No, no, no, you can't do that,' he said. That's the way Charlie was. He was honest to the day and didn't want anyone to think that all we wanted to do was go and get money. He knew what he wanted to do: he wanted to get Ali to come to Australia. That was the main aim of the trip.

Ali did come out to Australia a few years later, as part of a world tour of exhibition matches, and he visited some Aboriginal people in Melbourne, but we didn't know whether it was because of us.

* * *

Two weeks after Ali's fight with Joe Bugner, Brenda was ready to have the baby. Just like last time, the day she went into hospital, Charlie turned up. 'Cop, I've got to go here. I've got to go there.' The time I should have been down at the hospital with Brenda I was with Charlie.

The next morning I got up early and rang the hospital. I found out Brenda had had a beautiful boy, who we called Vincent. After me, of course. I had to run Charlie to the airport to catch a plane home. Then I went straight back to the hospital. So I didn't desert Brenda altogether. But it was a little bit difficult. That's how it was.

Being a father to a son was an unknown world to me, not having had my dad around and not being close to Allan, and then going to the boys' home when I was eleven. Having lost my dad at such an early age, and then losing Colin and Maureen and my mum at an early age, it was important for me to keep the connection with the boys.

Each of the boys from St Francis has their own story of the different things they did and how they did it, and this is mine. How I see it is, we never ever passed each other by. If one of the boys was in trouble or needed something, you'd go out of your way to help him. And your wife came second all the time. The wives became accustomed to that happening. You wouldn't want it to happen, but it happened. It was a strange world for them.

Brenda was okay with that. She played a much larger part in Kara and Vincent's lives than I did. That's something I think back on now and wonder about. There were other people around who helped us. Brenda's mum and dad were still alive when Kara and Vincent came, and they had time with them when we lived in Adelaide. Then once we were in Canberra, we'd come back to the farm every Christmas time. Everyone would be there, Brenda's sisters and their kids too. And Uncle Cecil and Aunty Doris Graham used to come to Canberra sometimes and spend a bit of time with us. They had fifteen kids, so they knew a bit about being parents.

Still, the kids grew up with all the boys, and the boys were all 'Uncle' to them. Uncle Charlie, Uncle Morey – that's John, Uncle Biggo – that's Gordon, and all the rest. They got to know them all, and all the stories too. When Vincent was baptised, it was Father Smith who did it and all the boys were there.

* * *

In November 1975, a few months after the Kuala Lumpur trip, Gough Whitlam, the Labor prime minister who was doing a fair bit to make things happen for Aboriginal people, was sacked. Malcolm Fraser from the Liberals was elected. He ended up being there for about seven years. The budgets for a lot of things Whitlam had started to set up were cut. But a lot kept going too.

We met with different prime ministers a number of times. Charlie said years later that the only bloke he ever thought was any good was Fraser. He was in power when Charlie was in the Department of Aboriginal Affairs and working on the bill for land rights in the Northern Territory. Whitlam had been in power during the initial negotiations then Fraser and the Liberals took over. The *Land Rights Act* covered all of the Northern Territory. It went through in 1976, and it had the support of both parties. It meant some First Nations people could finally claim their land back.

It was around this time that Eddie Mabo started his case for land rights for the Meriam people of the Murray Islands in the Torres Strait. That's what led to the end of 'terra nullius': the idea British people had when they arrived that none of the people already living here owned the land. I can remember Eddie at FCAATSI meetings. He'd come along and that's all he'd hammer. It took such a long time – until 1993 – for the *Native Title Act* to go through. And we're still not there yet. There's been amendments that the politicians have made and different things keep coming up. Eventually we'll get it right.

27

'The Germans ended up being served last'

When we'd first lived in Canberra when Kara was a baby, I was working as an executive officer in the Department of Aboriginal Affairs, as well as working on the hostels. I'd also give Charlie a hand with different jobs when he needed me, which is how I ended up going to Nigeria a few times.

Nigeria got its independence from Britain in 1960 and a decade or so later the Nigerian government wanted to have a big event to celebrate black culture. They sent some of their people around the world to meet with black people in different countries. When they came to Canberra they met with Charlie. John, Gordon and I were all working for the department at the time, and Charlie got us to come and meet them. Next thing we were on the international planning committee for a festival of art and culture to celebrate black, African and Indigenous people. It was going to be like a mini-Olympics of art and culture.

We had to find artists, musicians and dancers from all over Australia to take to Africa for a month. As well as John, Gordon and me, we had Chicka Dixon and Wandjuk Marika on the organising committee. They'd both been chairs of the Aboriginal Arts Board on the Australia Council at different times.

One of my jobs was to go to the capital cities, talk to the Aboriginal organisations there and let the people know what the festival was all about. Some people nominated themselves and some nominated others who were making a name for themselves. Plenty of Aboriginal and Torres Strait Islander people were on the record as being talented, so it wasn't that hard to find people. Some of the people who ended up going were Thanakupi, a top potter from Queensland; Lin Onus, a lovely painter from Victoria; Jack Davis, the playwright from Perth; and the Mornington Island and Aurukun dancers.

We'd also been working at the Lagos end to make sure the accommodation and transport was all right, and we went there a few times for planning meetings. It was the first time I travelled outside of Australia, and it gave me a chance to see different things. That first trip I was on a big jumbo and we stopped on the way at Singapore, Bombay and Bahrain. On one trip we stopped overnight in Rome and met up with the Australian Embassy people. The next day, before we flew out to Lagos, we went into the old part of the city and saw the Colosseum and the Forum, then St Peter's Basilica and the Spanish Steps. All these places I'd seen in the movies, and there we were.

The first time we were in Lagos, I started to see how some countries do things a bit differently to the way we do them at home. When the British had moved out of Nigeria in the early 1960s, the new Nigerian bosses had moved in. Because it was an oil country, they had heaps of money. They were living the high life and wanting to be treated exactly the same as the British rulers who'd been running the country before.

When we arrived at Lagos Airport, we were treated like dignitaries. They took us from the plane to the airport building, into a car and off to a hotel. The city seemed to be all islands and bridges, and the roads were chock-a-block with traffic and people walking. After a few days I could see that Lagos pumped twenty-four hours a day. Things were happening all the time, and you could feel the African beat they had day and night.

We also got to see racism in reverse to what we were used to. At the hotel we stayed in, one morning we were at breakfast in the dining room and some white businessmen from Germany were sitting at a table near ours. The waiters were all Nigerians, and black of course, and they all waited on us first. As they walked past the German blokes, the Germans would say, 'Where's our breakfast?'

'Don't worry, master, it's coming, it's coming,' the waiters would say.

The Germans ended up being served last. We could see the little smirks on the waiters' faces as they dropped off our food and took off.

We had our own car with a driver and an army bloke with a machine gun. They were with us all the time, wherever we went. At one stage in the long lead-up to the festival, there'd been a military coup and the president had been thrown out. They changed the CEO of the festival and brought in a navy general to run it. But I never felt like we were in danger. Having that army bloke with us all the time was a good deterrent.

The festival finally happened in January 1977. At the opening event, all the countries had to walk around the arena. While we were waiting to go in we were alongside the Watusi people – the tall people who dance standing in one place and jump three or four feet off the ground. On the other side of us was a group from another part of Africa, all done up in lovely costumes. All we had were shirts with a little design and a pair of slacks. We walked into the arena and it was full of people. The whole thing was so spectacular. A big bloke was leading the parade and carrying a torch that he held up high all the way around.

Going to the festival was about doing something for our mob. A lot of them hadn't travelled out of their community, let alone outside the state or out of the country, so it was really exciting for them. And for me it was exciting and new and adventurous – all of that all rolled into one. I was lucky to be there. Never in my wildest dreams had I ever expected to be walking around a part of Africa and having a good look at what was going on. Seeing the sad side of it and seeing the funny side of it. It was educational and broadened my outlook about people. After Lagos, when I'd watch the news and see wars going on and people starving, while I was shocked about it I could understand a bit more about why those things happened in some places.

In Nigeria, what I saw happen was that when the Nigerians got their independence from the British they carried on in the same extravagant way the British had, until they lost all their money. It got me thinking about what I'd seen happen for us

Aboriginal people over the years with government policies. It wasn't the same of course, but it made me think about when you've been controlled by someone for a long time, what happens when that all changes? We'd gone from segregation in the missions and reserves to assimilation in the 1940s and 50s and then to self-determination in the 1960s and 70s. That seemed to go all right for a while, but the government would only give you a certain amount of power and not go any further. The government would say, 'Well we've set this system up for you to do on your own. You should be able to cope and do what you want to do.' But it really doesn't work that way. I'm still thinking about how it does work.

* * *

In Charlie's early days in Canberra working in the Office of Aboriginal Affairs, he'd been involved in setting up a national Aboriginal sports program. He'd seen how well FCAATSI worked in bringing Aboriginal people from all around Australia to talk about what was happening in their part of the country. The annual conferences in Canberra back then were held at places like the university during holidays, so people could stay in the vacant student accommodation. Everybody would meet up in the big halls and discuss the different situations within their states and territories, which gave them the opportunity to hear what was going on in other places. When they'd return to their communities and cities and towns, they'd take that knowledge of other places back. That went on for a while. It was a good gathering of people, and we all came to know each other.

Then FCAATSI went through a lot of changes and the annual conferences were winding down. Charlie was worried about how people from across the country could keep meeting up and talking to each other, and he came up with the idea to hold a national sports carnival. He brought in top Aboriginal sportsmen and -women from all over Australia to what they called the National Aboriginal Sports Foundation: people like Lionel Rose, Roy Carroll, Tony Mundine, Darby McCarthy, Marcie Ella, and Bobby Huddleston, who was Wilf's nephew. They'd meet every so often, usually in Canberra or Melbourne, and work out where the next carnival was going to be then recommend that to Charlie, and from there we'd go through the government processes to make it all happen. At different times over the years the carnivals covered Australian Rules football, netball, rugby league, basketball and cricket.

All the states went through the process of selecting a state team, and then we'd hold the national carnival in a different place each year. Players had to pay part of the cost towards their airfares and accommodation – not a great deal, but enough to show the government that they were willing to do that rather than just rely on government funding.

There'd be seven teams from the states and the Northern Territory, and we'd pick an eighth team from the community of the place hosting it. If it was in Darwin, we got the Arnhem Land people to come over. In Alice, the Western Desert and Pitjantjatjara mob came in for it.

Charlie would tell us what he wanted and we'd make it happen. One year I wrote to all the state football clubs on his behalf. He wanted to see if they'd be willing to hold a local sports carnival for young Aboriginal people in the lead-up to the national carnival. There wasn't one bit of interest. The Victorian Football League sent Charlie a football and a hundred dollars. Charlie sent them back with a letter saying, 'By the looks of things you need it more than we do.' We'd write to all the clubs in the league competitions to let them know about it and suggest they send some scouts along to have a look at the players. Over the ten years the carnivals went on for, I think only one person from a professional club came to watch the games. I was disappointed in that lack of interest. I was at every carnival except one, and the talent at that time was just some of the very best you could see. A big part of the disappointment for me was that the broader community missed watching these talented people in action. The young players were probably disappointed too. But at least they had a reason to play, which for many of them wouldn't have been possible without the carnivals, not at that time anyway.

The carnivals worked like a snowball. You'd have your local competition, then your state competition, then the national one. People got to know about it, and from the cities to the remotest communities, they'd all be training for it. Communities would hold their own local carnival and select a team. Say like in Western Australia – they'd bring together people from the remote communities in the northern region to places like Broome, Derby and Wyndham. Then down in the Pilbara they'd do the same, and then south in Esperance and Bunbury. They'd take them all to Perth, and they'd play off against each other and a state team would be picked. That happened in each state.

Local communities all knew how to conduct the competition and make a selection. This was all part of Charlie's vision of connecting communities and finding ways to bring them together so they could learn from each other. It was doing other things too. If you picture a community in one of the remote areas, where people are smoking and drinking and things like that, the people there would be thinking, *Well I can't make this team if I'm gonna be a drunk.* It wouldn't stop those problems, but it would break them down a little bit. Those carnivals had effects that most people didn't see or notice, but they were there. In Charlie's mind, he knew exactly what it meant. His experiences playing soccer overseas and then coming back and coaching Pan Hellenic and other teams had given him a different way of thinking about it all.

Sometimes it was hard for Charlie to be at the carnivals. When he was there he was available. People would all have their problems and they'd all want to talk to him about them. It was tiring for him, and he still had his kidney problems. In the end, we had to make it that he wasn't so prominent. Being a sportsman himself, sometimes he just wanted to sit back and enjoy the games.

It wasn't all smooth riding. One time we were in Perth for the national carnival, and all the Victorians and Western Australians wanted to do was fight each other – even at breakfast. When they got out on the ground they were just punching each other up.

At half-time Charlie went into the clubrooms. 'If there's any more fighting, you're all on the plane home. You're here to play footy.'

The whole thing changed. People got to know the reasons why we'd got them there, and they started to think about that. Charlie had set it up so people could exchange ideas and talk about their different situations, and the fun of playing against each other was an important part of that.

The Carnival Ball was another important part of it all. As well as the actual sporting matches and meeting at mealtimes, over the weekend of the carnival we wanted people to mix socially and get to know each other. On the last night of the carnival we'd host the ball in a really nice place, and people would get dressed up in tuxedos and gowns. Charlie's thinking was it had to be one of the best facilities the city could offer, somewhere like the Hilton. He wanted to highlight that it was a pretty special event and also show that Aboriginal people could do this sort of thing as well as anyone.

The carnivals went on through the 1970s and into the early 80s. They highlighted the talent of Indigenous men and women and the competition among the players became stronger each year. I remember saying to Charlie one day that if you looked back to before the carnivals started, there were only a couple of pockets of high-profile black players in the country.

Towards the end, the lack of interest the top leagues had shown in the beginning had changed. States were starting to notice the players and recognise their talent. It took ten years to get that happening. Some state carnivals still happen, like the one in South Australia where people play for the Winnie Branson Memorial Cup, named after my sister.

How that came about was that when I was working for Hostels, we'd bought a building in South Terrace in Adelaide and had to do it up a bit. A company that made windows got a fair bit of work out of that, and at the end of the contract the boss of the company said to me, 'Can we get you something in return for all the work?' I asked him if he could buy us a trophy cup for the national carnivals. So he bought a beautiful cup. We had to name it, and I came up with Winnie's name for it, because she was connected to the beginnings of it all.

When she and John had set up the Nunga footy team with the Aboriginal Progress Association in the mid-1960s, they got the Adelaide matches happening. Then in 1968, Point Pearce turned one hundred years old and as part of marking that they held a football match against Koonibba, another mission near Ceduna. The next year the Nunga footy team played a round-robin carnival with Point Pearce and Koonibba. After that we had the first interstate carnival with three states playing against each other. It all grew from there. Winnie had been a big part of Nunga footy, so it's good we have that cup for her.

28

'She didn't care if the Queen was there'

Ever since 1955 when I'd lived with Doug Nicholls in Melbourne, I'd run into him here and there at FCAATSI conferences and sports carnivals. Then, in 1976, when we were living in Adelaide, the South Australian premier, Don Dunstan, appointed Doug to be the state governor. Charlie had wanted Dunstan to make me Doug's aide so I could take him round the state and introduce him to all the Aboriginal communities, but that didn't happen. I still saw a lot of Doug, though. I'd be at the office and the phone would ring. 'You'd better come down for a cup of tea,' Doug would say.

I'd say okay and down I'd go. We'd talk about whatever he was doing and where he'd been, then we'd go out walking in the garden.

One day the staff at Government House couldn't find Doug anywhere and there was a bit of panic. Eventually they found him in Rundle Mall having yarns with people. That's just how he was. Doug took it in his stride being the governor. He was a people's man, and wherever he went he'd be chatting away and finding out about people and what they did and where they came from. It was the same when he used to travel around Victoria giving those talks for the Advancement League – he'd always stay after and talk to people.

A few months later, the Queen visited Australia, and Doug of course was her host in Adelaide. He met up with her one day, then on another day he was meant to have lunch with her at Government House, but he got crook. The lieutenant-governor, a bloke by the name of Walter Crocker, rang me to see if I could stand in for Doug and bring my wife and a couple of my aunties.

So that's what I did. There were twelve people altogether: the police commissioner Harold Salisbury, the army, navy and air force hierarchy, and us four – Brenda, me, Aunty Glad, and Aunty Maude Tongerie, who was married to George Tongerie. Maude and George were fairly prominent in South Australia by then. They'd been in the Aboriginal Progress Association from the beginning, and George ended up looking after the first Aboriginal Lands Trust. Maude had worked with Aunty Glad on the women's council too.

We were all waiting in the lounge for the Queen to come and join us. We could hear her coming down the hall because she spoke really loudly even before she came into the room with us. The people in charge had spoken to us before about how we had to speak with her and Prince Philip. You had to wait for them to ask you a question before you talked. And there was what you had to call the Queen if you spoke to her: Her Majesty.

We were seated around a long table. The Queen was on one side with Prince Philip. One of the armed forces people was sitting on her other side. The police chief was at one end, and Aunty Glad and Maude were at the other. Brenda was the closest of us four to the Queen.

I was beside Lieutenant-Governor Crocker. He was a lovely old man, and we talked about things in general and also about what was happening with Aboriginal people at that time. He said he'd love to be able to go out to a community one day, and I said to him to let me know anytime he wanted to go and I'd take him around.

Another thing I noticed about the Queen was that her soup was chilled to somewhere between cold and warm. I love soup so I took a big mouthful. I thought to myself, *Cripes, it's cold.* For a start, I didn't know what to do with it, but of course, I had to swallow it. Afterwards they told me that the reason the Queen doesn't have her soup hot is to stop her nose running. That was fairly commonly known.

Another little incident happened with Aunty Glad. I was watching her, but I'm not sure if anyone else was. She was in her seventies then, and before she went to eat she took her teeth out and stuck them in her bra. She didn't care if the Queen was there or not – she did what she normally did and that was it.

At one stage Prince Philip was talking about the stock in Australia – cattle and things like that. I knew a bit from my experiences as a farmer, so I could talk to him about it. The talk didn't last long, but it's something I remember.

What did it feel like, meeting the Queen? First of all, I felt sorry for Doug not being there. The Queen had just knighted him and he deserved that recognition because he was a great worker and a great man. All the time I was sitting there I was thinking, *Well, I'm only just sitting in for Doug.* I felt sad about it for him.

In the end Doug wasn't in office for long. He had a stroke and he got over that, but he wasn't very well after. He retired the next month after the Queen's visit. Had he spent his full term in office, he would have made a great deal of difference.

* * *

Through all those years, first with football and then in the public service, I was lucky to meet people like Doug and be able to learn so much from them. As I got older I saw myself as trying to do the best I could for the people I was working for, which was Aboriginal people.

I had my own way of operating, but I also got to see one of the best operators up close. That was Charlie, of course. He could be in the office of the prime minister talking with him one minute, then sitting in the sand with a group of Aboriginal men, and be on the same level with each of them. That's not easy to do.

One time, Charlie and I went to a leprosarium just out of Darwin. I'd seen movies about leprosy and I was thinking I'd better stay home, or if I had to go to not shake hands or hug anyone. Charlie and I went in and he just sat down and shook hands with people. They were really happy, those old ladies and old men. He had the courage to do that.

Charlie had some big jobs in Canberra and if he had to travel somewhere, usually one of us boys from the home would be with him. He'd make sure of that. We were company for him – someone he could relax with and talk about old times and have a laugh – because he had a lot of work pressure on him and he was battling his kidney too. Somebody had to be around him to look after him. Charlie wasn't scared of anything, and you had to stand by and be ready for trouble – one good punch in the kidney and he'd be gone. He'd have some pretty tough men around him at conferences and meetings to protect him, in case some idiot wanted to make a name for themselves. People like Roy Carroll, Tony Mundine and Bobby Huddleston. Lionel Rose looked after him too. Charlie loved sportsmen, especially Aboriginal sportsmen, because he was one himself.

Sometimes people would want to argue with Charlie that they knew more than he did, and they'd ask him why he was doing different things, and why he had a flash car and they didn't, and some would call him Uncle Tom. Things got fairly heated sometimes. You'd never know if somebody might go off their head and start swinging and punching.

One time in Darwin, I was at a conference with Charlie, and as we were walking along a bloke bumped into my chest. I had my wallet in my inside coat pocket and the bloke thought it was a gun. He was telling everybody I had a gun, and so they kept a wide berth. I'd become Charlie's bodyguard! People might have wanted to fight him, but they knew Charlie was as important in his own way as the Queen or the governor-general or any other leader.

29

'This must be a dangerous operation'

Brenda, the kids and I moved back to Canberra again in 1977. A lot of Aboriginal people from all over the country were by now working there, which was probably a shock for Canberra. And a lot of us had connections going back to the early FCAATSI conferences. I had a few different jobs, and sometimes when Charlie couldn't get to meetings I'd stand in for him then let him know what people had talked about. The Aboriginal Hostels work kept going, and then in the early 1980s I was helping Charlie with the Aboriginal Development Commission, which was set up to buy properties back for groups of Aboriginal people on their Country. Ideas like the Hostels and the ADC had all come about from those FCAATSI meetings. So things had been slowly changing over those years.

One day in late 1982, I was on my way back to my office after a meeting in another building when I had a sudden pain in my chest. I was smoking and I thought, *It must be that.* So I threw the cigarette away. But the pain got worse and worse.

I stumbled up to the office and sat down. It wasn't getting any better, so I drove home. How I did, I don't know.

I lay down for a while. 'No, this is no good,' I said to Brenda. 'I've got to see a doctor.' We drove to our doctor's clinic, which was across town. I was sitting in the waiting room and the pain was getting worse. 'You better go and tell them it's piercing,' I said to Brenda.

Straight away my doctor took me into her room and called an ambulance. They took me to hospital and put me in intensive care. Things calmed down with the medicines they gave me. I was in there for twelve days, and they told me I'd probably need a heart bypass at some stage.

I was forty-five, so Kara would have been nine and Vincent seven. For a start, I didn't know what to do, and it frightened the hell out of Brenda, of course. I'd probably told her my dad had died of a broken heart when he was young, and she might have been thinking the same thing could happen to me.

As time went on I realised I'd let myself get unfit. I'd been pretty active when I was young, playing sport and doing hard physical work. But when I got the job in Canberra I was travelling around in cars and planes a lot, and sitting on my bum in meetings, smoking and putting on weight. It was eventually going to happen, and it did. I didn't really smoke or drink until I was in my twenties – a lot of us boys at the home had tried both when we were young, but we didn't like them. I think for a lot of us it just twigged in our minds that you don't have to do those things.

The doctor said if I kept smoking and drinking I was going to die. *That's it, no more,* I thought.

When I left hospital, I had to find out how to get well. The doctors had said, 'Just walk.' So that's what I did. Work gave me three months off, and I walked and walked and walked and walked, morning and night, and started to feel good. The heart attack seemed to go away, if that's possible.

It was coming up to Christmas time, and we came back to Curramulka to the farm. All the while since we'd got married in 1971, we kept going back regularly, often for holidays and celebrations but sometimes for sad times. Brenda's brother Robert had been killed in a car accident in 1974 when he was only twenty-five, which was pretty tough on his wife and three small children. Then Brenda's mum died in 1978, and her dad in 1980. The farm stayed in the family for a long time with someone share-farming it for them, so we could still go there. Brenda's sister Marlene was living in Curramulka with her husband Don, and Brenda's other sister, Pat, was in Elizabeth with her husband, whose name was Don too. We'd catch up with them and their kids, and we'd see Josie and her family pretty regularly too – they were still living in Taperoo.

I remembered that Frank Joraslafsky's birthday was coming up the week before Christmas. Pat didn't tell him I was coming, and when I walked in he got all teary and I got all teary. It was good to see them again.

We were at the Thomases' farm when, one morning, I was walking to the beach and felt a pain in my chest. It was a funny sort of pain and not like the one I'd had in Canberra. It felt like a blockage, and as I kept walking it went *fwoot* and that seemed to push the blockage away.

I turned around and went back to the house and told Brenda. The pain had stopped by then, so there wasn't any reason at that stage to get excited about calling doctors or driving to hospitals. And in any case, the nearest hospitals were the ones that had turned me away when I was a kid, and I didn't want to go there if I didn't have to.

Later that night the pain got bad again, so I called Frank, because he was the St John Ambulance man. He picked me up and took me to Minlaton hospital, and they kept an eye on me.

I'd been there for a few days when one morning I was lying on the bed and one of Brenda's cousins came in to see me. For some reason I started to get the shakes and couldn't stop. He must have gone and found the doctor, and when he came rushing in I thought it was my last hurrah. But he worked on me and stayed with me overnight and settled me down. That doctor, Peter Cameron, became a really good friend of mine. The next day I was in the ambulance on my way to the Royal Adelaide Hospital to have open heart surgery. Of course, it was Frank who drove me.

Charlie came over to see me before the surgery. The day of the operation I remember a few other blokes around me who were waiting their turn to go into the operating room for the same business. I was lying there watching them, and when they were being wheeled out of the ward they'd burst out crying or go really quiet.

Gee whiz, I thought, *this must be a dangerous operation.*

When I woke up later someone was saying, 'Mr Copley, we're going to take the tubes out.' It was all over and finished. That was in February 1983, on the day the big Ash Wednesday bushfires happened in South Australia and Victoria.

In those days you stayed in hospital for a fortnight after the operation, until you had your stitches out. Brenda and the kids mainly stayed with Pat and Don, and they'd come in and visit every day. After hospital you had to exercise for another three months.

There was no reason for me to lie down and die. The kids were still young, I was heavily involved in sport and hostels, and there were things I could still do that were of value for people. I did the exercises every day, and that's probably one of the reasons why I've lasted so long.

We went back to Canberra after a while, and I went back to work. I was driving and flying again, but I was doing a lot more walking too. While we'd been in Adelaide, the kids' teachers had sent over schoolwork for them to do, so they were ready to pick up the pieces again. They went back to school, and Brenda kept on looking after us.

Through it all, Charlie had been great to us. When I first had the heart attack it was Charlie who looked after Brenda. When I had to take time off work to go back to Adelaide and the farm to recuperate, it was Charlie who made everything possible. When I was in hospital having the bypass, he rang Brenda up every day. 'Are you okay?' he'd say. 'Have you got money? Do you need anything? Just say so.' That's how he was. He looked after her. He and Brenda just seemed to click. He made sure that if there was anything she wanted and it was in his power to do it, he would do it.

* * *

Charlie sometimes asked me to go to conferences on his behalf. Back in 1981, the World Council of Indigenous Peoples conference had been held in Canberra at the university, and we'd all gone to it. Three years later, I represented the department for Charlie at the next one in Panama City. About ten Aboriginal people from different organisations were heading over.

The conference ran for a week, and Indigenous people from all round the world were there, including a lot from South American countries. We'd meet for major sessions in a big hall and go to smaller sessions on education, housing and health. A couple of people from our group gave talks about what was happening in Australia.

I learned that some of the people had come to the conference against the wishes of their governments. They'd had to sneak out of the country to get there, and if they went back home they'd be shot or taken away by the people in power. I think that was mainly from some of the South American countries.

It was really good to see different people and their different cultures and customs too, and to see what was the same and what was different between them and us, and what you could learn.

After the conference we all headed to Los Angeles for the flight home. I was staying on because I'd organised before I left for Brenda to bring the kids across. It had been nearly two years since the heart attack, so by then Kara was eleven and Vincent nine.

We had a few days at Disneyland then we went to Las Vegas and San Francisco, then on the way home we went to Hawaii.

All the time on the trip I was hoping the kids weren't bored and were taking notice of things, but I wasn't sure. After we got back home, I'd hear them talking together sometimes. 'Do you remember this ...?' and 'Remember that ...' they'd be saying. When I heard that, I thought, *Well, it was worth the trip.*

* * *

Work carried on in Canberra, and in 1984 Charlie became the head of the Department of Aboriginal Affairs – the first Aboriginal person in the job. But I was starting to think about where I needed to be living. Brenda and I talked about it, and one day I said to Charlie that I thought I'd better go home to my family in South Australia. He changed my Canberra position to one in the Adelaide office, and in 1985 we moved back to Adelaide for good.

In the department's Adelaide office my main job for a while was to work on different sports programs we were running. I'd visit communities and see how they were going and help out with anything people needed. Life went back to normal. Sometimes Charlie would ring up and say he was coming through Adelaide on his way to somewhere and he wanted someone to go with him.

When we first came back, we rented at Newton. Brenda hated the house, but it was good for me because I could walk out the front door, get on the bus, and the bus would drop me in front of where I worked. Brenda got cancer while we were there, and I think that caused her to not like the house. Her doctor found it early and they didn't mess around – she went straight to hospital and they fixed it up.

We'd been looking to buy a place of our own, and one day when I was in Coober Pedy, up in the desert, I got a phone call. 'I've found the house, I've found the house!' Brenda wanted to buy it straight away.

I said to wait until I got back. 'No, no, no, other people are looking at it and it'll be gone. If you don't say yes, I'm leaving you!' she said.

'Well let me think about that,' I said, and waited a second. Then of course I said, 'Yes, go ahead and buy it.' That was the house we bought in Modbury.

The kids had moved between a few schools in Canberra and Adelaide. Vincent was getting on okay. He was easygoing, made mates easily and he was part of a group of kids. Sometimes he'd cop racist stuff, like being called the 'n-word'. But he didn't seem to have any problems with being bullied. Nobody would want to punch him because he'd punch them back.

Kara had a few problems, though. She was bullied at school. I won't go into the details. She never said anything to me about it until later. If she had I would have taken her to a different school, like Le Fevre where I'd gone, where there was a good program for Aboriginal kids. When I was there, we boys from St Francis didn't go through bullying to the same extent that Kara did because there was a whole group of us and that softened the blow. But Kara was by herself and it was hard for her.

She had one really good friend, Holly. They'd come out of school holding hands – Holly, who was lily-white, and Kara, with her lovely dark olive skin. Later on, Holly was one of Kara's bridesmaids.

Early on Brenda and I didn't really discuss what it was going to be like for the kids. Then, when they went to school they were copping all this rubbish because they had dark skin, and when I found out about it, I'd be angry. The trouble was I was busy with work and on the move fairly often, and Brenda had to deal with a lot of it. 'This has got to stop and I'm going to stop it,' she'd say. And that's what she did.

When the kids were a bit older, another one of their friends started doing the 'black' thing, calling them all the bad names. I heard him one time. 'If you keep that up I'll come round and I'll spear you and I'll eat you,' I said.

For a while he couldn't sleep and he couldn't eat. His mum ended up saying to Brenda, 'Can you tell your husband to come and say he's not going to eat him?' It didn't happen again.

We got on with life in Adelaide. We saw a lot more of our families, and the kids were at school and doing things with their friends. We still had lots of visitors coming – the boys, and different people I was working with from Canberra and other places. Vincent and I had sorted out that we had some different feelings about football. He was playing but after a while he didn't want me to go and watch him. He said I was putting him off a bit. I'd be yelling on the sidelines, 'Do this! Do that!'

'I can't do everything, Dad,' he said one day.

That was okay. Whether it was the right or wrong approach, I'd made an effort. We'd play golf together on weekends and he was pretty good – he did really well in the junior Aboriginal state golf championships.

In some ways Vincent was following in my footsteps and in other ways he was making his own. One way he did follow me, for a while anyway, was with suits. I was always dressed in a suit for work and when Vincent was a little kid, he liked wearing them too. He had two different ones and when we'd go out to different functions for work, Brenda would dress him up and he looked really smart.

Sometimes I'd tell the kids stories. One time Brenda wanted me to tell them about the facts of life so I invented Herb and Herbertina. I started with how they met in a tree and then fluttered around, and Herb kept chasing Herbertina until he caught up with her. Then along came all of these little babies from the catching up. Kara and Vincent were sitting there wide-eyed, then they started asking me questions about this and that. The story got longer and longer.

After a while I turned around to Brenda and I said, 'Is that right?' She was giggling away. My niece Shendelle was living with us at the time – she'd come over from Currie to start work, and she was standing outside the door listening. She told me after she couldn't stop laughing.

Opportunities to be able to make things better for Aboriginal people were coming left, right and centre, and Charlie and the rest of us were running with them. So Brenda had to look after Kara and Vincent a lot on her own. That's something I think back on now. But we seem to have worked it out. Something clicked.

30

'The proverbial hit the fan'

Nineteen eighty-eight was a big year. It was the bicentenary of the time the tall ships brought white people to Australia, and there were a lot of re-enactments and commemorations happening, as well as lots of protests. Bob Hawke, a Labor politician, had been the prime minister for about five years, while Charlie had been head of the Department of Aboriginal Affairs for going on four years.

Behind the scenes, Charlie was having a few differences with Hawke and some of his ministers about how Aboriginal Affairs should be run. That ended up playing out through most of the year.

One way we came up with to mark the bicentenary was by doing a re-enactment of the first ever Aboriginal cricket team to tour England in 1868. Hawke was keen for it to happen. So he joined forces with the Aboriginal Cricket Association, which Charlie had set up.

Forty cricketers were picked, but they could only take

thirteen. Charlie wanted me to do something with the ones who didn't make that group, so I suggested taking them to New Zealand to do a tour of the South and North Islands. I'd been in New Zealand before for a conference, and I'd seen Maori people at the opening ceremony singing and dancing, something that hadn't been done much in Australia at the time. I talked with Charlie about taking some traditional dancers with us. Doug Nicholls' son Ralph had been working with traditional people in Arnhem Land, so we worked with him to bring three traditional dancers on the tour. They danced in response to the welcome ceremonies put on by the

The cricket team we took to New Zealand in 1988. I'm second on the left at the back. On the building behind us you can see some Maori carvings. We met with a Maori chief that day.

Maori people. This was in the early days of doing things like that in Australia.

Before the Aboriginal team went to England, they played a match at Manly Oval in Sydney in January 1988. Bob Hawke played in the opposition team, in a prime minister's XI, while his wife Hazel, who was lovely, sat with Charlie and me in the grandstand.

Aboriginal people had been protesting against the commemoration of the bicentenary all over the country, and I thought we might be in for a bit of flack at the Manly match. In the end there was only one bloke who protested about the cricket team going over to England. Harry Penrith was his real name, but he called himself Burnum Burnum. He thought we shouldn't be dealing with the white people. He was at the oval in an old dilapidated bus, and he drove round and round with a loudspeaker, making his protest loud and clear. Just before the match was about to start, he went quiet. Next minute, he was lying in the middle of the pitch and wouldn't move. People were scratching their heads and wondering what to do. Then along came four big policemen, who picked him up and carted him off. He was yelling and screaming as they took him away.

Burnum Burnum was a funny man. He had a great big beard, and if he'd see you coming along the street and he didn't want to notice you, he'd put the beard up over his face and just walk on. He was the first bloke to go to England and claim Britain for the Aboriginal people. He used to go to FCAATSI meetings too, so we all knew him, of course.

Once he rang me from Melbourne. 'Listen, you haven't got a left thong, have you?' he asked.

'What?' I said.

'Have you got a left thong?'

'Why?'

'Because I lost mine. If you find it, would you send it over? Or better still, send me over two pounds and I can buy a new pair.'

'You gotta be joking,' I said.

He wasn't joking. He was a real character.

In the bicentenary year we also took a cricket team to play at Edenhope and Harrow in Victoria. Those two towns are pretty close to each other, and that's where a lot of the blokes who played in the 1868 team came from. In Harrow, they have an oval named after the leading player on the tour, Johnny Mullagh, as well as a statue of him. He's buried there and the people look after his grave and they've also got a museum about the English tour that tells you about how the team members were smuggled out of Australia and taken over there.

It took a long time for those cricketers and that tour to be recognised. Finally in 1951 some people put up a monument at Edenhope that the famous cricketer Victor Richardson unveiled. Then in 2002 a plaque was added to mark the 1988 tour. I unveiled that one.

* * *

The Barunga Festival was coming up in June, and it was going to be an extra-special occasion. Barunga's in the Northern Territory, not far from Katherine, and since 1985 the community has put on a cultural festival, with music, dancing, art and sport every year. The Central Desert people and the Yolngu people from Arnhem Land had joined together to make what they called the Barunga Statement. It had artwork from the two areas and it followed on in a way from the Yirrkala bark petitions back in 1963, in asking Australia to respect Aboriginal people's rights properly. The people behind it had invited Bob Hawke to come so they could present it to him. Two of the main people were Wenten Rubuntja, an artist and Arrernte bloke Charlie knew from the Central Land Council, and Galarrwuy Yunupingu, who'd been a pretty good dancer in his time and now was a leader of his Yolngu people.

A big crowd from all over Australia was there: people from the Central Desert, Arnhem Land and other places in the Northern Territory, and politicians from Canberra. A lot of people I knew from South Australia went up and camped. It was a big deal for Aboriginal people, and Charlie wanted to be there as the secretary of the department. But he was under a bit of a cloud with Hawke and his Minister for Aboriginal Affairs, Gerry Hand, so he and I just sat in the outdoor grounds with all the other people, watching quietly. After the festival, Hawke took the Barunga Statement to Canberra and eventually hung it up in Parliament House.

Charlie had been fighting hard for land rights legislation, but all the time the new laws were being discussed and debated, he could see that the parts that were really important for Aboriginal people were being watered down. Which he was pointing out to the politicians and whoever else he could. I saw what was happening and that people were trying to get rid of him.

Five months later, in November 1988, Charlie resigned, under pressure from Hand. He'd been accused of some things that, later on, would be found to not be true. It was all pretty hard on him.

Not long after Charlie left, the government closed down the Department of Aboriginal Affairs and started up the Aboriginal and Torres Strait Islander Commission, or what they called ATSIC, instead. The line seemed to be, 'We'll make a new organisation that looks like Aboriginal people have a say in it. But then once you have your say, or if you don't want to talk to the minister because you can see that he won't listen to you, we'll just say, "See you, mate," and it's goodbye.' And eventually away it all goes. Away the Aboriginal Development Commission goes, away the Department of Aboriginal Affairs goes, away all the funding goes.

With the Aboriginal Development Commission, which the government had set up in 1980, the idea was that Aboriginal groups that couldn't get land rights could get funds to buy their land back and do things like run businesses and set up housing. That happened in a couple of places, but the people who got the funds soon found out that they didn't have enough money or staff to do things properly. They were trying to do a good job, but they weren't trained in finance, and they weren't trained in how you look after a place.

I want to include all this in my story, because people can't be thinking, *Here's a bloke who lived in a utopia all his life.* There has to be something I listened to and thought about more than just that life is a wonderful thing.

* * *

In the early 1980s, John Moriarty had moved back to Adelaide to be the boss of the state branch of the Department of Aboriginal Affairs, which is where I was working after we'd moved back in 1985. John had married his wife, Ros, a few years before, and the two of them had this idea for making designs based on Aboriginal art. They started with ideas from Borroloola, where John was from, and they set up a label called Balarinji. It took them a bit of time, but they ended up having their designs turn up on company uniforms and bed sheets and aeroplanes. In 1988, John left the government job and went into his business full time. He was still in Adelaide, though, and he helped out with things he'd been involved in before, like Tandanya, a new national Aboriginal institute of arts and culture.

I can't remember how the idea for Tandanya came about. It might have been Charlie or it might have been one of those things that people had been talking about for a long time. However it happened, I had lots of connections with people nationally through the hostels and sport, and I became the first chair of the board.

The state government appointed a director and the first job we had was to find a suitable building for the institute. John and I did a lot of fighting to get one we found near the city centre that had been a power station supplying electricity for trams and streetlights. It was a fairly solid old building with a big inner hall that we refurbished with new floors and a lift, and with space for a gallery and restaurant.

We had a big opening for the centre with a few hundred people there. Being the chairman, it was my job to welcome everybody and talk about Tandanya and what we were looking to do with it. That was in 1989.

A few months later, in early 1990, the Adelaide Fringe was on, and Tandanya had put together a little play for it in the old East End Market, just across from our building. It was called *Up the Ladder*, about the 1950s boxing champion Elley Bennett. It won a prize, and our director got the idea to take it to the Edinburgh Festival Fringe later in the year. I thought that if he thought it was good enough for the world, we should take it to the world. We decided we'd take a couple of dancers and some Aboriginal paintings as well.

We had regular meetings with the Minister for the Arts and their staff, and they were asking if we had enough money for it. The director said we did, because as well as the government funding, Tandanya had sold a few paintings. I took his word for it and everything was set up. The team going over was the director, another person from Tandanya, and myself. On the way home we decided to visit the Australian embassies in a few European cities to let them know about Tandanya.

My niece Kathy was studying at the South Australian School of Art, and I said to her that I thought it would be a good idea for her to come along and experience some of the art capitals of the world. She didn't have much money, but her sister paid her fare and travel costs. Kathy worked really hard for us, organising things and being at the door of the venue to take money. That's how it worked at the Edinburgh Fringe – you had to do all that yourself.

The whole festival went for about eighteen days. The play we put on was tucked away in a little out-of-the-way place, like a lot of the shows there. Then we had a second little space where we exhibited the paintings we'd brought over, and where the dancers performed.

I had a day off, and Kathy and I caught a train to Glasgow to have a look around. When we got there we went into a cafe and there was Yothu Yindi. They were just starting as a band, and they'd been taken to Glasgow to perform at a big European folk festival. I knew Mandawuy Yunupingu, the lead singer, from when I'd been in Arnhem Land working on setting up the hostels. All these things clicked together as time went on.

When we got back to Edinburgh, I told the director we'd run into Yothu Yindi, and he got in touch with the bloke managing them and arranged for them to come to Edinburgh after they'd finished in Glasgow, to be part of our show. We secured a fairly large tent and people came to see them. Kathy helped us out with that one too, and it went pretty well.

When the festival ended, we travelled to the Australian embassies in Paris, Vienna and Rome. We met up with the people there and they all thought we could bring the play and exhibitions to their cities one day.

On the way home, we had an overnight stopover in Singapore. A friend of mine, Benny Mills, had been appointed the first secretary of the Australian Embassy in Singapore and he and his wife, Yvonne Haines, invited us to tea at their place. Benny was from the Torres Strait Islands and Yvonne came from Ceduna in South Australia. They had a baby son called Patty, who's a pretty famous NBL basketballer these days.

Sometime after we got back to Adelaide, the proverbial hit the fan. The Edinburgh trip had gone over budget, and we ended up in the red by $80,000. At the time, South Australia's

State Bank was about to collapse. When it did, in 1991, the state ended up with a $3 billion debt.

Some people in government tried to compare Tandanya's $80,000 loss to the bank's $3 billion one. It was a way to take some of the heat off the government, blaming the blacks for overspending. The newspapers were quick to rubbish the trip too, and also that Kathy had been there, though when they found out she'd paid her own way, they quickly backed off.

There was a big kerfuffle, and people were stood down. I resigned.

Back then, Aboriginal people working in business hadn't really had much training, apart from a handful who'd studied at university. People were put in management positions and often they were flying by the seat of their pants. It was a learning period for all of us.

Tandanya kept going. A few months later they went ahead with their first big art exhibition, with batik designs from the women from Utopia. That's an Aboriginal community a few hundred kilometres north-east of Alice Springs and it was just starting to become well known for its art. Janet Holmes à Court had bought a collection of their work and loaned it to us for the exhibition. At the opening they closed the street and had a concert on the back of a trailer, and Yothu Yindi were one of the performing acts. That first exhibition was pretty successful.

John Bannon had been premier of South Australia at the time and years later, when I got to know him better through some cricket work we did together, I had the chance to talk to him about Tandanya and the kerfuffle after Edinburgh. I asked him what the go was.

'There had to be something to take the heat off me and the government at that stage,' he said. 'You got caught up in it.'

In the end, he and I became very good friends.

* * *

Not long after we'd got back from Edinburgh, before the kerfuffle, Don Dunstan rang. Nelson Mandela was coming to Sydney and Dunstan wondered whether I'd like to go to a talk he was giving especially for Aboriginal people. Mandela had been out of jail a few months and Dunstan had been one of the people in Australia working towards getting him freed.

Of course I said yes.

The talk was held at the Intercontinental Hotel. There were about sixteen of us there, with me the only one from South Australia. We all shook hands with Mandela then sat down and listened to him speak.

Mandela talked about his dreams for South Africa, the changes he wanted to make, and the hardship he'd had in that island jail. To hear him speak about that and how he had suffered was very moving.

We only had the afternoon with him, because he had other things to do and places to go, but it was great that he made time to see us. I was thankful to Don Dunstan for doing that. Great people have an aura about them. Muhammad Ali had it, the Queen had it, certainly Mandela had it. You could feel their greatness. They rose above others.

It was around that time that the ATSIC people in Canberra decided to employ a bloke to run an Aboriginal cultural awareness program and teach some of us how to do it, so we could take it to the wider community. I was one of the Adelaide people selected to spend a week in Canberra with him and go through the process of learning it. His name was Chip Morgan and he was a white man, but he'd spent a lot of time working up in the APY Lands. He'd got to know the languages and had a fair idea about what was happening on the Aboriginal front.

After the training in Canberra we came away as qualified cultural awareness program trainers. When I got back to Adelaide, we trained all of the ATSIC staff within the office, and after that they were much more clued up on the history, and the different Indigenous communities, and what to do and what not to do.

A while after the cultural awareness training, the work bosses were handing out redundancy packages. I decided to retire from the public service and set up a little business with a bloke called Gilly from New South Wales. He'd gone through the training program too, and we joined up with Chip Morgan. Chip would organise where we went and who we trained. Gilly was a nice bloke and we got on well together. We did some big training jobs, like one with the Australian Federal Police, where we trained all their staff, all around the country.

We'd been doing a lot of training, then all of a sudden it collapsed. A job we had with Telstra was the one that really killed us. At the time, interest rates were pretty high. Telstra took a long time to pay us, and Gilly and I both suffered. Brenda and I had a mortgage on our house at Modbury, and we were battling. We ended up selling. I'll leave the rest of that story there.

31

'So many little things about Charlie'

Back when Charlie was head of the Department of Aboriginal Affairs and I'd been working in another office in the building, he'd rung me one day. 'You'd better come up here,' he said.

I went up to his office.

'Righto, we're going to the dentist,' he said.

'You've brought me here because you want me to go to the dentist with you?

'Yeah,' he said. 'I've got to go and I'm scared.'

'Things have changed,' I replied. 'It's easier now – they don't hurt you as much as they used to.'

'You're coming with me. That's it.'

'Hey, Cop,' he said when he came out after. 'You know, that didn't hurt a bit.'

That's how he was and how we were. He could have asked Gordon, he could have asked John – they were working there too. But no, he had to ring me up and drag me along. I don't know why he asked me, but his very last words to me probably said it all.

In 2000, Charlie was pretty crook with his kidney. He was at the Prince of Wales Hospital, and Brenda and I came over to Sydney to see him for a few days. Eileen had a sleeping bag and was staying with him in the room, and his kids were there too, Hetti, Adam and Rachel.

One day a few of us had been there and we all started to leave. Brenda and I were heading back to Adelaide. Charlie turned over in the bed, and grabbed hold of me. 'Wait on, Cop. Stay here. Listen, you've stopped with me all this time.'

'Yeah, of course I have,' I said. 'You're my mentor, you're my trainer, you're my friend and you're my brother. That's why I'm still here.'

'And I'll never forget it,' he said. And he just had hold of my hand.

I walked out, and Brenda and I got in the car and started the drive back home. We got to Narrandera and Eileen rang to say Charlie had passed away. We turned around and went back to Sydney.

The family had all gathered at Charlie and Eileen's house at Newtown, and the kids wanted to know stories about him. We sat there for half a day and told them things about their dad we knew they hadn't heard before.

It was a pretty moving moment for me, when Charlie grabbed me and told me to stay. I think what was in his mind was a thank you for the times we'd spent together. That I was someone he could talk to, and that whatever he told me stayed just with me if it needed to.

Apart from that, in our lifetime I'd seen him go through all the other business. That's what's amazed me, about how so many people overlooked him and what he did. I've talked to Eileen about that a lot since. People forget that Charlie was the man that stuck his neck out when nobody else would. I'm still not happy about some of the things people say about Charlie.

At his funeral I said something like, 'I don't hear the phone ring anymore.' When Charlie was alive, so many times I'd be home and the phone would ring and it was him. 'Cop,' he'd say, 'be in Sydney tomorrow.' 'Right,' I'd say. 'Who's organising it?' 'Everything's fixed up,' he'd say. 'Just go to the airport and get your ticket. We're going here.'

So the next day I'd be in Sydney. Other people would say to him, 'I can't make it, sorry, I've got this on.' I always made sure I was available for him.

There are so many little things that stick with me about Charlie. When we were working on the national sports carnivals, we'd visit places like, say, Port Lincoln on the Eyre Peninsula, when they'd be having their selection matches for the state event. We'd meet up with the local Aboriginal sporting club people, and they'd tell us they needed lights on the oval or something like that. Charlie's parting words would be, 'Cop, fix that up.' I'd follow up with people in the department and make sure the team got lights around their oval. I did things that made Charlie's job easier.

I'd seen Charlie at his worst and I'd seen him at his best. Sometimes he'd get wild with me. I wasn't much good at doing reports. I'd talk to him after a meeting or some other event and tell him what happened and who was there and what they did. He'd get a bit of an idea from that. But if he was having a bad day, he'd say, 'Where the bloody hell's that report?' And I'd tell him I didn't write a report because I didn't know how to.

But we didn't argue a great deal, and not about anything that was of real importance. If I was driving him somewhere out in the country, sometimes I'd be driving on the middle of the white line and he'd tell me all about it. 'Well that's the way I drive so don't worry about it,' I'd say. 'I'm not going to kill you.' Then we'd be staying in a twin room at a little pub in a small town, and I'd be snoring my head off and he wouldn't be able to sleep. Next morning I'd wake up with all these clothes on top of me that he'd thrown to wake me up. 'Next time get your own room,' I'd say.

When we'd been at the boys' home, one time they had a fundraising fete and we were going to put on a play called *William Tell*, and we'd be singing some songs. The singing teacher was a nice lady, but she had green teeth and the worst breath. When we were learning it, she was right in front of our faces. 'This is what you do,' she said, and she took some big breaths and let them out. You could see the kids all making faces, especially Charlie, because he had to sing a song that he hated on his own, and he had to stand in front of her. I can remember how the song went: 'Once in the dear dead days beyond recall, when on the world the mists began to fall, out of the dreams that rose in happy throng, low to our hearts love sang an old sweet song.'

All the locals turned up to the fete, and as Charlie sang the song the teacher was breathing all over him again. We couldn't stop laughing after. That's how it was – if we wanted to turn a serious thing into a joke, that's the way we'd do it.

Years later, when Charlie and I were working together, sometimes we'd be going along in the car and he would start singing. He thought he was Charley Pride, and every time he'd break into a Charley Pride song I'd say, 'Remember this, Charlie?' And I'd start singing the boys' home song. He'd burst out laughing.

A lot of people thought Charlie was just a stirrer. Lots of times when you were out at different events and parties, that would come across loud and strong – from some white people and even some of his own mob. They were misinformed.

Brenda was Charlie's most famous supporter. People learned not to ever say anything bad about Charlie to Brenda – they'd feel the wrath of her come straight down on top of them. 'Don't you ever say that again,' she'd tell them. I knew that sometimes when people said bad things about Charlie it was because they didn't understand what he was up to.

I'd try and explain things to them, and Brenda would say to me, 'What are you telling them that for?'

'They don't know any different,' I'd say. 'I'm trying to explain the reasons why he did this or he did that.'

'I don't put up with that rubbish,' Brenda would say.

'All right, that's your go,' I'd say.

Wherever Brenda was, if you said anything bad about Charlie, look out. She didn't care who was there or what she said. She certainly straightened a few people out.

With Charlie, you've got to keep in mind that the man was on a kidney machine for a long time, and he battled through and never missed a day's work. People don't realise that for a good part of his early public life that's how he had to live. He'd look like a big bullneck frog a lot of the time. Can you imagine a slim bloke with plenty of energy turning into one of those blimps they let go in the air? Then testing the man as far as he could go, to the point where he thought he might kill himself. And yet he was able to make jokes about it and he kept going.

I suppose in the sort of situation he was in, you've got to have somebody to trust and talk to. He had his wife, Eileen, and that was good of course – there's certain things that passed between them. But when your wife's not there and there's things that you don't want anybody to know, and yet you want someone to know – who do you tell? Probably that's the part I played. I was always there with him as best I could.

Charlie was just pure determination. No matter how many times he was knocked down, he was going to get up and just keep going. That was his great courage. I think that was his greatest gift. He couldn't fight his way out of a wet paper bag, but he just wasn't ever scared to have a go. I saw him so many times get knocked down and get up again. There's different ways that happens, of course. Politicians do it in words, and other people do it in physical ways. Charlie weathered the whole lot.

It was just something in his makeup. I think he got a fair bit of inspiration from his old mum, Aunty Hetti. She talked to him about his heritage and what that meant. Later in life he took the time to become initiated, and his responsibilities from that became entwined with his life. Right from the very beginning he was so determined in the things that he did.

32

'Done up in their suits with a Jimmy Pike tie'

After things had gone bad for us with the cultural awareness business and high interest rates, Brenda and I sorted out a new place to live in Hillcrest, another Adelaide suburb. I'd been retired for a while and was helping out with some sporting programs again. One job was with an Aboriginal sports group in Adelaide set up by Wilbur Wilson, who used to be a senior Australian Rules football player for Central Districts. One time we went up to Ernabella in the APY Lands to run a sports carnival with the kids and young people. There were going to be football, netball and basketball matches, and we got there a day or two before to set up.

It was wintertime and pretty cold at night and in the mornings, then during the day it would get really warm. One morning, a bloke flew in on the light plane at eight o'clock all dressed up in his white shorts and white shirt and long white socks. He must have been a government bloke there for a meeting – generally you don't dress like that unless you come from the government. We were just watching him while we set up for the carnival.

The bloke walked over to the outdoor stage where the meeting was going to be held. He set his things up and put his briefcase down, then he stood up ready to start. And of course he was waiting, waiting, waiting. Because nobody there wants to get out of bed until the sun comes out and warms things up. Gradually everybody started to arrive. Around eleven, everybody was sitting on the ground in front of the stage, and he started to spruik his stuff. We couldn't hear much of what he was saying, but we could see he was doing a lot of talking.

After this bloke had talked for a while, a dog broke wind. It was the foulest smell and all the community got up and walked away. But the bloke kept talking.

Then it was lunchtime. The mob didn't come back until two o'clock. The government bloke had to catch a plane out at five o'clock and there he was, still trying to get his message across to everybody and get an answer back from them before he left. At four o'clock, everybody headed off again to light the fire and get ready for tea. He was still there, waiting for someone to answer. And of course that's not the way they operate – the way they operate is that the community turns out and listens, and after that the people who you *think* are the heads of the community take off to see the elders and discuss what's been said with them. It takes two or three days before anything comes back. We could see this bloke getting twitchy, then the plane turned up and he had to take off. We were laughing away.

It was like some of the people Gilly and I came across when we were running the cultural awareness training courses. Some get it and some don't. I'd say this bloke didn't.

It was good doing that work with Wilbur and the kids. Whenever there was a chance to do something to help more young Indigenous kids be able to play sport, I was pretty keen to get involved.

Back in 1988, when we'd sent the Aboriginal cricket team to tour England, we had some good corporate sponsors, but most of the money for it came from the Department of Aboriginal Affairs. We'd been in touch with the Australian Cricket Board to see if they'd support it too, but they hadn't given us a hand with anything. I was pretty disappointed about that.

Now, a few years later, they started making some big changes. Their name became Cricket Australia, and they began getting involved in Indigenous cricket, as well as women's and school programs. With Indigenous cricket, they appointed a project officer and an Aboriginal cricketer from Western Australia called John McGuire, who travelled around the country talking to Indigenous people known to be interested in the game. They knew about me from the national carnivals I'd done with Charlie over the years, and one afternoon they came round to my place to talk about what I'd done with cricket. A month after, they invited me and others from around the country to Canberra for a meeting to talk about what might happen next.

At the beginning of the meeting the chairman and a few of the other Cricket Australia people were talking about all they'd done for Indigenous cricket.

When they finished talking I stood up. 'Listen,' I said, 'you blokes did nothing for us.'

They all looked surprised. I told them I'd been involved in the 1988 tour to England and that we'd gone to the old Australian Cricket Board and asked for some assistance and they'd given us nothing. I told them that, as well as that tour, I'd taken another group of Aboriginal players to New Zealand and the Australian Cricket Board sold us jumpers for the players, and when we asked for a discount they wouldn't give us any.

'Oh. Oh. Oh. Hang on, wait on!' the chairman and the others were saying.

'Don't get up there and say you did this and you did that. Because you did nothing,' I said. That shocked them all. They had to rethink their approach.

That was the beginning of the National Indigenous Cricket Advisory Committee – NICAC. About ten of us were selected to be on the committee: men and women, all Indigenous. After the first committee was selected, when the time for the election of a chairman came, they nominated me and a couple of others. It ended up that I got the job.

Cricket Australia gave us good support, and we set it up so we had two co-chairs – an Indigenous person and a non-Indigenous person with experience in admin and an appreciation of cricket.

Back in the early 2000s when we were starting up, Indigenous cricket had been going really well in the Northern Territory, and it was pretty well structured, so we built on that. First up we held a national carnival in Alice Springs over a weekend. We visited Alice before to talk to the Imparja mob – that's the television station run by Aboriginal people for remote communities – about being a sponsor, which they did. We had a major ground to play on and all the states sent teams to play.

Then the Indigenous women's cricket competition got going, and we ran a community competition too. That brought more people in from the remote communities, and they'd watch and sometimes join in. They'd bring some of the Elders along for the trip too and that was always good to see.

Another change the advisory committee brought about was to have the Aboriginal and Torres Strait Islander flags flown at every Test match played around Australia. We also advised them to hold a Welcome to Country given by a traditional owner, and that took off. My sister Josie gave some of the first in Adelaide. She was in her sixties by then and she gave the Welcome to Country in Kaurna language. Up until then, Welcome to Country had been done in little pockets around the country, but the committee and Cricket Australia made it uniform at the Test matches, along with flying the two flags. Now it's much bigger, of course.

I think Cricket Australia was surprised that very few Aboriginal people played cricket up until this push started with NICAC. One reason was that it's expensive to play. With football, especially for people in remote communities, you can play it without any shoes – all you need is a pair of shorts and you're given a guernsey. With cricket, you have to have proper boots, pads, gloves, white trousers and a white shirt.

I knew of another reason too. We'd been running cricket clinics for Aboriginal kids and finding it hard to get them to sign up. When we were in the APY Lands one time, I asked the community manager why they didn't play it. 'Because you use an unfriendly ball,' he said. I suppose that says it about right. If a cricket ball hits you it hurts, especially if you've got fast bowlers bowling at you.

In 2009 we took an Indigenous team to England to play a tournament while the Ashes were being played at Lord's. We had a function at Australia House in London with the Australian team. A fair few dignitaries were there wanting to meet the Test team, so they met us as well. There we were, the Australian Indigenous Cricket Team. Everyone was done up in their suits with a Jimmy Pike tie – we looked pretty good. We played quite a few games and won our fair share.

Back at that first meeting with the cricket board, after I'd jumped up and said they'd done nothing for Indigenous people, I saw that they were willing to listen. The whole feeling changed. So that was good.

Something I made sure of all through my time with Cricket Australia was to be there when anything was happening. If the medal count was on, I was there. If we wanted to talk to the Lord's Taverners, a funding body for local cricket in South Australia, I was there. Anything that happened, I would go. I'd be introduced as the chairman of National Indigenous Cricket, and people in that world would know there's a blackfella who you're going to see every time you turn around. When arrangements were made for me with planes and cars, I was on time. That was my contribution. Plus having a little bit of knowledge about cricket! In time people got to see that Indigenous cricket was up and running.

In 2011, I decided to retire from NICAC. I was seventy-four by then, and ten years is a fair time. It was time for others to take over the reins and see what they could do.

* * *

My time with the committee had put me in touch with Ashley Mallett, who'd been a Test player in the 1970s. After his cricket career he became a writer, and one of his specialties was writing books about sportspeople. He'd written a book about the Aboriginal cricket team that had toured England in 1868, and it gave me an idea.

I'd been hearing stories on the news where people were saying that black kids didn't want to go to school. I was getting sick and tired of it because a lot of the time they made it sound as if all black kids were like that and it was all their fault, and I knew from my own experience that wasn't how it was at all. That's when I asked Ashley if he'd write a book about the St Francis boys.

Ashley came round to our house, and we had a cup of tea and I told him a bit about the boys' home. How six of the boys were recipients of the Order of Australia. How five had played sport internationally and made their own way overseas without any assistance. How Wally McArthur had run the fastest time in the world for a hundred yards when he was only fourteen. How four played Australian Rules football at league level. How one of the boys was the bloke who designed the Aboriginal flag, and another one was the highest ranking Indigenous officer for the NSW Police Force and won a medal for bravery. How there were three university graduates, all with doctorates.

That was the easiest way for me to say to him and other people that this was a talented group of boys. And those kids hardly ever missed a day of school. I wanted people to know about the talent the boys had, and that St Francis House helped bring that talent out.

Sixty-six boys went through St Francis House from 1946 to 1959, when it closed. A lot of us kept in touch over the years. We'd meet up at reunions with Father Smith and Mrs Smith, and we'd be on the phone to each other or visiting and staying with each other. We knew a lot about each other's lives. I'll tell you a bit about the boys I was closest to and what became of them and what they did.

This St Francis reunion took place in the late 1970s. From the left at the back are Ken Hampton, me, David Woodford, Charlie Perkins, John Moriarty, Des Price and Les Nayda. At the front are Gerry Hill, Father Smith, Ken Nayda and Wally McArthur. *(Courtesy of the P. McD. Smith MBE and St Francis House Collection: www.stfrancishouse.com.au)*

Charlie Perkins, well you know a lot about him already, including that he wrote a book about his life called *A Bastard Like Me*. But there's a bit more to the picture of what he did after he left the department in 1988. He often went back to Alice and his traditional lands, and he headed up the Arrernte Council of Central Australia for a long time. He was on the boards of outfits like SBS Television and the Australia Council Aboriginal Arts Committee, and on the Sydney Olympics committee in the lead-up to the 2000 Games. For a while he was deputy chair of ATSIC, the organisation that took over once the Department of Aboriginal Affairs was closed down. He had a biography written about him too by a historian called Peter Read. That came out in 1990 and then an updated version came out in 2001. When he died he had a state funeral in Sydney. He's had some things named after him too, like the Charles Perkins Centre at the University of Sydney, where he got his degree back in 1966. Every year the uni has an oration in Charlie's honour, and there's a trust in his name that gives out scholarships to Aboriginal students to study at Oxford University after they've got their degrees. So that's Charlie. Not a bad record.

Morey – that's John Moriarty – you know a bit about him too now. He was a soccer star and could have been one of the big players for Australia, he was that good. He played for top clubs in Adelaide then he was selected something like seventeen times for the state team. He got picked for the Australian team that was about to tour overseas, until the tour was stopped because of some hiccups between Australia and FIFA. Then he had a bit more bad luck and copped an injury to his knee so bad that it never really healed and he had to let his soccer dream go when he was still pretty young. As well as working hard for the Aboriginal Progress Association and FCAATSI, he went to university, did different government jobs, and then set up his Aboriginal design business. These days he and his wife, Ros, run a foundation that helps Indigenous kids get into education and sport. Morey's written a book too. It's called *Saltwater Fella* and it came out in 2000.

Biggo, or Gordon Briscoe, went on to become an academic and he's written a book too. His is called *Racial Folly* and it came out in 2010. It's about his life but there's lots in it too about politics and all the changes that were happening in Aboriginal affairs. He worked really closely with Fred Hollows on the trachoma program, and he did a lot over the years behind the scenes with things like the Tent Embassy, and health services and legal services for Aboriginal people.

Coop – Malcom Cooper – didn't write a book, but he's been written about a lot in other people's books. As well as being my godfather, Coop was one of the frontrunners at the home – one of the older boys leading the way on how the rest of us boys could do things. Coop and his wife, Aileen, had three kids. After Coop did his electrical trade, he switched over to working for the government as an employment officer for Aboriginal people, helping them to find work. Later on he transferred to Alice Springs and worked there. Coop died when he was still young of a brain haemorrhage and he was buried in Alice Springs. It rained and rained that day. It was a really sad occasion. Aileen and I still talk to each other every couple of days. She's eighty-five now.

I'd better stop here or I'll be writing the same book Ashley's already written. His is called *The Boys from St Francis*. If you want to find out more about some of the other boys like Wilf Huddleston, Peter Tilmouth, Bill Espie, Ernie Perkins, Kenny and Cyril Hampton, David Woodford, Harold Thomas, Wally McArthur, Brian Butler, Jim Foster and plenty of others, then Ashley's book's a good place to start.

Before I stop talking about the boys, though, there's one I haven't talked about much who I'd like to tell you a bit more about, and that's Laurie Bray. He was my best mate at the home and at primary school, and he looked after me in the early days. Laurie was from a family of big men. His old dad was a big man, and his brothers were big boys. If anybody was picking on me, Laurie would come in and move them aside and look after me. That's how we became really good mates.

Laurie never went to high school. When he finished primary school he took off, and I think that's when we lost track of each other.

When the boys' home closed in 1959, I went looking for him. I thought he'd gone back to Alice, but one day I was in Port Augusta and somebody told me he was living at the Aboriginal community there at Davenport. I went there, and he was in his front room with his paints and a canvas in front of him. He was looking out the window at the Flinders Ranges, but the picture he was painting was of the Todd River in Alice, near the Cottages where we used to live.

'How do you remember what to paint?' I asked him.

'I just paint how I feel,' he said. 'If I'm thinking about the ghost gums along the Todd River, I paint them.'

Laurie became a well-known landscape painter – not as well known as he should have been, because at that time Albert Namatjira was the landscape king. Had Laurie gone to high school I think he would have stunned the teachers by how good an artist he was.

Laurie died early, when he was about thirty, I think. I don't know what from. Years later, Brenda and I were at a conference at Port Augusta, and I was talking to some of the local people about him and they said his daughters still lived at Davenport. We had a St Francis reunion coming up, and Brenda and I went around and knocked on their door. A young woman came out, and I could hear kids in one of the rooms. I looked at her and said, 'You're Laurie Bray's daughter.' And she said she was. I told her we were holding a reunion at St Francis House, and if she wanted to come I'd make sure she was looked after and given some money to cover her costs. We didn't see her again, but I'm pleased we met her and made the connection.

A lot of the boys decided they wanted to have a go at what they wanted to do, and they did it. They spent five years battling away to get their trade while they lived in sewer-rat conditions. Then life started to change, and they did different things. A lot of them used sport as a way to help get work and accommodation – that would open doors for you. Some of the boys married early, and then they were battling to get work and keep a family, but they had the courage to do that. To stick with life. While things may have got hard for them, it didn't break their spirit. It didn't make them think differently about where they wanted to be.

After Ashley's book was published in 2018, he said that getting to meet some of the boys and telling the story of St Francis House was one of the most important things he'd ever done.

Reaching eighty years of age is pretty unusual for an Aboriginal person. Most of the boys from the home were still alive into their sixties and seventies, and still some of us in our eighties – there was something about the home that kept us going so long. It interests me in terms of why.

These days when I talk about the boys, memories come flooding back, and I get a bit sad and I get a bit happy. All of those feelings are there. I can see everybody in my mind – Charlie, Laurie, all those blokes who have passed away now. They're all still here in my memory.

33

'There's still a lot more we're finding out'

I mentioned that my dad was Frederick Warrior and he died when I was one. I don't know much about what he did and what sort of man he was, and whether I'm the same or whether I'm different. All those questions need to be answered, somehow. But whether they can be, I'm not quite sure. I keep trying to piece things together.

All along, I've known at the back of my mind that there was my dad's family. And I've never forgotten the time Winnie sang that country song and said to me, 'Don't forget you have another side to your family.'

But then a lot of years went by and all of a sudden there I was, a bloke in middle age, and I still didn't know who they were. For a while I didn't know where to start. Then different things started turning up.

I found a bit from the newspaper archives. Dad ran in lots of famous athletic competitions like the Underdale Gift and the

Appila Gift. They were called Gifts because in the early gold-mining days when they started, the prize was a piece of gold. There's a story about someone called The Great Warrior who won the Appila Gift, but whether that was Dad I'm still not sure, because the records for the Appila Gift were burnt in a fire years ago. One of my cousins, Bobby Wilson, was a good runner too, and I found out that he ran barefoot and won a big race. In the newspaper story about that there's a photo of Bobby standing next to Grandfather Barney. Whether Barney used to follow his son's races, I'm not sure, but it looks like he might have.

Another piece of the Warrior picture turned up one day in the late 1980s, when I was at work in the Adelaide office of Aboriginal Affairs. This older white bloke came up to the front counter. The receptionist wasn't there, and I noticed him looking around.

He saw me, walked straight over, and plonked a photograph of an old man down in front of me. 'I don't have to ask who you are,' he said. Then he turned around and was gone before I had time to ask him who he was.

I was stunned. The photo was of Grandfather Barney. It was a small square photo about seven or eight inches wide. It was just of Barney's head.

Around the same time, a historian called Tom Gara came across something in the archives at the South Australian Museum about Barney – sometimes Barney's surname is spelled Waria. Tom found out that in the 1930s and 40s, Barney had met up a lot of times with three anthropologists and talked with them about Ngadjuri Country, his traditional lands. Tom had come across my nephew Freddie, whose other name was Warrior, and wondered if there was a connection. They soon worked out there was. Here was Barney again.

Back when Mum used to take me to Light Square when I was a kid and I used to see the older Aboriginal bloke there talking with some young white bloke, I didn't make any connection other than thinking that the Aboriginal bloke was probably from Raukkan. Later on, after that white bloke dropped into my office with the photo of Barney, I twigged who they both were and what the connection between them was. The old Aboriginal man in Light Square was of course my grandfather, Barney Warrior, and the bloke who gave me the photo at the office that day was an anthropologist called Ronald Berndt.

The story of Barney Warrior talking to Ronald Berndt is an important one for us Ngadjuri people, but there are some problems we're still trying to sort out. Grandfather Barney gave a lot of information about Ngadjuri culture to three anthropologists: Berndt, Norman Tindale and Charles Mountford. All three of them wrote down a lot of what he said.

You can easily find Tindale and Mountford's articles and field notes in libraries, but Berndt's field notes about Ngadjuri are another story. He was a young bloke when Barney met up with him. As well as meeting at Light Square, they used to go to the South Australian Museum, and Barney would point out different artefacts and tell Berndt all about them. Berndt wrote down what Barney told him in notebooks and he ended up with a fair few. But as far as I know Berndt only published one article about Barney and Ngadjuri.

Berndt died in 1990, not long after he dropped off the photo of Barney to me at work that day. Then his wife,

Catherine, who was also an anthropologist, died in 1994. They left their field notes and other information to the University of Western Australia. But they put a thirty-year embargo on some of it, including the information Barney gave them. That embargo has meant that we, as his grandchildren and great-grandchildren, can't read it. When the time's up, in 2024, someone will get to read it. But of course, I'm thinking of my time and my family's time, and I would like to be able to read it now. I tried a few times to go to Perth to see the people in charge of it, but each time we hit a brick wall. So my chances of being able to read my grandfather's words aren't looking too good.

Someone did get to see Berndt's field notes, but not a Ngadjuri person and not an Aboriginal person. As part of a native title claim, we wanted to go over and look at the notes, but instead they sent a white bloke and he wrote a report and he copied out some of Barney's words. Why did they send him and not us? I don't know. I'm sure we would have read them in a different way to how that white bloke read them.

One thing we found out from his report was that Barney had told Berndt he was very upset when my brother, Colin, died and that Colin had been his favourite grandson. Barney would have been around sixty-five then and taking it in that he'd lost both his eldest son and his eldest grandson.

Now when I think about it, Barney might have been pinning his hopes on Colin and passing on all he knew to him. But of course with Colin dead that was all gone, then Grandfather Barney died a few years later. Whether he'd wanted to pass on stories to me when I was old enough, I don't know. Mum and us kids were on the move for a few years, and then I was at the boys' home. These are some of the questions I have.

* * *

Some of us descendants of Barney started getting together to talk about our different memories. Then we came across a schoolteacher called Fran Knight who'd been living in the Mid North on Ngadjuri Country since the 1980s and doing a lot of research of her own so she could teach her students about the traditional owners. She'd written a lot of it down, then she teamed up with another teacher called Adele Pring, who knew a fair bit about coming up with activities for kids to be learning from. They started putting together a book and around then Freddie started working with another lady called Sue Anderson, who was a historian and archaeologist. Adelaide being small, Freddie and Sue heard about Fran and Adele, and they all got together. Then they joined up with some of us other Warriors and put together a really good book for schoolkids to learn from. Another photo we found of Barney is on the cover of that. The book's called *Ngadjuri*. Back then it was a big deal to have that book come out, because very few people remembered even that Ngadjuri was the name for the people who are the traditional owners of the Mid North.

Truth is, when I'd been a kid going between Point Pearce and Adelaide, we didn't really talk about the different Aboriginal nations we came from – not in the way we do now. At that stage all I knew was there was the Narungga mob on the Yorke Peninsula, and the Ngarrindjeri people at

Raukkan. What I know now is that my ancestral connections are to the lands of the Ngadjuri, Narungga, Ngarrindjeri and, possibly, the Ramindjeri and Kaurna nations. We're still working those last ones out.

But back when I was living in Point Pearce, the way I knew myself was: 'I'm a Narungga'. That was it. I mentioned earlier that I'd noticed that some of my aunties at Point Pearce were different in their ways to the local Narungga people. Most people might think there was no difference, but when I listened to them I noticed they sounded more Ngarrindjeri. Some of them had a real Raukkan slang. That would have been from their mum, Mary Warrior, who was Barney's wife. She was called May, too, and she used to be a Wilson. If you go down there today, some of them still talk a bit like that – it's a different type of language from Point Pearce. I can't quite put it into words, but you pick it up as soon as you hear it. You'd have the normal words coming out in English, but with a different accent.

Living on Point Pearce we only knew a few words of our old languages that we picked up the way that you do when you're on missions. Nobody was saying, 'Look, we're the so and so language group.' I can remember having a bit of Ngarrindjeri language tied in with a bit of Narungga language. That's all that existed then of the languages. Not only because people weren't on their proper Country anymore, but because the managers and the government didn't want you to have your language at that time anyway.

In Point Pearce and Raukkan there were remnants of the language probably still around in the 1930s. There was enough of it left to pick it up and run with as far as recovering what had been lost and putting it back together so that the people could speak it properly again. Narungga and Ngarrindjeri have a lot of their language back, but so far with Ngadjuri, we don't yet. We didn't have anyone with any remnants of the spoken language. Barney would have still had it in his time, and he and some other Ngadjuri people left a few hundred written words with the anthropologists.

Linguists have been working with some of us Ngadjuri people to revive our language, and that's really good. But I found it hard to pick it up. When they first put some of it back together I went to a workshop they ran and had a go at learning it. The people training us started off with: 'What's a verb? What's a noun?' You already know that when I was at school I failed English very badly. Now here I was thinking, *What do all these nouns and verbs have to do with a bloke talking?* I was hopeless at it. And yet when I visited different Aboriginal communities over the years and people were talking, I could understand what they were saying. It was a much different type of language than the one you get when you're sitting in a classroom. If there'd been a place on Ngadjuri Country where the old Ngadjuri people were still living, I could have gone there and been a part of it even for a short time, and I probably would have picked it up a lot more easily.

I'm disappointed now that when I was old enough I didn't take the time to get to know my aunties on Dad's side better. In the small moments I had with them, they always showed me that they wanted to hug me and do all those things aunties do. They had that love for me, just because we were connected. They had it without even knowing me very well. They cared for me.

If I could say something to my young self now, what would I say? I should have had more respect. Not knowing more about their history and their feelings about who they were as a family makes me wonder. How do you try and pick up the pieces and put them all together? Especially now, so late in life? It takes energy that I haven't got anymore. Now it's become more of a thinking time for me, imagining what it would have been like if things had been different. My father dying when I was young left a great big hole that I'm still trying to fill.

34

'This is my Country'

Around the time we were first finding out more about our connection with Barney Warrior, a lot of other things started to happen. The local council for the Burra area, which is on Ngadjuri Country, put out some feelers to see if there were any Ngadjuri descendants left, because they wanted to take better care of Red Banks, an ancient riverbed near the town, and they thought we could help. People on motorbikes had been tearing up the banks and ripping up the land, and the council reckoned one way they could stop it was by confirming with the traditional owners that it was probably a burial ground.

Josie and I went up to Burra to a meeting in the old courthouse. People from the council and a few other locals turned up. We thought it probably was a burial ground, and we said that as far as we were concerned, if they wanted to protect it and fence it off, then yes, go ahead. Later on, we did archaeological work there and found evidence of old gravesites, so it was the right decision.

Sometime after the Burra meeting, a few of the families connected to Barney formed the Ngadjuri Walpa Juri Lands and Heritage Association. We started going up to the Mid North regularly to try and find a place either to set up a cultural centre or a place where a Ngadjuri person could go there and live and be on Country.

One day our Ngadjuri group was in Burra again looking at some accommodation either to buy or rent for an office. The town's fairly small, and we ran into a group of people who were doing the same as us, looking for accommodation. We had a bit of a yarn about what we were doing and what they were doing, and it turned out they were archaeology lecturers and students from Flinders University. They were looking at old Welsh miners' huts in the creek bed.

That was our first meeting with Claire and Jacko. Claire is Professor Claire Smith, who was in charge of archaeology at Flinders University for a long time, and Jacko is Gary Jackson, an anthropologist. Around this time, the government was running the Indigenous Heritage Program, and universities could apply for money to do research. Claire applied, and soon we had our first proper field trip to the Mid North to look for Ngadjuri sites.

In the archives there was some information about rock engravings in the Mid North. We started making contact with people who owned properties and had sites we could look at. We covered a lot of the top part of the territory: around Orroroo, Plumbago, Mount Victor, Ketchowla, Bimbowrie, Red Banks, Burra – places like that. We found creek beds scattered with rocks, and engravings on a very large one. On an old station near a dilapidated house, we saw a rock face that was covered with engravings. Cattle and sheep had been brushing against it and wearing it down, so we got money from the government to put a grille in front of it. On another trip we walked further out and found more mounds of rocks with engravings on top. Some of the sites went on forever. Claire said they'd never seen big sites like that before.

Over five or six years we did about a dozen field trips. After we'd been working with Claire for a while, I knew a lot more about what to look for. One time I was standing next to a rock engraving site at Panaramitee, just out of Yunta.

One of the many ancient Ngadjuri rock engravings we've found on our field trips. This rock was one of several that were close together and had similar engravings. *(Courtesy of Ngadjuri Elders Heritage and Landcare Inc.)*

We were up on a hill, and when I looked across the country I could see through to some of the other sites we knew in the distance, and they seemed to be in a straight line. There was Pitcairn, then you went from there to Ketchowla, then down to Red Banks. *That must mean something*, I thought, *that all these sites are in a straight line.*

Other things I noticed got me thinking differently too. One day on a field trip I bumped into an old cricket mate who owned a property, and he had some sites he wanted me to see. Near them was an old shepherd's hut made of mud that hadn't all fallen away. In the olden days of the station, the bosses used to send shepherds out to look after the sheep, and they built huts for them.

Claire and I were looking at a rock nearby that had Ngadjuri engravings on it. Alongside the Ngadjuri design was a scratching of a schooner – one of those boats with a couple of masts and sails that used to carry small loads between ports. One of the shepherds must have decided to add his own art to what was already there. Claire asked me if I thought there was any similarity between European art and our traditional art. At that stage I'd never really thought about it. It got me asking questions like, *Where did this shepherd come from, for him to sketch one of these boats like this?* I was thinking he might have lived at Wallaroo or Port Victoria for a time and seen them coming into port. Or he might have been in England and seen them there.

The field trips opened our minds to Country. Before all this I'd been through the Mid North on lots of occasions but had never stopped and thought about Ngadjuri Country. Here was my father's and grandfather's Country that I'd known nothing about. My feeling was, this is my Country and I'm going to learn as much as I can about it. Vincent was coming on the field trips too, and he ended up studying archaeology at Flinders University. Brenda sometimes would come too and help out with cooking, and after a while my niece Kathy came along too and took photographs for us.

Other times, Brenda and I would go for drives around the Mid North and in the different towns, and we'd buy any books we came across about the local history to find out what they'd put in them about Aboriginal people. I was trying to see as many places as I could so I could let those pictures sink into my mind. I remember everything I saw and all the changes of Country, and I visualised what it would be like if the people now there weren't there and my grandfather's people still were. It was all a big learning curve, and it hasn't stopped.

* * *

When I first got to know Claire and Jacko, Claire was the president of the World Archaeological Congress — that's WAC for short. They held conferences at different universities around the world, and Claire invited me to go to a few. The first one I went to was in Auckland. That was in 2005. I went to a few of the sessions, but at that stage I wasn't really sure what these archaeological discussions were all about.

The next year, in December 2006, Claire and the Flinders archaeologists organised a local symposium on what they called 'Cultural Heritage and Indigenous Intellectual Property Rights'. It was about the Berndt embargo, and we held it in Burra, on Ngadjuri Country.

In the lead-up to it I'd been thinking more and more about what happened to all the Aboriginal people who gave the anthropologists their information. You had people like Berndt, Tindale and Mountford, who picked the brains of the local people and published articles about them, and those articles are all around the world, at universities and in museums and libraries. They made careers out of it. But what happened for our people, who the knowledge belongs to and who are still battling to get it back?

At the Burra meeting there were international lawyers talking about Grandfather Barney and Berndt's field notes and the question of who owns them. They came out with the most stupid things: 'If the pencil belonged to Berndt, then the property belongs to Berndt.' And 'When he bought the journal, was it blank?' I was amazed at some of the things that came out of their minds and mouths. *What rubbish*, I thought.

When the symposium finished, it turned out that nobody seemed to know anything and you couldn't get around Berndt's embargo. It was so strange to hear educated people talking like that.

The second WAC I went to was in Dublin in 2008. That's where I did a presentation. There must have been about seventy students in the room, and I talked about my grandfather Barney Warrior and Ngadjuri Country. Then we had a discussion about Barney and the battle over the Berndt embargo.

I've been working with academics for thirty years, and when it comes to how they work with us, I can say that their attitudes are slowly changing. In the early days of anthropologists and archaeologists, back in the 1930s and 40s, they didn't seem to care much about us – my parents and grandparents and great-grandparents. They thought of us as their subjects that they were studying. For them it was all about getting the information they were after – they didn't seem to care about the relationship. If you look at my grandfather, Ronald Berndt went away as a wealthy man, from what I can tell, and Barney stayed a pauper. That seems to be the kind of approach people took, with very little thanks to Aboriginal people. Like I said, it's changing now.

The next WAC conference was in Jordan in 2013. I was seventy-five by then. Claire, Jacko and I left here in the summer, and I was wearing a pair of jeans, a short-sleeved shirt and a pair of sandals. When we landed in Amman, it had been snowing for two days. We stayed in a pretty basic boarding house, then travelled each day to the convention centre twenty kilometres away. It was on the banks of the Dead Sea, and you looked across and there was Israel.

The King of Jordan opened the conference. There were functions each night, and the King's daughter came to one of them. I presented another paper on Barney Warrior and the Berndt embargo. Towards the end of the conference, Claire organised a trip for us to a Bedouin camp and then to Petra. After that we flew to Cairo and had a few days there. I saw three of the pyramids and the Sphinx, and we did a boat trip on the Nile.

That was my last trip overseas. It was another great experience. Any time I was about to jump onto a plane and head to another country, I was always excited about what we were going to find. There are so many good things out there to pick up on and think about.

When I travelled anywhere I always loved to go to the old cathedrals and other buildings and see how they were built and how people used them. I'd imagine what it would have been like in that time and I'd be thinking about the sort of talent the stonemason must have had. And the people who built the scaffolding. It opens your mind. They were really talented, and they didn't have the tools people have today. I'd think, *How did they do that?* and *Why did they do that?* I was always looking out for those things that affect people and the way they live. That travel then got me thinking differently about things at home.

When we'd first visited sites where my ancestors had made engravings, I'd look at them and think about the fact they didn't have any instruments or tools like we have now – all they had was one rock bashing against another. Then I'd think back to when I'd seen a stonemason in Italy sitting there with a chisel and a hammer, and I'd compare them. I'd think about the time it would take for our mob to engrave rocks in a creek bed compared to the stonemason.

Then I'd be up on Ngadjuri Country and I'd picture people sitting down next to a rock and using a stone to go *bang-bang-bang* into it, and out would come designs that had a meaning for them. Orroroo is a long way from Red Banks and yet the markings are the same. I got the impression they were telling other people where there was a good place to camp, or water in the area, or food. That made me think about the connections they must have had with each other. When you think about how the engravings were done and the size of the sites, you just have to marvel at people. When I compared them with what I'd seen in Asia and Europe, I thought, *Well, Ngadjuri must have had that same talent as other people around the world.*

When a few of us Ngadjuri people started going to the Mid North regularly, as far as we knew, Ngadjuri people hadn't knowingly been on their Country as Ngadjuri for fifty years or more. The government's Indigenous Heritage Program meant that we could start doing work there to recover some of what had been lost. People in the Mid North were starting to understand that the area had traditional owners, and they wanted to work with us. Then in 2014 the government cut the program. They're the silly sorts of things that happen.

* * *

Since we reconnected with Barney Warrior thirty or so years ago, a lot of good things have happened. The book about Ngadjuri was published in 2005. The same year a couple who have a property halfway between Terowie and Ketchowla gave some of their land back to us Ngadjuri people.

Then in 2016 a life-size sculpture of a Ngadjuri woman and child was put up in the town of Riverton. It was made by a local artist, Robert Hannaford – he donated it because he's really interested in Ngadjuri and has been all his life. When the governor of South Australia, Hieu Van Le, unveiled it, I spoke at the ceremony. I said a few words about Ngadjuri Country and the rock engravings, and how I hoped the statue would help people embrace Ngadjuri culture a lot more. I'm really pleased the statue's there – it's something visible for locals and people travelling through to let them know that the traditional owners of this place are Ngadjuri.

The local councils around the Mid North are getting more and more involved now too, and we've been doing some good

This is another time I met the governor of South Australia, Hieu Van Le.
In 2014, he presented me with the Member of the Order of Australia.
It was a surprise to me when I found out. Some people I'd worked with
over the years made it happen.

work with them. We've got good relationships with different
people there, and they know we want to keep working
together with them. We've started a couple of projects that
will take some time, maybe years. They may not all be done
before I die, but there's good people working on them and
they'll go on without me.

Whenever I go back to Ngadjuri Country, I'm always looking for people I have a little bit of connection with, like knowing one of their friends or a relation. I visited Jamestown one time and worked out that someone I knew lived there. I went to see them, and that led to someone else, and the next thing we were invited to the Bundaleer Forest Weekend. That was a cultural event with music and art, and they wanted Ngadjuri people to be there too and to let people know about us.

Things like that open doors. I like it that people take pleasure in getting to know me and want me to visit them again – it means I've got connections back on my Country.

I know a few station owners now. One owns a sheep station near Burra and he was the first landowner I was aware of who got in touch with Ngadjuri people to set up an Indigenous land use agreement. He opened up his station to us, and we had a signing day with him. They have claypans and other Ngadjuri heritage sites on the property that I've now been able to see.

Meeting him was good – I could talk to him about farming and sheep, which he really appreciated. We have that in common. It's important to me to honour what other people know. I never want to rush in like a bull at a gate and talk rubbish to people. I never want to start off by saying, 'You blokes shot three hundred people here,' or something like that. It puts people on their guard straight away. It's then easy for them to say, 'These blokes don't know what they're talking about', or question what proof there is.

I think the right way to approach it is to get to know people first and who they are and what connections you might already have, whether that's people you know or interests you've got. You want people to be calm and not be hostile. Then people might say to you, after that first chat, 'You'd better come up another time and have a cup of tea, and you can have a look around the farm and we'll show you some of our history.' Straight away you know that the change is happening. They're starting to appreciate you as a person, and not as a blackfella or whatever.

And don't be angry when you go in, because there's no need. At some of the farms and stations I've been to, I've met people who've battled their guts out all their lives, and their parents did the same before them, and their parents before them. I've got to know them and their stories, and they've got to know me and mine.

Other people who haven't wanted to meet with me – well, sometimes I wonder if what they're wondering is whether I've been eating snakes or goannas!

When I'm on Ngadjuri Country, I think about my people and where they would have roamed the area and how they made a living from it. For me it's an open question.

35

'On the veranda'

Out the front of my home, where Brenda and I lived for eighteen years, I have an old grey office chair parked on the veranda. I started going out there when Brenda and I first moved to the house. I'd sit there and I'd be looking at the trees and looking at the birds and looking at the kids running around the playground of the school over the road, and while I'd be doing that all sorts of memories and feelings and thoughts would come out. It became my singing chair, my whistling chair, and my story chair. I could sit there on the veranda and be nice and warm for the day. All I'd say to Brenda was, 'I'm outside,' and she'd know where I was. The chair was a haven for me.

When I started working on this book, the chair booted me into gear. I'd sit there and start to have all these memories, and I'd ask myself questions and work out what I wanted to say.

It was Brenda's idea that I should write this book for our kids so they'd know more about their dad and what I got up to. After we'd got to know Lea, Brenda and I asked her

Here's Brenda and me in our house at Hillcrest in March 2019.
You can see the edge of the dining table where we sat over the years,
enjoying Brenda's cooking, and cups of tea with all sorts of good
people. *(Lea McInerney)*

if she'd work on the book with me. So in March 2020, Lea
came over from where she was living in Melbourne to start
the interviews. When Covid happened, she had to go back,
so we switched to doing it by phone.

Then in May, Brenda suddenly died. She'd been sick for a
while, but we didn't think she was that sick. Lea and I talked
about it, and I decided to keep going. We'd talk on the phone
a few times a week about different parts of my life, and Lea

would write it up and post it over to me to check. Then she'd work on it a bit more and check it with me again, and now here it is.

* * *

Five o'clock one morning, when I'd nearly finished working on this book, Brenda started tapping me on the head, so I got up. Of course Brenda wasn't there, because she'd died a while before. Anyway, Brenda tapping me on the head got me thinking about some things. One of them was how in my life I've mainly been around people who care. That thought led to other thoughts that flooded into me, about whether people care or not.

Like with Kudnarto, one of my ancestors on my mum's side. She was a girl when Europeans arrived in South Australia, and she had a lot to do with them. When she was a young woman she met an Englishman called Tom Adams and they married. Kudnarto must have been pretty smart because she learned to speak English and then she learned pretty quickly to read and write in English. Kudnarto and Tom had two sons, Tom Jnr and Tim, and they farmed some land near Skillogalee Creek in the Mid North that the government said Kudnarto could keep, as a gesture of what they saw as goodwill towards the Aboriginal people at the time. But Kudnarto died when the boys were young – she was pretty young too, only about twenty-four – and the government kicked Tom and his sons off the land. Tom Jnr and Tim ended up at Poonindie, an Aboriginal mission on the Eyre Peninsula, while their white dad lived near them and tried to get work wherever he could.

Tom Jnr and Tim and their dad fought for years and years to get the government to return Kudnarto's land to them, but it never happened. When the boys were old enough they ran the farm at Poonindie and did a really good job. They kept writing to the government to give them land for themselves, because all the money that the Poonindie people made went back into consolidated revenue rather than to the Aboriginal people working hard there.

Later on, some of the local farmers who happened to be white wanted to take over the land because they could see the Poonindie people were getting better yields than they were. The farmers thought it must be better land, but it was the local knowledge Aboriginal people had that made it that way. Poonindie started with six thousand acres and it dwindled down to three hundred, then eventually in the 1890s it closed, and the people there were moved on to Point Pearce, and Tom and Tim had to start over again with their families. It was only ten or so years later that Mum and Dad were born there and started their lives on a mission.

When I was young I learned a lot by observing what happened to Aboriginal people at Point Pearce and other places. How they were treated, how they handled the racism, how they treated themselves, how they thought they could overcome the problems, whether they reacted with hostility or with the opposite of that. I watched how people dealt with life on a mission where you're being controlled. In the time that I knew Point Pearce, the women were the strong point there, because for the men, no matter what they did, they couldn't get away from government control and couldn't look after their families the way they wanted to. If they got an exemption they thought that meant they could go to Adelaide and get a job and a house, but they couldn't. If they were a good sportsman and they got work locally as a shearer or as a farmhand, it was only while the football season was on – then they had to go away until the next season.

The men became really despondent because every time they tried to get work or housing they were turned away. They'd hear things like, 'You're Aboriginal, we're not employing you.' Or, 'You can't have this house because you're Aboriginal.' So what a lot did was turn to drink. They had a big hole in their hearts. And it was embarrassment too – they were the head of the family and yet they couldn't do things. Even other possibilities were very scarce. No matter how you look at it, people just went back in their shells and said, 'To hell with it. We're not bashing our heads against a brick wall anymore.'

It took the women to do the business of finding a house and looking after it and making sure the kids went to school, because the men just got so sick and tired of being shunned wherever they went. And that could have been my life. The same thing could have happened to me each time Brenda and I were looking to rent or buy a house. If I'd had to be the one to go in and negotiate, we wouldn't have got it.

I was a failure at school, a real failure, and yet I managed to travel a lot in Australia and overseas, and I noticed different things and I listened a lot. Like when I was with governors or premiers or kings and queens of countries, I'd listen and notice that they each had a different language, a different way of talking about things, and I'd pick up a little bit here and there. I became confident enough to not be afraid to talk to anybody. I'm better educated now in that sense than I was then. I'm grateful for the opportunities I've had to travel and meet so many people.

I also learned to do some things differently, and I came to know when to pick my fights. One time I was in Alice Springs with a bloke who was a boxer. We were on our way into a hotel to watch Ted Egan sing when two white blokes came walking up the passage towards us. They weren't going to move out of the road, and it looked like we weren't going to move either. When they got close enough for us all to bump each other, I just stepped to the side and went round the bloke on my side. They moved on and we moved on.

'Why didn't you just bump that bloke?' my mate asked me later.

'What for?' I said. 'What's that gonna prove?'

He was scratching his head for a while.

These were some of the thoughts that came to me after Brenda tapped me on the head that morning. Why did some people care about others and some people didn't? Why hadn't people cared about Kudnarto and Tom Adams and their kids all those years ago? They had to battle to make a living on their farm, and when Kudnarto died, the government turned around and took the land back off her husband and young sons, which was unfair. What would have happened if Kudnarto and Tom Adams had been treated not as a whitefella marrying a blackfella, but instead as a couple who were welcomed and assisted by the people around them? What effect would that have had?

Would it have meant my wife wasn't pushed to the back of the line at the bank because she was with a blackfella? Or that my daughter wasn't bullied at school because a white kid didn't like her skin colour?

If being welcomed and assisted had happened in the 1830s and 40s at the start of things in South Australia, how easy and simple it would be now. We wouldn't all be sitting here trying to work things out. The connection would be much easier and nicer.

Every time I think about this and how life would have been different if that had happened, I end up thinking that we're still not there. You hear things like, 'Let's close the gap, let's have reconciliation.' And we're still not there, because I don't think everyone is thinking that positively yet. Say, for instance, you're a blackfella and you walk down the street and you run into some people who are whitefellas who you know quite well and they're actually good friends. Why can't it be that when you meet up in the street, neither of you is frightened to put your arm around the other one and give them a hug? Nothing spectacular, but you know you're genuine friends. One's white, one's black, but you don't see the skin colour – all you see is a friend. That's the world we'd be looking at. That's the world *I'm* looking at. Whether that exists, I don't know. People might think I'm getting carried away.

What do I really want from reconciliation? Something has to happen. Because white people aren't going to move from this country and Indigenous people aren't going to move. You can put signs up where you live about the local Aboriginal people, about how we've been here forever, and you can do other things like that. But unless it's black and white working together on those things, you're not reconciling. Reconciliation is working together. And if you can't do that, you're only making out.

Some big companies want you to give a talk during NAIDOC week, and then after you've said your bit someone from the company gets up and says something like, 'The company has set up a planning committee for reconciliation.' But what's that even mean? That they'll meet with you every now and again and give you a sitting fee? Or do they make you the CEO of the company?

With the top leaders, as much as they say it, I don't know how many of them have their hearts sitting there with you when they do. They say it in a way that means it might put money in your pocket, but I don't think they say it to make people's minds change.

People keep saying they want to reconcile. But the reconciliation process has been going for a fair while now, and there's still not a great deal of things happening between black and white – not as much as there needs to be anyway. Surely people have to look at each other and say, 'Well, wait on a minute here, is this working between us or not?'

What I want to see is the difference we can make in the feelings of black and white people towards each other. Do people really believe that things can change and get better? Are you feeling that deep under your skin? Can you put me on one of your local committees where I'll be working with a lot of white people, and will we both have the same idea of what's really needed to work together and do things together?

I don't know that that's in most people's minds yet. What do I think might be on their minds instead? That people – Aboriginal and white people and other people – still can't say to each other, 'I don't mind living alongside of you.'

What if I could say to you, 'Listen, why don't you come

over tomorrow morning and we'll have a cup of tea and we'll just sit and talk. Not about anything in particular, just to get to know each other a bit.' What if you're not frightened to come to my home and sit around and talk, and I'm not frightened to go to your home and sit around and talk? Even though some of us will be chalk and cheese.

Or what if we had the situation where people see you as a workmate or a friend, and you see them the same way. Where you don't see each other as a black person or a white person. I think that's the key to what can happen with true reconciliation. If that does happen then people will enjoy life.

Maybe some of what I think about this is airy-fairy stuff. Does it fit in today's world? Sometimes you think that the way you think about things is different from other people. But there are so many simple ways for reconciliation to happen. Projects where we're working together, black and white, kids and adults. Learning from each other, enjoying each other's company.

* * *

Looking back over my life, one thing I often think about is how I've got a few families. There's Brenda and the kids, there's my mum and dad and my sisters and brother, there's the boys from St Francis, and there's Currie. The Curramulka people and the feeling in that community – well, I just love it. I love it every time I think about them. Like the kids there always calling me Uncle Vin. And now all the older ladies and men are gone, but I still see them in my memory, and sometimes I'll be laughing and sometimes I'm crying. Curramulka became so important to me as a person. Whenever people have interviewed me about football, every chance I've had, I talk about them. They were the people who changed my whole life around. Currie gave me a different vision of life. I'm forever grateful for that.

My way in life became to push the bad things aside and only look for the good things. Time will tell – well, it's nearly told now. At eighty-four, you can't get any more time to make big changes, to twist your life around and start again. I don't know a lot about my dad and Grandfather Barney, but I've tried not to let it upset me. It's the same with the life that Brenda and the kids and I had. People would say to me, 'When such and such a bad thing happened, how'd you handle it?' Well, it never really took centre stage. We'd just make some crazy joke about it and get on with life. I probably didn't let things get me down to the point where I became somebody else. If there was something that you thought was bad, you'd just get over it. That's how we were. I had bad times with racism, and Brenda did as well, but we got over it.

Over the years I've been asked to give talks to people, and when I've told them stories about when I was young and the sort of control that the government had over us Aboriginal people, they've been really surprised. Well, the majority of them. Different ones would say to me that they hadn't ever heard about it or even thought about it. 'Well, one reason you probably haven't is that you had your own problems at the time,' I'd say. Because back then for a lot of people, everything was Struggle Town. They didn't have time to be worrying about what had happened to Aboriginal people.

Often at those talks someone would come up to me after and say, 'Why aren't you angry?'

'What's the good of being angry?' I'd say.

If you want to put bad thoughts onto things you can soon do that. But I don't want to waste my time on that. I'd rather sit out on the veranda and think about good things.

I'm pinning my faith on young people that they'll ask the right questions when they get up to being able to do that. Then the changes might happen.

One day when I was sitting on the veranda, I watched the schoolkids across the road build a couple of wurlies. When they finished, they were running in and out, in and out. That made me think that someone is trying to teach them a little bit about Aboriginal people and who was here first, and things like that. They probably didn't have an idea of what it was all about, but they were enjoying it, building the lean-tos and putting it together.

Then there's my niece Shendelle's three young kids in Brisbane. One of them was doing Aboriginal studies at school, and she had to do a talk for her class. She asked me a few questions that I answered for her, and her mum helped her write out a good script about who I am and what I've done. She took that to the class and talked about it with the other kids.

Another time, one of the kids rang Brenda's sister and she was all excited. 'Uncle Vin's an activist! Uncle Vin's an activist! I read it on Google!' Later on they were in Adelaide for Christmas at their grandparents', and they all came around to see Brenda and me.

The youngest one said to me, 'Oh, you're one of them *Abonijonees*.' That was how she said it.

'Ye-e-e-s, I am,' I said.

She never said anything more about it – she was happy that she'd cleared that up. And she was happy that we were related. Even at their young age they were seeing that I was an Aboriginal person and also that I was their uncle.

It started them thinking. And they did think. And they've kept on thinking. Every time I see them, they want to know more and more.

When I was at school, it wasn't like this. We'd be sitting in the classroom and the teacher would be saying that a bloke sailed down the River Murray and all of a sudden he was attacked and speared by blacks, and the black blokes were eating goannas and snakes. We'd be sliding down in our seats, and all the other kids would be looking at us to see whether that was true or not.

Those young kids running around in the schoolyard, my niece's kids, all the other young kids their age – they're the ones who are going to make the change. We haven't got it right yet, but eventually we will. When those kids are older, I think that's when the time's going to come. The good people in the world far outweigh the bad, and you don't waste your time mucking around with bad people. You spend your time with nice people. And that's what I've done. I think it's probably the right choice.

For me now, I've enjoyed remembering the life I've lived. I thank goodness for all the wonderful things I've seen and done, all the wonderful times I've had with Brenda and the kids, all the people and all the little things that make the world wonderful. I look at it all now and I go, *That's my life.*

Afterword by Lea McInerney

On the tenth of January 2022, Vince died at home, his family around him, as they had been day in, day out, for the previous week.

By the time he died, Vince and I had finalised the manuscript that became this book. He and I had first met in 2016, when he was seventy-nine. I'd grown up in South Australia in the 1960s and 70s, but I'd lived overseas and interstate for many years, and by this stage I was living in Melbourne. One day, at Melbourne's Bunjilaka Aboriginal Cultural Centre, it occurred to me that I knew a lot about the Wurundjeri Woi Wurrung people of the area where I lived, but nothing of the people on whose lands I'd spent the first eighteen years of my life. It became important to me to learn about them.

I read a book about Ngadjuri people and culture, and, while I loved it, I felt that just learning from a book wasn't enough. I contacted one of the book's authors and she put me in touch with Vince. I took a deep breath, rang him and asked if we could meet. Vince being Vince, he soon worked out that he knew my brother and that my mum lived in Adelaide. Then he said, 'Come and have a cup of tea with us next time you're in town.' And so I did, again and again, and we became friends.

Three years later, Vince and Brenda asked me to work with Vince on his story, at that stage as a record for their kids. I wasn't sure how I'd fit it in around my day job, but by then

I knew Vince and his way of telling stories was unique, and I figured I'd find a way. I had no idea we'd end up where we are now, although fairly quickly I'd come to see the larger significance of his life. We talked about sharing his story more widely and Vince wanted to do that.

A few months into the work, with Vince in Adelaide and me in Melbourne, he was admitted to hospital for a few days. The day he came home, he rang me to get going again. He knew time wasn't on his side, but he was optimistic. 'I'm here to get the book finished and publication started,' he said. 'That's what I'm dreaming about.'

Once he'd seen a few chapters, he had a sense of how it was shaping up. 'I'm the storyteller, you're the writer, and this is our book,' he said to me. From early on, he wanted to include my name on the book's cover because he saw it as work that neither of us could complete without the other. This for him was reconciliation in action – black and white working alongside each other on shared interests and projects.

By March 2021, Vince had finished telling me most of the stories he wanted to include. In Melbourne, where I was still living at the time, the city was coming out of one of its lockdowns. I came over to Adelaide for a few weeks and Vince and I met up often and worked on the book. On my last visit with him before heading back to Melbourne, as the afternoon turned to dusk, I switched the recorder off and we just chatted. About friendship, cups of tea, Brenda, what she'd started – the draft in a big orange folder there on the table. Vince said lovely things about what it meant to him. We talked about the different people we'd introduced each other to over the years, and how lovely they all are. It was a gentle hour. Then, as the dark settled and I got up to close the curtains, he said, 'The whole story's more than the story in the book.'

Those words speak volumes: of the connections being made as we worked on the book, and of all those stories that aren't in the book. One reason for that is that Vince told me enough stories to make a book as big as *War and Peace* and with more characters. He had stories of family and friends that went back fifty, sixty, seventy years. And so, to Vince's many friends and big extended family, we're sorry we couldn't fit you all in the book, but you'll all know what your connection meant to Vince and what he meant to you.

Vince also told me some stories that, after some reflection, he decided weren't his alone to tell, and so they didn't go into the book. Others weren't ready to be told yet. One day he said to me that what was in the book were all the stories he wanted to tell for now, and he hoped people would accept the book as it is.

In weaving together stories and history, we both tried our best to get the details and timing of different events right. Often after Vince told me a story I'd ask, 'When did that happen, Vince?' He'd go quiet and I'd wait. Finally he'd say, 'Sorry, Lea. I'm a bit skew-whiff with the dates.' Brenda had been our lifeline to dates, and that was another of the many ways we missed her in the days after she died.

Slowly, Vince and I pieced it all together, with help from family and the archives. I *think* we got it all sorted in the end. But if you find any errors, please be gentle with us and don't hesitate to let me know – I'll be delighted to have another piece in the puzzle to pass on to Vince's family.

During 2021 Vince had been needing more and more support and eventually couldn't live independently at home anymore.

His family shared his care. In the last months of the year, he was mainly at his niece Kathy's place, with her and her husband, Steve. They have a big lounge room and Vince had a favourite armchair he was comfy in. His son Vincent lived just around the corner and he popped in and out. His daughter, Kara, lived an hour or so away and came regularly and rang often.

By September 2021, we'd finished a major draft and we had a publisher. In December, the editor sent through twenty-one questions for us, to fill in extra details about people and events. Vince and I spent two days going through them. His memory was as sharp as ever but he'd become frailer. He'd tire at times, have a little nap, then be smiling and ready to go again.

Vince felt the cold and he usually sat with an electric rug wrapped around him. One day, not long before he died, Kathy was sitting next to him and she noticed that the rug had become unplugged. 'You must be cold, Uncle,' she said to him, plugging it back in. Vince looked up at her and smiled his beautiful smile. 'I can't be cold. I've got all this love around me keeping me warm.'

Over Christmas, many of his big extended family came to see him. A few days after, he became ill and needed to go to hospital. The doctor's news wasn't good. Vince's medical problems had worsened and there was little treatment the hospital could offer now. He came home to be cared for by close family. A stream of family and friends came to see him.

I spent time with Vince and he talked about the book and what he wanted me to do once he was gone. He'd done what he'd dreamed of eighteen months before – the book was finished and on its way to being published. He handed over the reins to me, and to Kara and Vincent.

Earlier he and I had spoken about who he wanted to include in the thanks at the back of his book. Straight away he spoke of Kara, Vincent, and Kara's husband, Callum, of how they'd cared for him during the past few years and how he couldn't have done all he had without them. Then he spoke of Kathy and Steve. 'I can't find the words to describe what they took on and what they did for me,' he said. 'They put a lot of work in. They're just so lovely.'

* * *

Brenda was the inspiration and powerhouse behind this book. On Vince's eightieth birthday card, she'd called him 'the love of my life'. She knew his story was important, because of both who he was and the times he lived in. Vince used to say she bullied him into writing the book, but of course he loved that she had.

'The kids don't know what you did,' Brenda would say. They both understood how that had happened, that when the kids were growing up Vince had been travelling a lot for work, and then the kids were off living their own lives. Kara and Vincent knew many of the stories in the book, but only as fragments, not as a whole story. This book is Brenda and Vince's gift to them, of the remarkable families they come from and the stories they share.

For Kara and Vincent the last few years haven't been easy. Their mum died only two years ago, and their dad this year. Vincent's partner Andrea died in 2018. It has been a heartbreaking time of life for them, and they've shown grace and courage in carrying out their mum and dad's wishes for this book.

* * *

Vince had a big life. He knew he'd been part of making history through the Aboriginal rights movement. He saw firsthand the different ways people operated and how each way had its place. He came to know his own way and he carried that through with confidence.

Over the five years I knew Vince, I learned a lot. I came to realise that he seemed able to see the whole, when many of us can only see our own small bit in that whole. He was a master of finding the connections that make up the big picture. And as well as enjoying his own sporting talent, Vince loved watching other people's talents in action and he loved nurturing talent and building people's confidence. He did that for me too.

Being able to walk alongside someone in their eighties while they look back over their life, examine the choices they've made, look deep into painful times in their life, laugh again at funny events, remember tender moments and kind gestures, and feel their way through all these experiences towards a sense of the whole of their life and what it has meant is a great gift to be given. To be honest, I'm only just beginning to comprehend the extent of the gifts of these past few years with Vince and his world view.

Vince's lightness of spirit was powerful. He would talk of serious things, like racism, reconciliation's shortcomings, the Berndt embargo, and native title's flaws, and once he'd said his bit there'd be a smile. From what I saw, Vince's way was to tell you stories and then leave you to make your own connections and insights. I learned to listen, even when I wasn't sure where he was going with a story. He always went somewhere interesting.

As with the question Vince asked me not long before he died: 'Lea, can people write their own eulogy?'

I knew he'd already made up his mind. 'Shall I turn the tape on, Vince?'

We got rolling.

Vince spoke of Brenda, of the people at Curramulka, of St Francis House, of the importance of structure in his life, of what was most lovely to him. Kara read his words at his funeral. Two sentences became the inspiration for the book's title and cover:

> *What a wonderful life I've been able to live …*
> *All these little things may not mean much to anybody else,*
> *but to me they're something.*

Vale, Vince, and thank you.

Vince and Lea in 2021.

Further reading

Dear reader,

Vince thought you might like to have some more details at your fingertips about the laws and famous events he talks about in his story. We've put together a few things here for you: a timeline and potted history, books that Vince and I read and talked about and referred to, a little bit more about a few other people who feature in the story, and the names of all the boys who went through St Francis House.

Lea McInerney, July 2022

Timeline

This summary of events and laws that affected Vince's life and the lives of his people is centred mainly on South Australia, but it also touches on national events. The early 1900s through to the 1970s in particular was a time when many laws and government policies were being made that deeply affected, and often harmed, First Nations people. In the face of this, as Vince's story shows, their immense courage and strength shone through.

As you make your way through these pages, you might find it helpful to see the 'big picture' of Australia's long history shifting and changing across overlapping stages or eras:

- Before 1770
- Colonisation
- Protection
- Assimilation
- Self-determination

YEAR	WHAT'S HAPPENING AT THE TIME

BEFORE 1770

For tens of thousands of years Vince's ancestors, among them the people of the Ngadjuri and Narungga Nations, hold sovereignty of their lands, and live under their own laws and culture.

1600s and 1700s People from Britain and Europe are sailing the world's seas. Some sail along parts of the coast of Australia, no doubt noticed by the people already living there. They possibly have contact with each other. Some of the visitors travel in a spirit of curiosity and adventure, but some come looking to seize land on behalf of their own nations. The people already living here wouldn't necessarily have been aware of these intentions.

Makassar people, from what is now eastern Indonesia, sail annually to Arnhem Land to trade goods with the Yolngu people.

COLONISATION

1770 A British man sails a ship along the east coast of Australia, charting it for the British Crown.

1788 Another British man steers his fleet of eleven ships into a bay on the east coast of the Australian continent. On board those ships are about 1500 people, 700 of them convicts. They are expecting to come across local people and have been told by their king's representative back in Britain to open talks with these people and 'conciliate their affections'. The British see this land as *terra nullius* – Latin words for 'land belonging to no one', which the British interpret as 'owned by no one' – so they establish a colony and run it according to British law. There is no attempt to find out about the laws of the people already living here, or to negotiate a treaty with them.

Early 1800s

After the place now known as Sydney is founded in 1788 on the lands of the Eora people, other European settlements follow and are also given European names: Risdon Cove (Hobart) in 1803, Brisbane in 1824, Swan River (Perth) in 1829, and Port Phillip (Melbourne) in 1836. Darwin will come a bit later, in 1869. All these places already have names and stories connected to the people already there.

More and more Europeans are arriving in boats and ships. A number of them sail along the coast of what will become known as South Australia. As well as more adventurers and more colonisers, seal hunters from Europe and America are setting up camps on that same coast.

There's contact between the people already living here and all the different groups arriving. Sometimes it's friendly, at least to start with, but often there is conflict and violence.

1834

The British Parliament passes what it calls the *Foundation Act*, also known as the *South Australia Act*. It's described as 'an Act to empower His Majesty to erect South Australia into a British Province or Provinces and to provide for the Colonisation and Government thereof' and is dated 15 August.

1836

Nine ships leave England and sail for South Australia with about 600 people on board. The last of the ships, carrying the person the British have appointed governor, arrives at a place the newcomers call Holdfast Bay on 28 December, joining the other eight ships that arrived in the preceding months. The governor proclaims the Colony of South Australia, to be controlled by the British Crown.

As well as the *South Australia Act*, two other documents relevant to First Nations people set the terms for what the British are up to: the *Letters Patent* of February 1836 and the proclamation read out by British officials when they land in December. The documents are all a bit contradictory. On the one hand 'the native inhabitants' are recognised as having occupation of the lands and the right to continue to occupy and enjoy them. On the other, the territory marked out for settlement is said to consist of 'waste and unoccupied lands ... fit for the purposes of colonisation'. Land isn't meant to

1836

be taken up by colonists unless its original owners voluntarily cede ownership and are awarded compensation. But early settlers who have bought preliminary land orders in Britain claim they have first choice over the original inhabitants.

What the local people call this influx of settlers spreading over their land isn't readily available in written records. But the disruption of First Nations sovereignty, law and culture is now well underway in this part of the continent, and soon reaches beyond the Adelaide settlement.

While the colony officials talk about how the land will be surveyed, carved up and sold, they also talk about setting aside areas of land to keep for the people already living here. It happens, briefly. But it never quite holds. There's also talk of taking care of the people already living here and protecting them from harm. The year before, officials had created a position called 'Protector of Aborigines', who is expected to learn the local languages, and the first formally appointed one does. The role of protector will continue intermittently, in changing and often malevolent forms, for more than 120 years.

1837

While there is no government policy to move Aboriginal people off their lands, from 1837 onwards they find it increasingly difficult to access places where they've always sourced water, food and shelter. Blankets and rations of flour and sugar are provided to some, but many get sick and die, and others are killed in violent conflicts. Some humanitarian colonists complain about the way Aboriginal people are being treated.

1838

The second governor of the colony, in power from 1838 to 1841, swings between defending the rights of Aboriginal people to their land and regarding them as inferior and not capable of entering into treaties.

1839

Rations continue to be distributed to Aboriginal people at selected sites.

A couple of English men separately explore the lower north and mid-north of South Australia, looking for suitable grazing and agricultural land. They travel through the lands of some of **Vince's ancestors**.

**1840s
and 1850s**
Increasing numbers of the Europeans now living in South Australia are leasing large areas of land through occupation licences and, after 1851, pastoral leases. European-style villages and towns are being set up in the colony's fertile districts. Some local Aboriginal people make requests to the government for their land to be returned, or for them to be given other land to live on and farm. Some of the new incomers publicly complain about the way Aboriginal people are being treated. Within a few years of European occupation, many Aboriginal people are working on stations and farms as shepherds, shearers, labourers and domestic help. They're often paid in rations. Sometimes they're offered wages but then not paid.

1844
The *Aboriginal Orphans Act 1844* allows the Protector of Aborigines to apprentice out Aboriginal children who are orphans and, with parental consent, other Aboriginal children. It also gives the protector the right to visit children and to penalise employers who mistreat the apprentices.

1848
In January, the first legal marriage takes place between an Aboriginal and a European person, **Kudnarto** and **Tom Adams**. Kudnarto was born in what is now known as Crystal Brook in about 1830. **Vince** is descended from Kudnarto through his grandmother **Maisie May Edwards** (née Adams). Kudnarto and Tom will soon have two sons: **Tom Jnr**, born in 1849, and **Tim**, in 1852.

1850s
Influential Christians set up the Poonindie Native Training Institution on the Eyre Peninsula, while the Aborigines' Friends Association open the Port McLeay mission in the lower Murray River region, on a site the locals know as Raukkan.

1856
South Australia's *Constitution Act 1856* is passed. All men over twenty-one can vote, including Aboriginal men.

1860
A select committee appointed by the state government investigates the conditions Aboriginal people are living in. Its report notes that, as a result of colonisation, they have 'lost much, and gained little, or nothing'.

1868	The townspeople of Moonta, Wallaroo and Kadina work with Moravian missionary Julius Kühn and **'King Tommy'** and other Narungga people to set up the Point Pearce mission on the Yorke Peninsula. Run by a committee made up of representatives from the three towns, it never becomes a single denomination mission and is not controlled by any missionary organisation.
1877	**Joe Edwards**, Vince's grandfather on his mum's side, is born at Point Pearce, on Narungga Country.
1878	**Mary (May) Wilson**, Vince's grandmother on his dad's side, is born at Encounter Bay, south of Adelaide.
1879	**Barney Warrior**, Vince's grandfather on his dad's side, is born at Ororoo, on Ngadjuri Country.
1882	**(Maisie) May Adams**, Vince's grandmother on his mum's side, is born at Poonindie.
1894	Poonindie mission closes. Some of the people living there are moved to Point Pearce, among them **Tom Adams Jnr** and his family. Others are moved to Point McLeay.
1895	South Australia's *Constitutional Amendment (Adult Suffrage) Act* becomes law. All women over twenty-one can vote, including Aboriginal women.
1901	In January, the Parliament of the United Kingdom passes the *Commonwealth of Australia Constitution Act 1901*. It brings together the existing states and territories under one federation. According to Westminster law, the nation of Australia has come to be. The written Constitution is a set of rules for governing the country. It can only be changed through a referendum in which a majority of citizens and a majority of states vote for change.
	One clause in this new Constitution says 'in reckoning the numbers of people … Aboriginal natives shall not be counted'. Another clause says that the Commonwealth will pass laws for any race except Aboriginal people. This leaves the power to make laws affecting Aboriginal people in the hands of the state governments.

1901   In December, the Commonwealth government passes a law called the *Immigration Restriction Act 1901*. It effectively bans any person who isn't Caucasian from entering the country and becomes known as the White Australia policy.

1902   The federal government passes the *Commonwealth Franchise Act 1902*. This gives women, as well as men, the right to vote in federal elections – unless you're what is classed as an 'aboriginal native' of Australia, Asia, Africa or the islands of the Pacific. This is a backwards step for South Australia and the local Aboriginal people.

1907   Vince's parents, **Fred Warrior** and **Kathleen Edwards**, are born at Point Pearce mission.

PROTECTION

1911   *The Aborigines Act 1911* creates the positions of Chief Protector and regional protectors. A government department is set up to provide for the custody, maintenance and education of the children of Aboriginal people and to supervise 'all matters affecting the wellbeing' of Aboriginal people.

The Chief Protector is the legal guardian of every Aboriginal child until they are twenty-one years old, even if a child has a living parent or other relative. Each regional protector is the local guardian of every child within their district. The Chief Protector has control of where adults and children live, and can confine them to a reserve or institution, and move them to other reserves or institutions. If an Aboriginal person refuses to be moved, they can be charged with committing an offence.

1913   A Royal Commission on the Aborigines is set up by the South Australian government 'to inquire into and report upon the control, organisation and management of the institutions in this state set aside for the benefit of the aborigines, and generally upon the whole question of the South Australian aborigines.'

Joe Edwards, Vince's grandfather, is one of five Point Pearce men who appear before the commissioners to speak about conditions where they live. The topics they cover include

1913   land use, farming, wages, rations and education for their children and young people. Vince's mum, **Katie Edwards**, is six years old. The transcript records this exchange between Joe and one of the Commissioners:

> *Commissioner:* Is there anything to prevent you going away and securing employment elsewhere?
>
> *Joe Edwards:* We always understood this as our land, and looked upon it as our home.
>
> *Commissioner:* Do you look upon this reserve as your own, and that it must provide for you for all time?
>
> *Joe Edwards:* I have always understood that.
>
> *Commissioner:* Your impression is quite wrong.

1915–1916   The South Australian government takes over the running of Point Pearce mission (September 1915) and Point McLeay mission (January 1916).

1918   Under the *Aborigines Act 1911*, an Advisory Council of Aborigines is set up to advise the government on 'any matter … affecting the interests of' Aboriginal people.

1923   The *Aborigines (Training of Children) Act 1923* is passed, which says Aboriginal children can be removed to institutions and detained there until they are eighteen if – in the opinion of the Chief Protector – a child is being neglected.

1924   The Oodnadatta Children's Home is set up in far north South Australia by the United Aborigines Mission, an organisation of different Christian denominations. Twelve children live there; most have been taken from their families. The building is very basic.

1927   In Quorn, the United Aborigines Mission opens Colebrook Home as an institution for Aboriginal children. The children from the Oodnadatta Children's Home are moved there, further away from their families. Over the years, many others are taken there.

1931   Nepabunna Mission is set up in the northern Flinders Ranges by the United Aborigines Mission.

1933	In Victoria, the Australian Aborigines' League is set up by Yorta Yorta leader William Cooper. The following year, he draws up a petition calling for improved living conditions for Aboriginal people, and for Aboriginal representation in parliament. In 1937, he sends it to Prime Minister Joseph Lyons, expecting it will be sent on to the British king for his attention. It isn't.
Early 1930s and 1940s	Adelaide-based medical doctor Charles Duguid and his wife, Phyllis Duguid, are involved in various organisations advocating for Aboriginal people to have their own land and govern their own lives. In 1935, Charles becomes president of a group known as the Aborigines' Protection League. Ngarrindjeri man David Unaipon, inventor, author and advocate for his people, is a member. In 1939, Phyllis becomes the leader of a women's Christian group and they set up the League for the Protection and Advancement of Aboriginal and Half-Caste Women. In 1946, these two organisations merge and form the South Australian Aborigines Advancement League. This signals a philosophical shift from protecting Aboriginal people to supporting their advancement. **Gladys Elphick** moves to Adelaide around 1940 and will go on to work alongside the Duguids for many years.
1934	In South Australia, the *Aborigines Act 1934* brings together the 1911 and 1923 Acts. It takes effect in 1937. There are no significant changes to the powers of the Chief Protector, who still has full control over where Aboriginal adults and children live.
1936	**Vince** is born at Wallaroo hospital, north of Point Pearce. He is the youngest of **Fred and Katie Warrior**'s five surviving children.
	Barney Warrior, Vince's grandfather, begins sharing some of his Ngadjuri cultural knowledge with three anthropologists: Norman Tindale, Charles Mountford and Ronald Berndt. He will meet up with them regularly over several years.

1937   Charles Duguid leads the setting up of Ernabella mission on Pitjantjatjara Country, in far north-west South Australia, by the Presbyterian church. Children are taught in their own language and Pitjantjatjara ceremonies continue with support of the missionaries. On some of the other missions, Aboriginal people are banned from speaking their own languages. Among the exceptions are the German Lutheran missions, which respect and advocate for local languages to be retained, and even teach in them.

A national conference of chief protectors and boards controlling Aboriginal people in states and territories is held. They pass resolutions on some twenty areas, including how Aboriginal people are to be defined or 'categorised'. They also resolve to aim for uniform legislation across the country.

1938   Following years of campaigning by the Australian Aborigines League and other activist groups, a 'Day of Mourning and Protest' gathering is held on 26 January at Australia Hall in Sydney. Its purpose is to protest 'the callous treatment of our people by the whitemen', and to call for full citizen status and equality for Aboriginal people.

With support from many religious groups, the League declares the Sunday before 26 January to be 'Aboriginal Sunday'. It is first celebrated in 1940 and continues annually until 1955, when it is moved to the first Sunday in July, eventually giving rise to the now annual NAIDOC Week.

In June, **Fred Warrior**, Vince's father, dies.

1939   In South Australia, the *Aborigines Act 1934* is amended and becomes the *Aborigines Act 1934–1939*. An Aborigines Protection Board replaces the Chief Protector, the regional protectors and the Advisory Council of Aborigines. The board's stated duty is to control and promote the welfare of Aboriginal people. Board members become the protectors and legal guardians of Aboriginal children, even where children have parents or other relatives. Legally, Aboriginal people can be board members, but they are considered unsuitable because they don't have what the government and its advisors see as acceptable education, training or professional qualifications.

1939 One section of the Act rules that marriage between an Aboriginal and non-Aboriginal person needs ministerial approval. Another section rules that a non-Aboriginal man with an Aboriginal woman must be married or they will be charged with consorting. The stated intent of laws like these is to protect Aboriginal people from fraudulent non-Aboriginal people and also to protect Aboriginal women from sexual assault. But, in reality, the powers given to the Aborigines Protection Board are easily misused and abused.

The Act also brings in the exemptions system, which states that, 'Where the board is of the opinion that any aborigine by reason of his character and standard of intelligence and development should be exempted from the provisions of this Act, the board may ... declare that the aborigine shall cease to be an aborigine for the purposes of the Act.' Exemptions could be conditional and revocable for three years, or unconditional and irrevocable. The first exemption is granted in 1941.

1940s The people of Point Pearce send petitions to the government to protest about their living conditions, such as overcrowding and exploitation, and their lack of control over their lives.

Assimilation is happening in practice, although not yet spelled out in policy. People are being moved off missions, where they've been living controlled yet regulated lives, into cities and towns. They're often separated from family and the community they've been part of their whole life. Their connection to culture and language is further disrupted. They face discrimination and financial hardship. Their lives are closely monitored and assessed against cultural standards that aren't their own. Children are being removed in increasing numbers.

1942 Darwin is bombed by the Japanese military. Aboriginal missions in the Northern Territory are evacuated and many children are removed to other parts of the country, mostly without their parents' consent. The mothers of some children go with them. Some children from South Australia and Queensland are also removed to missions during the war's disruptions. A large group is taken to Mulgoa mission, west of Sydney, at the foot of the Blue Mountains.

1942	Colebrook Home moves to Eden Hills on the outskirts of Adelaide. About fifty children live there.
1944	On 1 February, a letter written by **Barney Warrior** is published in *The Advertiser*. It says, in part: 'People are too ready to judge without understanding, and most of them like to think that anyone with dark skin can't be as good as they are themselves.' Then he writes, 'On one hand, white people talk of all races being treated the same way, but on the other hand they do not want to treat "dark" people as equals. We have found this to be true. If we are to be accepted as citizens of this community, we should not be treated differently from others, and we should not be debarred (as we are now) from so many aspects of life in the community.' On 5 February, **Colin Warrior**, Barney's grandson and Vince's brother, dies in the Royal Adelaide Hospital.
1945	A small Anglican children's home is set up in a private house in a suburb in Adelaide called Marryatville, to be run by Anglican priest Father Percy Smith and his wife, Isabel. They bring six young boys there from Alice Springs for schooling, something not readily available to Aboriginal children in Alice Springs. The boys' mothers give their permission for this to happen. Later the home will become known as St Francis House.
1946	**Vince** and his family leave Adelaide and head north to Leigh Creek and later to Alice Springs.
1947	St Francis House takes in more boys. The Smiths move them to a larger building and grounds at Semaphore, another Adelaide suburb. Vince is living in Alice Springs and, during the Christmas holidays that year, he meets some of the St Francis boys.
1948	**Vince** leaves Alice Springs and becomes a boarder at St Francis House.

ASSIMILATION

1951   While practices intended to assimilate Aboriginal people into the white world have been going on since colonisation began, the Aborigines Protection Board now formally adopts it as policy. The intention is to absorb Aboriginal people over time by removing children from their families and placing them in institutions where they can be 'trained' to take their place in white society.

1952   **Vince's mum, Katie,** dies in the Royal Adelaide Hospital.

1953   **Vince** starts his apprenticeship as a fitter and turner. He is still living at St Francis House.

An amendment to the South Australian *Summary Offences Act 1953* means that if a white person 'consorts with' an Aboriginal person 'without a reasonable excuse', they have committed an offence. This is a different Act from the *Aborigines Act 1934–1939*, and gives further reach to police powers on who can and can't associate with each other. The government states the amendment is meant to protect Aboriginal people from exploitation by white people, but the way police interpret it varies widely.

The British government conducts atomic tests at Emu Field. The local people call the explosions and their aftermath the Black Mist.

1954   **Vince** leaves St Francis House and his apprenticeship, and moves to his sister **Winnie Branson**'s home at Pine Point.

1956   The British government conducts atomic tests at Maralinga.

Labor MP Don Dunstan is in the state opposition and speaks in parliament about the conditions at Point Pearce. He also questions the government on the policies and practices of the Aborigines Protection Board.

A group of young women from Colebrook Home graduate as nurses from the Royal Adelaide Hospital, after having been refused entry for years because they are Aboriginal. Among them are Lowitja O'Donoghue, who goes on to be a much-admired leader of her people, and Faith Coulthard, who will play cricket at state level and for the Australian women's team.

1958   The section in the *Summary Offences Act* on consorting between Aboriginal and non-Aboriginal people is repealed after an intense campaign by Aboriginal people and their supporters.

The Federal Council for the Advancement of Aborigines (FCAA) is set up as a national body, bringing together state activist groups of both Aboriginal and non-Aboriginal people. Its first meeting is in Adelaide. In 1964 the name will change to the Federal Council for the Advancement of Aborigines and Torres Strait Islanders, known as FCAATSI.

1959   St Francis House closes.

1962   The *Aborigines Act 1939* is repealed by the *Aboriginal Affairs Act 1962*. The Aborigines Protection Board is replaced by the Aboriginal Affairs Board. The new board is no longer the legal guardian of Aboriginal children.

The Minister for Aboriginal Affairs is responsible for Aboriginal reserves, and general supervision and care of the welfare of Aboriginal people. The minister is expected to provide for the maintenance and education of Aboriginal children, and 'to promote the social, economic and political development of [Aboriginal people] until their integration into the general community'. Aboriginal children are still being removed from their families, under a different child welfare law.

The Act has new powers to set up a Register of Aborigines. The names of people who, in the board's opinion, 'are capable of accepting the full responsibilities of citizenship' – that is, people with exemptions – can be removed from the register. In 1968, this power will be abolished.

SELF-DETERMINATION

1963   A new Aboriginal Affairs Advisory Board is set up. It marks an official shift in South Australia from assimilation policies to self-determination. Aboriginal people are on the board, among them **Gladys Elphick**. In 1970, the board's functions will be taken over by a new state government department of Social Welfare and Aboriginal Affairs.

1963   In the Northern Territory, Yolngu people in Yirrkala send a bark petition to the House of Representatives in Canberra to protest against a mining lease granted without their permission. The government runs an inquiry, then goes ahead with the mine anyway.

1964   In South Australia, a group of mainly Aboriginal people, among them some of the St Francis boys, sets up the Aboriginal Progress Association. Members feel strongly that there needs to be an 'Aboriginal voice' within the community. They also plan to campaign vigorously at a parliamentary level 'to improve the lot of Aborigines everywhere.' The association is controlled and run by Aboriginal people. Soon its membership will be solely Aboriginal people.

1965   In New South Wales, the Freedom Ride led by **Charles Perkins** and other University of Sydney students brings attention to discrimination against Aboriginal people. Meanwhile, the students' staged kidnapping later in the year of Fijian-Australian five-year-old Nancy Prasad brings attention to the deeply flawed White Australia policy.

A new Labor government is elected in South Australia. Don Dunstan becomes attorney-general and Minister of Community Welfare and Aboriginal Affairs. In 1967 he will become premier and treasurer. Dunstan begins an era of significant legal and social reform.

1966   **Gladys Elphick**, along with **Maude Tongerie** and others, is setting up the Council of Aboriginal Women of South Australia. Its purpose is to provide welfare and support services to Aboriginal people, and also to lobby for social change. Gladys, by now in her sixties, is in regular contact with Don Dunstan.

South Australia enacts two significant laws. The *Aboriginal Lands Trust Act 1966* transfers the titles of Aboriginal reserves to Aboriginal people to hold and manage. The *Prohibition of Discrimination Act 1966* bans all types of race and colour discrimination in employment, accommodation, legal contracts and public facilities.

1966   The Wave Hill Walk-off by Gurindji people working on a cattle station in the Northern Territory begins and will last nine years. The workers strike over unfair wages and demand the return of a portion of their homelands from the people who hold the pastoral lease. In time it brings the issue of land rights to the attention of the wider Australian public.

1967   On 27 May, following a concerted campaign by Aboriginal and Torres Strait Islander people and their allies over many years, Australians vote in a referendum to change two clauses in the Constitution. Aboriginal people are no longer to be left out of the census, and the Commonwealth can now make laws for Aboriginal people, instead of there being myriad state laws across the country.

1969   In Canberra, the federal Liberal government sets up an Office of Aboriginal Affairs. **Charles Perkins** is recruited to work there.

1971   In July, on National Aborigines Day, the Aboriginal flag designed by **Harold Thomas** is flown for the first time, in Adelaide.

1972   In South Australia, the *Community Welfare Act 1972* is passed, repealing several Acts including the *Aboriginal Affairs Act 1962–68*. Its stated intent is to promote the cultural, social, economic and political welfare and development of Aboriginal people. It recognises that Aboriginal people have their own languages, traditions and arts, and that they should be supported to preserve and develop them. Aboriginal organisations and industry are to be supported and fostered.

     The law also marks a philosophical shift in how children are viewed: when there is any question of a child being removed from their family and placed in care, the interests of the child are to be considered paramount. Many Aboriginal children, however, continue to be assessed as 'neglected' by those in charge, and are removed.

     In January, in response to years of demands by Aboriginal people for land rights, the federal Liberal government announces that, instead of land rights, it will give some

1972   Aboriginal people fifty-year leases to some of their traditional Country. The day after, Aboriginal activists set up the Aboriginal Tent Embassy in front of Parliament House.

In December, a federal Labor government is elected. The new prime minister, Gough Whitlam, says Aboriginal people are no longer to be denied 'their rightful place in this nation'. Commonwealth policy shifts from assimilation to self-determination. Land rights are now firmly on the agenda. Whitlam sets up a federal Department of Aboriginal Affairs, with its own minister. The government officially brings the White Australia policy to an end.

1973   The federal government commits to having a National Aboriginal Consultative Committee (NACC) to advise the government on issues concerning Aboriginal and Torres Strait Islander people. It is to be set up and run by Aboriginal people.

1974   An Aboriginal Land Rights Commission recommends 'basic compensation in the form of land for those [Aboriginal people] who have been irrevocably deprived of the rights and interests which would otherwise have been inherited from their ancestors.' Work begins on an Aboriginal land rights bill for the Northern Territory.

For the first time, NAIDOC is run by a committee made up solely of Aboriginal people.

1975   The Labor government is dismissed by the governor-general. At the subsequent election, a Liberal government led by Malcolm Fraser is elected. Many of the programs set up under the Labor government continue although have their budgets cut. Law reform work continues.

1976   In South Australia, Yorta Yorta man **Sir Douglas Nicholls** is appointed state governor, becoming the first Aboriginal person in such a role.

The Commonwealth *Aboriginal Land Rights (Northern Territory) Act 1976* is passed. First Nations people in the Northern Territory can now legally claim land rights for Country where traditional ownership can be proved.

1977   The federal government replaces the NACC with the National Aboriginal Conference (NAC). While its members want to take on a more direct role in creating policy, it remains mainly advisory. They have little political power; however, they persist and over time influence policy and shape the thinking of both parliamentarians and the public on fundamental issues such as self-determination and treaty-making.

1980   The Aboriginal Development Commission is set up in Canberra to promote the economic and social wellbeing of Aboriginal and Torres Strait Islander people.

1985   The Hawke Labor Government winds up NAC, and begins work on creating a different body.

Uluru is handed back to its traditional owners, the Anangu.

After sustained advocacy by Aboriginal communities led by people like Yankuntjatjarra man Yami Lester, the Royal Commission into British Nuclear Tests in Australia releases its report. Among its recommendations are compensation for traditional owners, and that Emu Fields and Maralinga be rehabilitated and this be paid for by the British government.

1988   The Barunga Statement is presented to Prime Minister Hawke by leaders from Arnhem Land and the Central Desert. In the statement they call for land rights and self-management, and emphasise their desire to make policy and decisions that affect their people.

1990   The Aboriginal and Torres Strait Islander Commission, commonly known as ATSIC, is set up by the Hawke Labor government, in place of the NAC and the Aboriginal Development Commission.

1991   The Royal Commission into Aboriginal Deaths in Custody is released and makes 339 recommendations.

1992   The Mabo decision is handed down by the High Court. The colonial concept of Australia as terra nullius – land owned by no one – is overturned.

1993   The Commonwealth *Native Title Act 1993* is passed in response to the Mabo ruling.

1997   The *Bringing Them Home* Report is released by the Human Rights and Equal Opportunities Commission. It tells many stories of Aboriginal people taken from their families and communities, and the suffering they experienced. It calls for a formal apology and compensation to support communities to heal.

1998   The *Native Title Amendment Act 1998*, also known as the 'Ten-point Plan', is brought in by the Howard Coalition government. The Amendment Act makes it more difficult for Aboriginal people to be granted native title, and restricts the land that can be claimed.

2004   ATSIC is abolished by the federal Coalition government.

2005   Professor Tom Calma releases a report on Aboriginal and Torres Strait Islander people that shows the stark differences in their health and how long they can expect to live, compared to the rest of the population. In response, all governments across the country agree on a national strategy to 'close the gap' within twenty-five years.

2008   The Australian Parliament, under a new Labor government, apologises to Aboriginal people who were taken from their families during the 1900s. In the years to come, various states and territories will offer reparation payments and the opportunity for people to tell their stories.

2010s   The federal government sets up different processes over the decade to advance constitutional recognition of Aboriginal and Torres Strait Islander peoples.

2015   In South Australia, Labor politician Kyam Maher, a First Nations man, is elected to state government. He guides reforms to begin treaty negotiations with local Aboriginal nations.

2017   First Nations people from across the country present the 'Uluru Statement from the Heart' to the Australian people. In it, they invite their fellow citizens to recognise the unique place of First Nations people, and 'to walk together in a movement of the Australian people for a better future'. They set out three areas of attention, summarised as Voice, Treaty, Truth: a First Nations Voice to Parliament, treaty making, and truth-telling about our shared history. The federal Coalition government rejects the Uluru Statement.

2019	Liberal MP Ken Wyatt becomes Australia's first First Nations person to be Minister for Indigenous Australians.
2022	A new federal Labor government is elected and the prime minister commits to implementing the Uluru Statement from the Heart in full.
	Labor MP Linda Burney becomes the second First Nations person to be Minister for Indigenous Australians, and the first woman in the role.

The information in this timeline has come from many different sources, among them:

- overviews of Indigenous Affairs created by the Australian Parliamentary Library
- Find & Connect, a website of historical resources relating to institutional 'care'
- South Australian government timelines created by the health and education departments
- collections in the Australian Institute of Aboriginal and Torres Strait Islander Studies (AIATSIS)
- the Museum of Australian Democracy
- the History of Aboriginal Exemption website

Other books and papers

A while after Vince started telling his stories to me, we talked about how he might turn them into a book, and looked at other books for ideas. Some of the stories he read connected with his own life, which then sparked more memories for him, and more stories to include. Here are some of the books we read and talked about – in alphabetical order.

Barnes, Nancy, *Munyi's Daughter: A Spirited Brumby*, Seaview Press, West Lakes, SA, 2000.

Briscoe, Gordon, *Racial Folly*, ANU Press, Canberra, ACT, 2010.

Brodie, Veronica, *My Side of the Bridge*, Wakefield Press, Adelaide, SA, 2002.

Butler, Brian, and Bond, John, *Sorry and Beyond: Healing the Stolen Generations*, Aboriginal Studies Press, Canberra, ACT, 2021.

Clark, Mavis Thorpe, *Pastor Doug: The Story of Sir Douglas Nicholls*, Rigby, Adelaide, SA, first edition 1965, revised 1972.

Forte, Margaret, *Flight of an Eagle: The Dreaming of Ruby Hammond*, Wakefield Press, Adelaide, SA, 1995.

Graham, Doris May, and Graham, Cecil Wallace, *As We've Known It: 1911 to the Present*, Aboriginal Studies and Teacher Education Centre, South Australian College of Advanced Education, Adelaide, SA, 1987.

Mallett, Ashley, *The Boys from St Francis*, Wakefield Press, Adelaide, SA, 2018.

Moriarty, John, *Saltwater Fella*, Penguin, Melbourne, VIC, 2000.

O'Brien, Lewis Yerloburka, and Gale, Mary-Anne, *And the Clock Struck Thirteen: The Life and Thoughts of Kaurna Elder Uncle Lewis Yerloburka O'Brien*, Wakefield Press, Mile End, SA, 2007.

Perkins, Charles, *A Bastard Like Me*, Ure Smith, Sydney, NSW, 1975.

Read, Peter, *Charles Perkins: A Biography*, Penguin, Ringwood, VIC, first edition 1990, revised 2001.

Roach, Archie, *Tell Me Why: The Story of My Life and Music*, Simon & Schuster, Sydney, 2019.

This next list is history books, transcripts and other documents we used to check facts and dates. If you're interested in history, you might find some of these worth a read. You'll find a lot of them in public libraries.

Anderson, Sue (ed.), *J. D. Somerville Oral History Collection*, State Library of South Australia, various years.

Beeson, Margaret J. (ed.), *Some Aboriginal Women Pathfinders: Their Difficulties and Their Achievements*, Women's Christian Temperance Union of Australia, Adelaide, SA, 1980.

Brock, Peggy, and Gara, Tom (eds), *Colonialism and Its Aftermath: A History of Aboriginal South Australia*, Wakefield Press, Mile End, SA, 2017.

Foster, Robert, and Nettlebeck, Amanda, *Out of the Silence: The History and Memory of South Australia's Frontier Wars*, Wakefield Press, Mile End, SA, 2012.

Krichauff, Skye, for the Narungga Aboriginal Progress Association Inc., *Nharanangga Wargunni Bugi-Buggillu: A Journey through Narungga History*, Wakefield Press, Mile End, SA, 2011.

McGinness, Joe, *Son of Alyandabu: My Fight for Aboriginal rights*, UQP, Brisbane, 1991.

Macilwain, Margaret, 'South Australian Aborigines Protection Board (1939–1962) and Governance through "Scientific" Expertise: A Genealogy of Protection and Assimilation', PhD thesis, University of Adelaide, 2006.

Mattingley, Christobel, and Hampton, Ken (eds), *Survival in Our Own Land: 'Aboriginal' Experiences in 'South Australia' since 1836*, told by Nungas and others, Australian Scholarly Publishing, Melbourne, first edition 1988 (with Wakefield Press), revised 1998.

Perkins, Rachel, and Langton, Marcia (eds), *First Australians*, The Miegunyah Press, Melbourne University Publishing Ltd, Melbourne, 2010.

Raynes, Cameron, *A Little Flour and a Few Blankets: An Administrative History of Aboriginal Affairs in South Australia 1834 to 2000*, State Records of South Australia, 2002.

———, *The Last Protector: The Illegal Removal of Aboriginal Children from Their Parents in South Australia*, Wakefield Press, Mile End, SA, 2009.

Rintoul, Stuart, *Lowitja: The Authorised Biography of Lowitja O'Donoghue*, Allen & Unwin, Sydney, 2020.

Taffe, Sue, *Black and White Together. FCAATSI: The Federal Council for the Advancement of Aboriginal and Torres Strait Islanders 1958–1973*, UQP, Brisbane, 2005.

Traynor, Stuart, *Alice Springs: From Singing Wire to Iconic Outback Town*, Wakefield Press, Mile End, SA, 2016.

Vandenburg, Paul (ed.), *South Australian Aboriginal Football and Netball Carnival: A Focus on Our History*, Power Community Ltd, Port Adelaide, second edition, 2014.

Wanganeen, Eileen (ed.), *Point Pearce: Past and Present*, researched by Narrunga Community College, South Australian College of Advanced Education Aboriginal Studies and Teacher Education Centre, Adelaide, SA, 1987.

Warrior, Fred, Knight, Fran, Anderson, Sue, and Pring, Adele, *Ngadjuri: Aboriginal People of the Mid North Region of South Australia*, Humanities and Social Sciences SA (HASS), 2005.

More remarkable people

As Vince was telling me his stories, he'd talk about people he'd known and worked with over the years. Many of them had fought hard all their lives in South Australia to make things better for Aboriginal people. Often they'd done this work out of the public eye, chipping away year after year, quietly getting on with what they knew they had to do. Here are a few snippets about four people Vince mentions in his story: Gladys Elphick, Maude and George Tongerie, and Ruby Hammond.

Vince's Aunty Glad, **Gladys Elphick,** was born in 1904. She grew up at Point Pearce mission, married and had two sons. After her husband died, she and the two boys moved to Adelaide. It was 1939 and wartime. Aunty Glad worked in a factory making weapons, where she won an award for a tool she invented. In time she remarried and, through the 1940s and 1950s, she was active with the South Australian Aborigines Advancement League. In 1966, with other women, she set up the Council of Aboriginal Women of South Australia. They supported Aboriginal families who were struggling, and they campaigned for political change.

'In the old days we didn't speak up for ourselves,' Glad once said. The women's council met this problem head-on and gave its members a crash course in public speaking. The women came to the fore during the 1967 Referendum campaign, when they travelled around South Australia giving talks to mainly white people and encouraging them to vote yes.

In 1973 the Aboriginal women's council joined forces with Vince and others from the Aboriginal Progress Association, and together they started an Aboriginal-controlled community centre, with various services all under one roof. The centre – now called Nunkuwarrin Yunti – is still going strong.

Aunty Glad believed emphatically that it was Aboriginal people who were going to solve the problems they faced. She said, 'We understand our people. We understand our people's problems.' Aunty Glad was appointed a Member of the Order of the British Empire in 1971 and named South Australian Aboriginal Person of the Year in 1984. The annual Gladys Elphick Oration is held in her honour.

* * *

Vince got to know married couple **Maude and George Tongerie** while he was at St Francis House boys' home. They were about ten years older than him. Both were from around Oodnadatta and had been at Colebrook Home when they were children. George fought for the RAAF during the war, serving in New Guinea and Borneo. Maude initially worked for a family as a domestic help.

Maude and George were both active in the Aboriginal Progress Association, then Maude joined Aunty Glad and the other women at the women's council. As well as working with mothers with little children who were often isolated and struggling, she was active in the 1967 Referendum campaign. She'd say to people that all Aboriginal people needed was a little bit of a lift out of the discrimination they faced, and they'd then be able to take the next steps in life themselves. In the early 1970s, the state government was looking for people to act as a liaison between Aboriginal people and the wider community. Maude trained on the job to become a social worker, and George did similar work. They both worked a lot with young people caught up in the juvenile courts.

Around 1980, Maude and George returned to Oodnadatta. The railway line through the town was being re-routed and many white people who'd run businesses were leaving. George and Maude worked with local Aboriginal people to keep the town running and a good place to live in. 'We're here to do what you want us to do,' was the essence of their approach, and in time Aboriginal-run organisations and businesses thrived. In 1987 Maude and George returned to Adelaide to live and in 1988 both were made Members of the Order of Australia.

* * *

Vince met **Ruby Hammond** in the early days of the Aboriginal Legal Rights Movement. Ruby was born in 1936 near a small town called Kingston, in South Australia's south-east. Her family lived independently of a mission, and while Ruby was at school she didn't feel any different from the other kids. But when she left school, she saw discrimination in action: white boys and girls who hadn't done as well academically as she had got better jobs. When she worked in the back room of a grocery shop, filling up bags of flour and sugar, she asked the owner if she could work at the counter. 'No,' he said. 'The customers wouldn't like it.'

Ruby was ambitious and moved to Adelaide and got a job as a telephonist. In time she met Aunty Glad and joined the women's council too. Ruby took the council's crash course in public speaking and gave many talks in the lead up to the 1967 Referendum. She became well known for her influential style and, in 1972, she was one of several Aboriginal people invited to Canberra to meet with the Liberal minister in charge of Aboriginal Affairs at the time. After the next election, she returned to Canberra to meet the new Labor minister, this time as a member of the National Aboriginal Consultative Committee.

Ruby spent six years with the Aboriginal Legal Rights Movement, then she worked for the Land Rights Trust and was chair of the Aboriginal Housing Board. She became a public servant in different agencies, among them planning and the arts, and also worked on a program that aimed to employ more Aboriginal people in the public service. She was on many committees and professional organisations. 'We're always told discrimination is not there,' she once said. 'It is there.' She worked all her life to dismantle it.

* * *

The stories and quotes above come from Vince's memories, the documentary *Sister, If Only You Knew* (Film Australia, 1975), the pamphlet *Some Aboriginal Women Pathfinders* (listed above), Australian Dictionary of Biography entries, and oral histories gathered by historian Sue Anderson.

St Francis Boy's Home
The following are the names of the boys who were resident at St Francis Boy's Home from 1946 until 1959

William Briscoe	David Woodford	John Bray
Henry Campbell	Fred Turner	Clifford Bray
Francis Fejo	Des Price	Phillip Bray
George Kruger	Vincent Butler	Ken Wesley
Ken Nayda	Brian Butler	Les Nayda
Harold Thomas Jnr	Malcolm Cooper	John Palmer
Trevor Reid	Jim Foster	Gerald Tilmouth
Wilfred Huddleston	Clifford Garrett	Colin Tilmouth
Sam Wickman	John Howe	Geoffrey Miller
Richie Bray	Sonny Morey	Jack Campbell
Tim Campbell	John Moriarty	Peter Tilmouth
Charlie Kunoth	Peter Butcher	Max Wilson
Robert Bray	Peter Espie	Harry Russell
James Bray	John Horrell	Ernest Perkins
Walter Gardiner	Fred Kruger	Ivan Butler
Noel Hayes	Glen Roberts	Colin Butler
Harold Nayda	Robert Walker	Vincent Copley
John Spencer	Ron McCoy	Allan Furber
Richard Tilmouth	Gerry Hill	Ken Hampton
Brian White	Bill Espie	Walter McArthur
Ron Tilmouth	Laurie Bray	Gordon Briscoe
Cyril Hampton	Spencer Weetra	Charles Perkins

Australian Government · City of Port Adelaide Enfield · ANGLICARESA

Part of a memorial for the old St Francis House, which is now a function centre. Carved into the stone above this nameplate is a quote inspired by something Brenda said: *We were here. We came as boys and left as men.*

353

Acknowledgments

The Wonder of Little Things was created on the lands of the Kaurna, Ngadjuri, Ngarrindjeri, Narungga and Wurundjeri Woi Wurrung peoples.

* * *

Bringing this book into being has been a team effort. Our thanks to many wonderful people. Brenda for having the idea for the book, Kara and Vincent for being the reason for it, and Kathy and Steve Sutton for care and logistics. All of Vince's family and friends. All of my family and friends.

And many others.

Clare Forster read Vince's story when it was made up of about three hundred fragments, like scraps of material waiting to be made into a quilt, or three hundred bricks in a pile waiting to become a wall. She recognised Vince's distinctive voice and saw my enthusiasm, and agreed to become our literary agent. She gave us a way to start stitching the stories together. Then she put her heart and soul into finding us the right publisher. Clare has been beside us all the way – steady, immensely talented, big-hearted and good-humoured. Thanks also to Benjamin Paz, Clare's associate at Curtis Brown Literary Agency, who made all the things that were new to us easy to grasp.

Jude McGee, publisher for ABC Books at HarperCollins, took on two first-time co-authors, one in his eighties, the other in her sixties. She believed in Vince's story from the word go. She knew it was special. She also knew it needed work to transfer the intimacy of Vince's natural 'in-person' storytelling style to the pages of a book. Jude and Vince met on a video call and they were both laughing together within minutes. Jude's initial edit and questions helped Vince bring even more to the story. She played to our strengths and shepherded us through with brilliance and fun.

Jude also put a great team behind and beside us. Much gratitude to senior editor and project manager Scott Forbes, who did a thousand little things to help bring the book together, from editing to photo selection and much more. His calm patience and attention to detail were invaluable. Kate Goldsworthy did our second edit. She took great care to maintain the integrity of Vince's voice and her curiosity led to more good details being unearthed from Vince's stories. Proofreaders Nicola Young, proud Barkindji woman Allanah Hunt, and Shannon Kelly brought astute eyes and sensitivity to the story at critical stages.

Our thanks to everyone else at HarperCollins for helping to share Vince's story, many of them doing so behind the scenes, including typesetter Kelli Lonergan, marketing manager Kate Butler and campaign manager Hannah Lynch. Thanks to Darren Holt for the vibrant cover design, and to artist Venita Woods for her very beautiful artwork that speaks so fittingly to Vince's story. Thanks to First Nations actor Greg Fryer for narrating Vince's story for the audiobook version. Thanks also to all the wonderful booksellers and librarians who will place this story in readers' hands.

In early January 2022, Vince had this to say to you all: 'A great big thanks for your appreciation of my story.'

* * *

Four historians gave generously of their expertise and time, and we've been very lucky to work with them. Dr Skye Krichauff grew up on Ngadjuri Country and worked with Vince on several projects. Skye is an ethno-historian specialising in cross-cultural relations in South Australia's colonial era and how historical injustices are remembered in the present. Dr Tom Gara helped Vince find out more about his Warrior family connections and gave him newspaper clippings about his dad and grandfather. These meant a great deal to Vince. Tom specialises in Aboriginal history of the nineteenth century and, in the past twenty years, the twentieth century as well. Dr Cameron Raynes helped me understand the protection era and the policies and practices that affected Vince's family. Cameron specialises in the engagement between Aboriginal people, the South Australian government and the wider public, between 1901 and 1953. Twenty or so years ago oral historian and archaeologist Dr Sue Anderson interviewed many Ngadjuri and other First Nations people of South Australia and documented oral histories on their behalf. These were invaluable in giving us background material and further prompting Vince's memories of people and events. Skye and Cameron also checked the timeline in the book, and offered valuable additional material.

Thanks also to Andrew Wilson in the archives team at South Australia's State Records office, who located records about Vince's family that helped Vince make sense of different things he'd heard as a young person. Bec O'Reilly was also very helpful. Dr Christopher Wurm helped us interpret medical information on hospital records and death certificates. While heartbreaking at times for Vince, it helped him come to know more about his grandparents, dad, mum, brother and sisters.

Vince's appreciation of the work of academics is evident in what he said one day as we went through historical documents. 'Bit by bit, we've found more information in different archives and from historians. That's given me a better idea about the where and when and how of some of the things that happened.'

Vince and his son Vincent have worked closely with archaeologist Professor Claire Smith and anthropologist Gary Jackson for many years. Vince very much appreciated their help in recovering Ngadjuri cultural heritage, and also their friendship.

Two former school teachers have been good friends to us, and great collectors and documenters of historical records. Thanks to Fran Knight and Adele Pring for all they've done in education over many years. It was Adele who introduced me to Vince.

Vince's St Francis family has been there all the way through. Not many of the boys are left with us now. During the writing of the book, Vince arranged for Charlie's wife, Eileen Perkins, to meet me, and Eileen has been a great support in finalising the text. Her memory of the details of the history-making events that Charlie, Vince, Morey (John Moriarty), Biggo (Gordon Briscoe) and others were part of was a gift to us. It was also a joy to remember the funny stories with her. Morey and his wife, Ros, have also been close by. Vince and Morey spoke on the phone regularly, often about the stories going into the book. Since Vince's passing, Morey and Ros have been a much-appreciated presence and support. Biggo and his wife, Norma, also remained in touch with Vince, as did the other surviving boys. The bonds created through St Francis House go deep.

Special thanks to Pat Joraslafsky, Rex Watters, Greg Agnew and Robin Longbottom, who filled in some Curramulka details for us and also helped Vince go back to his beloved Currie in November 2021, to see old friends and leave some of Brenda's ashes on Currie soil.

First Nations author and editor Lisa Fuller helped us at early stages in the project. We're grateful for her suggestions and support of Vince's story from the beginning. It was heartening.

Vince's friend Trevor Woodhead helped us with cricket details, and one of Vince's oldest friends, Stewart Donnell, contributed details from primary school days. John and Mark Smith, Father Percy Smith's son and grandson, have also assisted us generously with photos and background information.

Glanville Hall and Port Adelaide Enfield Council have been wonderful in honouring the legacy of the St Francis House boys and their story. Vince wanted them to know how much this has meant to him.

In her role as CEO of Clare and Gilbert Valley Councils, Dr Helen Macdonald became a trusted colleague of Vince and his family.

Thank you to Kathryn Sutton, Vince's niece, for taking photos and videos as the book was being made. Thank you to Callum McEwen, Kara's husband, for his technical help with the photos we selected from the family collection.

Thanks to these people who helped out in many different ways: Meredith Appleyard, Billie Bakker, Jeremy Bakker, Steven Bird, Mikaella Clements, Michelle Deans, John Drislane, Melinda Dundas, Paul Fyfe SJ, Megan Hanley, Robert Hannaford, Penny Johnson, Earnsy Liu, Alison Manning, Julie Perrin, Angela Pye, Sarena Ruediger, Fiona Rutkay, Shendelle Strawbridge, Melissa Sweet, John Tague, Marlene Wallace. Also, to the many McInerneys, for so much: (the late) Steve, Mary, Marie, Paul, Monica, Maura, Stephen, and Rob. In particular, thanks to Mary, Monica and Maura for generous and practical support in so many ways; and to Marie for an ongoing conversation over many years about justice, and for all I've learned from you and your colleagues on what it means to be an ally.

Thank you to early readers of Vince's story: Phillip Adams, Tony Birch, James Boyce, Ali Cobby Eckermann, Adam Goodes, Paul Kennedy, John Moriarty and Bruce Pascoe.

Two pandemic-related thanks. To Zoe, Shally, Yun and Bo at my local post office in Melbourne, who during the city's many lockdown days, made my regular walks to post the growing chapters to Vince an enjoyable adventure, and their office a safe port of call in uncertain times. And to the librarian at the State Library of South Australia who, when I couldn't get over to Adelaide to research books for Vince in the not-for-loan collection, went out of their way to find material and put it in a format we could look at digitally. That was really kind of you. What you found had immense meaning for Vince. The wonder of little things …

Lea McInerney
July 2022